EARLY CHINESE ART
AND ITS
POSSIBLE INFLUENCE
IN THE PACIFIC BASIN

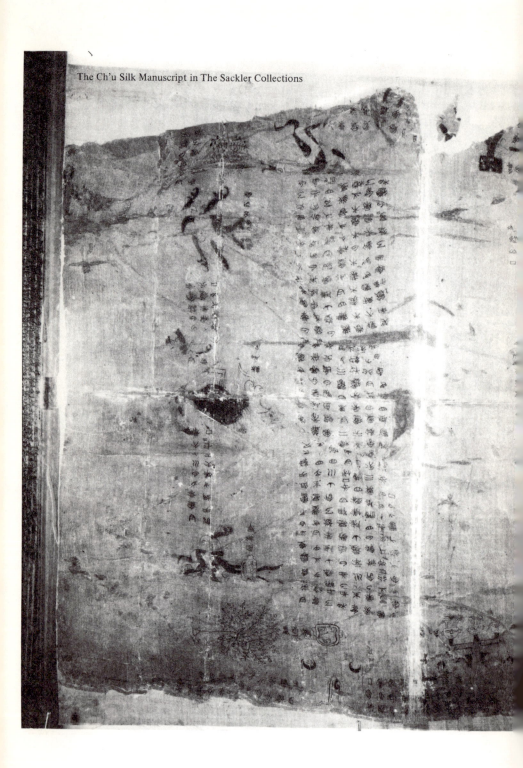

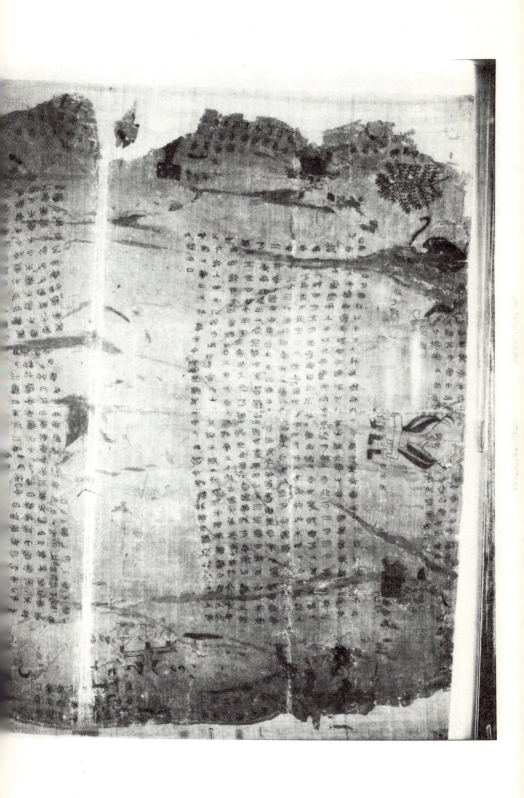

EARLY CHINESE ART
AND ITS
POSSIBLE INFLUENCE
IN THE PACIFIC BASIN

A Symposium Arranged by the
Department of Art History and Archaeology
Columbia University, New York City
August 21 – 25, 1967

Edited by Noel Barnard
in collaboration with Douglas Fraser

Volume One

CH'U AND THE SILK MANUSCRIPT

Intercultural Arts Press
New York

This symposium and the publication of
these volumes were
made possible by a grant from
the Sackler Fund
to Promote Central Asiatic Studies

THESE PROCEEDINGS ARE DEDICATED
TO THE MEMORY OF
ROBERT VON HEINE-GELDERN

Photograph courtesy Fayer, Wien.

ROBERT von HEINE-GELDERN, 1885-1968
Professor Emeritus of Prehistory, Art History
and Ethnology of Asia

Sad tidings of the passing of our highly esteemed colleague reached us just as these volumes were being prepared for press. It is therefore the unanimous wish of the contributors that our collection of papers— which has, indeed, come to take the form of a Festschrift to him—be formally dedicated to the memory of so distinguished a scholar whose stimulating pioneer work in the field of diffusionist studies will ever serve to encourage others to probe deeper still into one of the most fascinating problems in the story of mankind.

CONTENTS

LIST OF FIGURES, MAPS, AND TABLES

Figure captions are given below in as brief a form as possible.

THE LACH-TRUONG CULTURE

INTRODUCTION

1. General Considerations

In these volumes there is presented an assembly of 27 papers prepared by more than a score of specialists working in a variety of cultural areas and per medium of several markedly different disciplines — all are concerned with the subject of diffusion in the Pacific Basin and aspects of the thesis that numbers of art forms and artifacts extensively distributed in the area were, in all probability, anciently derived from China. As a starting point attention is focused upon the Chinese scene in the surveys by Chang Kwang-chih and William Watson which deal with the culture of the ancient State of Ch'u whence came the famous Silk Manuscript illustrated in the *Frontispiece*. This important archaeological document discussed in detail by Jean Mailey, Jao Tsung-yi, Hayashi Minao, and the present writer, was a major source of inspiration leading to the establishment of the Symposium. It has, by virtue of its contents and certain of the archaeological artifacts associated with the parent Ch'u culture, been instrumental in bringing to the fore new evidence datable in the closing centuries of the first millennium B.C. of possible Chinese influences upon Pacific cultures.

This is not the first occasion, of course, that the problem has been debated. Nearly two decades ago at the Congress of Americanists held in New York (1949) 'where 'diffusionism' spoke with renewed vigor in a disturbing exhibition entitled *Across the Pacific: Did the Ancient Civilizations of the Far East Contribute to American Indian Civilizations?* prepared for the occasion by the American Museum of Natural History ... an overwhelming mass of Asiatic-Pacific-American parallels"was presented, Miguel Covarrubias, from whose delightfully illustrated book *The Eagle, The Jaguar, & The Serpent* the preceding assessment is cited, had tackled the task apparently single-handed both to review and to illustrate the case as it appeared at that time. In the present volumes, however, we are able to proceed further and to bring together the individual views of a comparatively large number of scholars and to place these on record for the edification and interest of many people — academics and laymen alike — who are well aware of the fascination that this field of research holds to all who attempt to explore its various ramifications.

Since the early days of diffusionist argument the scene has changed remarkably. Previously conjecture largely held sway — there was a lack of dependable evidence and an often studied indifference to the necessity for systematic research methods. The opponents of the theory comprised hard-headed anthropologists and archaeologists who certainly advocated caution if not outright 'isolationist' views; however, we find now not only a tremendous increase in long-needed archaeological and scientific data but also the serious entrance into the field by archaeologists, anthropologists, linguists, and other humanistic scientists. No longer is it the domain of the dilettante or the old-fashioned art-historian who was so often concerned with the vagaries of art rather than with the exacting discipline required of a serious investigator. The field is one that now claims the attention of many highly trained scholars as the list of contributors and participants who were in attendance at this Symposium so well illustrates.

This opportunity which has allowed so many scholars to meet both formally and informally has, naturally enough, resulted in valuable exchanges of views and discussions covering many items of mutual interest — at least one aspect of the value of such direct contact has been particularly evident to me during the task of editing these papers: it is reflected in the numerous occasions where both minor and major revisions of crucial details in the original (pre-Symposium) form of the papers have been undertaken. Foremost amongst the factors which seem to have stimulated several of our contributors to re-cast sections of their papers is the better appreciation that has resulted in respect of some of the recent archaeological discoveries in China, Japan, Taiwan, and Southeast Asia. It is a matter of some importance to record, however, the observations made by several participants as to the difficulties besetting non-sinologists in consulting effectively the tremendous quantities of obviously relevant materials published in Chinese (and in Japanese) language reports and in numerous secondary studies. By some means or other, it was generally felt, the language barrier must be surmounted. Recognition of the importance of the wealth of archaeological data which has accumulated in recent decades in Mainland China was thus well attested by those least able to use the fruits of these excavations as freely as they would wish.

Similarly, specialists concerned with the various island cultures ranging from Melanesia to Polynesia were equally aware that a deeper understanding of many aspects of the now rapidly increasing corpus of archaeological materials — pottery in particular — cannot be achieved without constant reference, in the first place, to the Southeast Asian ceramic scene and thus ultimately to China. Possibly the publication of our 'Proceedings' may have the happy result of interesting younger scholars with reading ability in Chinese and/or Japanese to prepare themselves to enter one or other of the relevant fields to help in bridging this awkward gap. Or, perhaps students seeking to specialize in archaeology and with an interest in the Pacific area might be persuaded to include Chinese and/or Japanese as 'reading language' units in their undergraduate courses. It would seem unlikely that a programme of research and translation based on Chinese archaeological reports comparable with the valuable work in progress in the Japanese Prehistory Project at the University of Wisconsin under the direction of Chester S. Chard will be established anywhere in the near future.

One of the most significant features attending the papers tabled by our several archaeologist colleagues is the emphasis they have placed upon pottery shapes and décor. That this emphasis is notably strong amongst archaeologists whose special interests lie in the Pacific island groups is more than a matter of mere coincidence. The ability of pottery to resist the ravages of time and burial is an attribute common also to the products of lithic and bone industries and the latter are, of course, surveyed in some detail in these volumes. But there are limitations attending functional design and manufacturing methods of stone and bone implements which will not always allow one to justify diffusionist interpretations beyond certain bounds. In pottery, on the other hand, there is greater freedom in execution and design and in the manner in which decoration may be applied to the vessel. Accordingly a more extensive range of data is available and where one may choose to explore the possibility of diffusion – or even that of independent invention – the greater scope of information present may be expected to allow significant results to follow upon the application of systematic research techniques. There is, of course, nothing especially original in remarking upon this aspect of the materials – what is noteworthy, however, is the fact that our archaeologist colleagues faced with the request for papers touching upon the problem of diffusion in the Pacific area should edge away from the more aesthetically appealing wood sculpture and carving and other such perishable art media which one normally expects to be provided in support of diffusionist argument. The latter material is certainly striking in its apparent implications of cultural contacts yet one may appreciate two major disadvantages inherent in the majority of such commonly cited artifacts: (a) a large proportion is of recent manufacture (i.e. post-European contact) and (b) only rarely may adequate controls be obtained from archaeological discoveries. The distinct impression arises, therefore, that future enquiry will tend increasingly to centre upon the particular kinds of documentation which so extensively result from field archaeology throughout the Pacific island area.

Archaeological excavations over the past few years in the area have been progressing apace and their findings present new and much needed data which is especially important because of the time perspective that is becoming increasingly significant. However, we do not expect archaeological investigations (stressing non-perishable artifacts and technology) always to have direct links with art-historical studies (dealing with perishable objects and style, though interesting possibilities in this respect appear in several of the surveys e.g. those contributed by Mino Badner, Jack Golson, and Sidney Mead. Amongst the papers prepared by our archaeologist colleagues it will be observed that the practice is largely to work out connections in terms of their own material. These assessments should accordingly serve as a form of control of especial value to those interested in seeking interpretations upon the basis of a greater range of similar materials which, in many cases, may have to be derived from sources of uncertain provenance and indifferent reliability. It is here that the surveys of Chang Kwang-chih, Per Sørensen, Wilhelm Solheim, Roger Green, Jack Golson, and Bruce Palmer are together of specific value in providing us with a summary of the prehistory, as it is now known, of the area from southern China through Southeast Asia and Melanesia out into the Eastern Pacific. This is shown to be, in an original sense, a cultural area through which the effect of later developments on the continent becomes more and more attenuated. Some of these later developments are taken up in terms of the non-perishable material, bronze, by Emma Bunker and Magdalene von Dewall in their appraisals of the problems associated with the Tien and Dong-son cultures. Unfortunately, however, the art of metallurgy as such did not leave the Southeast Asian sphere and thus conveniently provide us with a further medium of data preservation in the Pacific island area. It may be granted, nevertheless, that influences from these metal-using cultures must have made some impact — and so it does, indeed, appear, when we turn our attention to the intriguing evidence known mainly from perishable artifacts.

The preceding observations should not, of course, be taken to imply that the more visually impressive data used in earlier surveys and in several of the present Symposium papers are to be regarded as of doubtful validity. Far from it. There remain important avenues of study here. The major problem is to find the earliest (and preferably pre-European contact) examples of the art forms under survey so as to confirm the validity of proposed cases of cultural contacts in antiquity. Although one might critically comment upon the dangers of comparing, for instance, the protruding tongue, split tongue, three-finger hand, joint mark, and other such motifs abounding in Maori carvings of 19th and 20th-century date with the comparable elements in Ch'u Culture artifacts, the fact remains, nevertheless, that an interval of as much as 2,500 years separates these two far-distant areas. If it were merely a correspondence of only one or two isolated motifs one might well entertain the possibility of independent invention but the comparable elements, singly and in combination, seem to require more than so simple an explanation. In the circumstances it may be rightly claimed that there is good ground for establishing a working hypothesis in terms of diffusion. However, this does not constitute proof of contact which, from our present knowledge of the Chinese scene, must be assumed to have commenced to spread from central/southern China not much later than early Han times (*circa* 200 B.C.) and not much earlier than, say, 600 B.C.

There are various ways in which data of rather recent date may be explored,; several important approaches are illustrated in these volumes. I select but four examples: first, the comprehensive and systematic assembly of visual evidence backed by relevant ethnographic, linguistic, and other such information compiled with the aim of illustrating distributional patterns of particular art motifs within a specific area and of assessing the possible factors governing such distribution. It is useful, in fact essential, to know clearly just what is meant when it is stated, say, that the protruding tongue motif is present in New Guinea art and when an accompanying illustration of one or more Sepik masks is provided. The impression that the motif is one to be found throughout the island immediately arises. Deeper investigation shows, however, as Douglas Fraser points out, that it is characteristic of a sector of the Sepik River only. The moment a peculiar geographical situation of this kind is ascertained the researcher is led willy-nilly to seek an explanation in the local environment. As a result an intensive programme of research is instituted to enquire into factors relevant to the distributional pattern often not immediately concerned with the art motif as such.

In this manner very valuable background information is brought to the fore. Detailed approaches of this kind should be found particularly useful when it comes to investigations of greater geographical scope concerned with the same motif. Secondly, one may take two distinct cultures widely separated but within reasonable distance of one another — one culture acts as the control area by virtue of the high antiquity of its art forms which are, furthermore, attested by extensive excavation. The other — a more primitive culture — manifests amongst its generally perishable art materials that are still preserved (none of which can date back more than a few centuries) certain motifs apparently derived originally from the other. This is, in several respects, the 'classical' approach but it would appear when applied within more modest geographical bounds than is usually the case that the resultant attention to detail, particularly in the intervening cultures, gives rise to quite acceptable conclusions. Mino Badner's paper illustrates interestingly how evidence may be brought to bear upon proposed connections between Dong-son and the Admiralty Islands. Thirdly, I should like to draw attention to Paul Tolstoy's approach which, in brief, is based upon a world-wide assembly of all relevant data in respect of a particular product, its material, and its mode of manufacture. This comprehensive survey makes its point not by sheer weight of evidence which must, indeed, be of monographic proportion but by the author's exhaustive analysis and extremely well thought out arrangement of the processed information. Here on a world-wide scale of study we may observe how data, which is almost entirely (though not exclusively) of comparatively recent date, may be systematically investigated with the fairly certain knowledge that worth-while results will be forthcoming. Fourthly, one may explore the variations amongst a particular group of artifacts within a relatively small cultural area along the lines suggested by Robert Bruce Inverarity in respect of Northwest Coast Indian totem poles. Such careful and detailed analysis demonstrates well enough that even comparatively recent examples of aboriginal art may furnish data of value if the materials are approached in a realistic and essentially 'scientific' manner.

In selecting the above four approaches for brief consideration here I have in mind the fact that there still seems to exist a certain degree of scepticism amongst 'pure' archaeologists, anthropologists, etc. in regard to the efforts and approaches of those of us who are more 'humanistic' in our disciplines. The term 'art-historian', for instance, is one which conjures up all kinds of opinion in respect of the forms of investigation concerned. However, it may be fairly claimed that 'art-history' today is rapidly developing into a field of research which aims to complement the specialised work of archaeologists, linguists, ethnologists, etc. Drawing heavily upon the evidence provided by those working directly in the field, the art-historian seeks to interpret the rapidly accumulating information in a wider perspective. The above papers illustrate the point both representatively and effectively.

Amongst the several more technically written papers will be observed frequent reference to radiocarbon (C14) datings from numerous sites wherein the associated ceramic evidence (amongst other) plays so significant a rôle. It is, no doubt, still rather premature to attempt to synthesize this scientifically derived data or to deduce tentative conclusions but during the process of editing the papers a number of particularly important points caught my attention. Because of the bearing they have upon the earlier mentioned problems of access to the contents of Chinese language archaeological reports, a few observations are pertinent. This is one reason for the discussion which follows; the other is more far-reaching – there is, so far as I am aware, practically a total lack of radiocarbon datings from the extensive excavations in Mainland China. Certainly there are no published datings amongst the various available archaeological reports which may have bearing upon the subject of Pacific contacts (i.e. Han times or earlier). By plotting on the Pacific map, in Figure 1, all the radiocarbon dates (associated with pottery) which are mentioned in these volumes, a patterned tendency results which accords remarkably well with migration/diffusion routes proposed or implied in several of the papers. This little exercise is intended, however, merely to check

KEY TO MAP ON FOLLOWING PAGES

	Site	Radiocarbon Date		
1.	Fukui	B.P. 12,400		10,000 B.C.
2.	Kamikuroiwa	B.P. 12,165		10,500 B.C.
3.	Yüan-shun			beginning 2500 B.C.
3(a).	Ta-p'en-k'eng	B.P. 11,000		9000 B.C. ?
4.	Feng-pi-t'ou			2000 - 200 B.C.
5.	K'en-ting			2500 - 2000 B.C.
6.	Hai-feng	B.P. 3,125	± 150	1300 - 1000 B.C.
7.	Ban Kao			1800 - 1500 B.C.
8.	Non Nok Tha			3000 - 2500 B.C.
9.	Palawan			2000 - 1750 B.C.
10.	Niah			2000 B.C.
11.	Viscayan			800 B.C.
12.	Gua Cha	1770 B.C.	± 140	1900 - 1600 B.C.
13.	Gua Kechil	B.P. 4,800	± 800	3600 - 2050 B.C.
14.	Samoa	B.P. 2,170	± 90	310 - 130 B.C.
15.	New Hebrides	590 B.C.	± 110	700 - 480 B.C.
16.	New Caledonia	1215 B.C.	± 120	1335 - 1095 B.C.
17.	Tongatapu	430 B.C.	± 51	480 - 380 B.C.
18.	Natunuku	1290 B.C.	± 100	1390 - 1190 B.C.
19.	Yanuca	1030 B.C.	± 90	1120 - 940 B.C.
20.	Marquesas	B.P. 1,270	± 150	550 - 830 A.D.

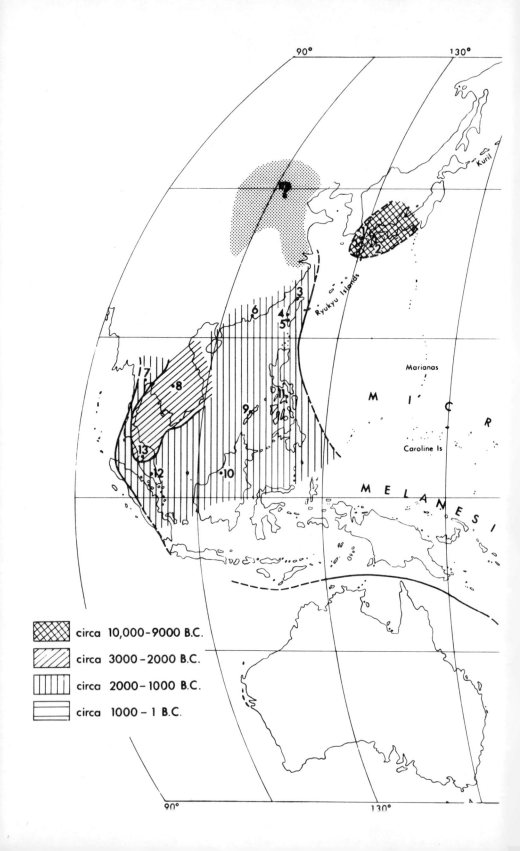

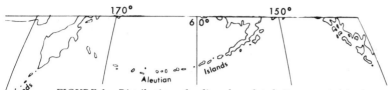

FIGURE 1. Distribution of radiocarbon dated sites reported in the present volume which have yielded ceramic materials; the data comprising the earliest examples cited is listed on p. XXV. The shadings and boundaries are rather idealistically rendered so as to accentuate the following aspects of the data: 1. the high antiquity of Jomon pottery sites; 2. the absence of radiocarbon dating in the Chinese 'nuclear area'; 3. Lung-shan ceramic influences extending into Taiwan and Southeast Asia which seem to have commenced their infiltration during the period 2500-1000 B.C.; 4. the notably early datings attending certain Thai and Malaysian areas; 6. the spear-head of 2000-1000 B.C. dated sites far to the southeast in New Caledonia and Fiji amidst later sites in the New Hebrides, Samoa, and Tonga.

Notwithstanding the incompleteness of this data and the fact that a highly fluid situation exists with new radiocarbon datings appearing now quite frequently, the pattern exhibited in this map does indicate reliably the nature of the problems which will occupy the attention of students over the next several decades.

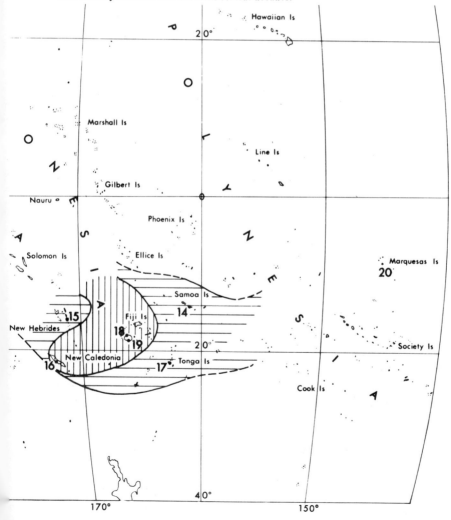

upon the immediately available radiocarbon data as a matter of interest and to supplement the very effective chronological diagram in Roger C. Green's paper (Figure 1, p.667). The observation which to my mind is of utmost importance is that arising from sites along the immediate periphery of China — radiocarbon datings of Lungshanoid Phases in Taiwan and of the quite marked Lung-shan Culture influences in the Ban Kao site area in Thailand. Regarding the former Chang Kwang-chih remarks: 'Radiocarbon dates are available for Taiwan only but these indirectly reflect the temporal ranges of the relevant cultures on the mainland.' Per Sorensen in his concluding sections hints at much the same idea — his ceramic evidence, albeit even further removed from its obvious source of inspiration, is actually the more strikingly parallel in measures of Lung-shan Culture influence. The fairly close correspondence of radiocarbon dates issuing from the relevant ceramic levels in the two peripheral areas — Taiwan and Ban Kao, respectively 2500 — 2000 B.C. and *circa* 1800 B.C. — as approximate 'arrival dates' of the Lung-shan contacts may be taken as a basis for tentative assessments of a probable date when the mainland parent culture area itself was at a well-advanced stage.*

So far as the Ban Kao finds are concerned the presence of an appreciable number of pseudo *li*-cauldrons in the early sub-phase is a matter of especial significance as this feature will, I think it may be granted, allow us to assume that it must have been the later phases of

* Upon reference to Per Sørensen's recently published report on Ban Kao, *Archaeological Excavations in Thailand* Volume II (pp. 110-11) it will be noted that the Ban Kao radiocarbon datings comprise two items only (Nos. K.838 and K.842) respectively '3720 b. 1950 or 1170± 140 B.C.' and '3310 b. 1950 or 1360 ± 140 B.C.' The former is of particular value because of its clear associations with the early subphase pottery; however, it is important to keep in mind that the range of the K.838 date is actually 1910-1630 B.C. With only this example available the necessity for caution is, of course, generally appreciated. In the case of the several Taiwan radiocarbon datings cited by Chang Kwang-chin the position is somewhat more secure in respect of the Taiwan Lungshanoid Culture of Feng-pi-t'ou ('Recent Advances in the Prehistoric Archaeology of Formosa', *Proceedings of the National Academy of Sciences,* 1966, 55.3: 539-43). Until an appreciably larger number of radiocarbon dates becomes available there will necessarily remain uncertainties attending interpretations attempted, but with the presently available data from two such widely separated site-areas coinciding so closely and centering upon the beginning of the second millennium B.C. we may seek to establish a tentative dating of the mainland Lung-shan Culture in its later phases with a greater degree of confidence than has been possible hitherto.

Lung-shan — wherein the *li*-type vessels tend to be found in greater quantities — which would, in all probability, have contributed the idea to Ban Kao potters to design vessels reminiscent of this Lungshanoid and uniquely Chinese vessel. With reference particularly to the Ban Kao materials it would seem reasonable to propose tentatively that this later phase of Lung-shan flourished at least as early as 2000 B.C. and possibly earlier. Radiocarbon dated sites of such significance should, it is to be hoped, inspire our estranged colleagues in China to take up the challenge and to institute a programme of radiocarbon dating covering key site-areas and, so far as possible, to extend the programme even into the historical sphere where very valuable controls exist.*

Perhaps even more important reason to plead for the commencement of a radiocarbon dating programme in China is the surprising antiquity of Japanese pottery sites reported in these volumes. Although apparently developed in isolation we now see located right next door to one of the world's most remarkable pottery cultures this seemingly independent ceramic tradition of which the earliest manifestations are radiocarbon dated as much as 12,000 years ago. As Chester Chard observes: ' . . . it seems necessary at the moment to derive the first ceramics, at something like 13,000 years ago, from the mainland — but from where we do not know.' What was the situation of Chinese ceramics, at so early an epoch? Did the Yang-shao tradition exist in some 'incipient' or 'initial' phase then? Should we assume that pottery was unknown in the Chinese 'nuclear area' at the time and look much further southward for possible routes of

---

* A particularly valuable form of control might be sought in regard to the radiocarbon dating of sites which contain written records incorporating dated entries. The latter seldom contain the year of reign and when the year is recorded difficulties arise as to which King's reign is involved. Nevertheless, there exists useful data comprising the month, the month-quarter (in Shang times, the 10-day 'week'), and the sexagenary day cycle. An appropriate programme of radiocarbon datings, conducted with the specific aim of defining the archaeological document dates in a precise chronological system (in terms of the astronomical day) would be a project well worth undertaking. Traditional data, too, could be put to the test and, no doubt, problems such as those mentioned in the section on Chinese Chronology later may possibly be solved.

entry — thus taking up Wilhelm Solheim's thesis (expressed in the concluding pages of his paper) of northern Southeast Asia as the area whence pottery spread to other parts of East Asia?

In this manner attention may be drawn to many such leading questions raised in these volumes some of which must await the resumption of archaeological activities in China and the extensive application of scientific methods of dating to Chinese key-sites before definitive answers can be attempted.

It will be observed that several of our contributors: Karl Jettmar, William Samolin, Olov Janse, Carl Schuster, and the late Robert Heine-Geldern have prepared papers which amongst other matters touch upon the possibility of Western origins of specific art forms, particularly those found, roughly speaking, south of the Chinese 'nuclear area' — as defined some years ago by Chang Kwang-chih — in lithic, ceramic, and other cultural contexts. It is useful to keep in mind aspects of influences from the Middle East and Europe which penetrating Asia, approached the Chinese scene towards the close of the Western Chou period and entered parts of Southeast Asia possibly somewhat earlier. The picture resolves itself more clearly into focus, however, as we pass into the Ch'un-Ch'iu and Chan-kuo periods so far as China is concerned. In this connection there are still occasional opinions voiced as to the Western origins of metallurgy in China far westward of the 'nuclear' area, somewhere in the Middle East. However, the situation as expressed archaeologically in China itself implies unambiguously an entirely different interpretation as the reports of acceptably and properly controlled excavations conducted over the last 45 years illustrate quite clearly.* Because of the centrifugal nature of the spread of metallurgy in China from a comparatively small inland area within the historical bounds of Shang (where the

---

* A preliminary note on the results of an extensive research project that permits tentatively at least, the expression of strongly isolationist views in respect of both the discovery and the development of metallurgy in China has recently been published by the present writer under the title 'The Special Nature of Metallurgy in China' in *Applications of Science in Examination of Works of Art,* Museum of Fine Arts, Boston (pp. 184-204) with a series of distribution maps illustrating the point.

earliest manifestations of the art are presently known) it does not come as a matter of particular surprise to learn of the recent discovery of metal artifacts and of certain casting equipment in Thailand sites in strata associated with radiocarbon datings ranging from 3000-2000 B.C. These materials are, if anything, strongly 'Western' in character and exhibit nothing that suggests intercommunication with the nucleus of Early Shang metallurgy far to the north.

The preceding observations lead us to a problem which has not been adequately touched upon in this volume although it occasionally came to the fore in both formal and informal discussions during the course of the Symposium — a subject which is deserving of a symposium in its own right: to what extent is man, individually or collectively and at any particular time or place, to be regarded as a being (or beings) capable of invention? Obviously a new idea or artifact has to be created somewhere by someone in the first instance before it can be transmitted to other individuals or communities. Given that the process of invention can take place in one community over a range of time and result in, say, a socketed axe where hitherto axes were simply lashed to their handles, is it necessarily the case that another community — separated by vast expanses of land or ocean, either at the same time or later (and without direct or indirect contact with the other) — should *not* be able to 're-invent' the same or a functionally identical idea for attaching a similar implement to a handle? No doubt an interminable argument could arise from a question of this sort. However, what can be attempted in a practical manner in regard to this problem? Will the research involved lead to conclusions that might jeopardise the concept of diffusion? To answer the second question first is best as it is the easier: not necessarily — it would be equally unrealistic to assume that most fundamental knowledge and functional artifacts have been independently discovered and re-discovered in community after community at various times and in various places.' So far as the first question is concerned, the problem which is to be investigated might be more precisely stated: to what extent are the materials of construction, the methods of manufacture, shapes, sizes, functions, etc. of artifacts "pre-ordained"? To illustrate this: a container is to be invented — the idea may arise from simple cupping of the hands, a gourd, etc., but this is not our immediate concern — the material to be used for the purpose is clay (which we may assume is universally available). What will the object look like after generations of due trial and error? We know it will sooner or later tend to be made semi-globular in shape — the material employed and the several possible methods of manufacture (see relevant section of papers by Wilhelm Solheim and Bruce Palmer in these volumes) combine to allow, only a globular, oval, or other such curvilinear structure. It will have a mouth, for obvious reasons. The mouth may take various forms within the limits allowed by the material in its plastic-damp state, the shape of the vessel constructed, the container-use to which it is to be put, etc. but we may be sure that a circular shape of mouth would nearly always result because of the combination of such factors as: the material, the method of manufacture, the function of the mouth, and the nature of the contents which the container is to hold. For certain cooking purposes it will be found necessary to raise the container somewhat above the fire-level. The addition of legs to form part of the vessel structure is one of several alternative methods. If legs are to be attached to the vessel (and also to be made of clay) there are certain practical limits that are to all intents and purposes "pre-ordained". Firstly, there is the number of legs that a round container will require — and consequently the number that the inventor will settle for after due experiment. One leg is feasible but this must take the form of a pointed extension of the vessel bottom (rhyton style) and the idea is simply to press the vessel into loose sand, embers, etc. so that it will remain standing in vertical position. Two legs are useless and the second one redundant because the two can only function in the same way as a single leg. Three legs are perfect and are easy to trim so that the vessel will stand level on a flat surface. Four legs are feasible but offer a number of disadvantages in the case of round containers — a square or rectangular container, however, has to have four legs. The legs will be made of solid rod-shaped pieces of clay if the bases of the legs are to be flat; if pointed the shapes will tend to be conical and to splay diagonally from the vessel-body. In the case of splayed conical legs the possibility of future invention of the *li*-cauldron will arise, but the invention will be made only if the need for it exists — only in China apparently was there a call for the invention of this peculiar form of vessel. For ease of pouring attention must be given to the manner in which the lip is curved, its thickness, the diameter of the mouth, but better still, a beak may be fashioned in the rim, or a spout of tubular shape inserted in a perforation in the vessel wall.

Dozens of features of this kind are known to us all and many are so simple and obvious that we barely realize that they comprise, in effect, quite rigid principles underlying the construction of artifacts. Providing the principle is properly understood and correctly incorporated in the general structure of the artifact then the associated function will operate efficiently.

A comprehensive assembly of such 'principles' and careful observation and analysis of their shape-structure-function associations may well be expected to help in many aspects of interpretation of the peculiar, as well as the commonplace, in artifact construction. For instance, Wilhelm Solheim mentions a radiocarbon dated bronze-working site at Non Nok Tha which apparently is earlier than the dates we normally assess for the emergence of bronze casting in China (*circa* 1500 B.C.). Crucibles from this site which he showed me last year are very small and have pouring beaks — in every respect they are typically European or Middle Eastern in construction. Chinese crucibles of the earliest phases at Cheng-chou (and right through to Chan-kuo times) lack pouring beaks, are bucket-shaped, and would hold 30 or more times the quantity of molten metal. That there can be no connection (regardless of the degree of reliability of the radiocarbon date on the one hand, and the total lack of such dating on the other) becomes evident when we investigate the construction principles and consider these in terms of casting methods in each culture: the presence or absence of the beak or spout in crucibles in relation to the size of crucible becomes a key point. What is commonplace to us as Westerners was not necessarily so in China, in the 'nuclear area'. Similarly, comment upon the pseudo *li*-cauldrons (Type I) from the Ban Kao site-area is called for. It is not a *li*-cauldron from the Lung-shan point of view. The true *li*-cauldron which is thought to have developed from the practice of standing three elongated vessels neck-to-neck over a fire or as I have suggested above — a development from splayed conical legs — is a cooking vessel whose function is perfectly clear. The inventor was aware of the fact that the more surface area to come in contact with the fire, the quicker the vessel contents would heat and boil. But his interest was probably not so much in merely bringing water rapidly to boil as it was to produce steam effectively. Even today the basic principle in Chinese cooking is largely that of steaming. Up to the Han period it seems that most cooking was done in vessels placed over the flame in an open fireplace but with the introduction (or the invention?) of the stove in Han times the *li*-style vessel soon fell into disuse.

With an appreciation of such background it is accordingly evident that although the Ban Kao potters were familiar with the *li*-cauldron — amongst other Lung-shan vessel-types — they did not understand the function of the hollow legs. This is perfectly evident when we observe that not only do the legs not open into the body of the vessel but also they contain perforations. The latter, too, is a Lung-shan feature, but such perforations occur only in ring-footed vessels and usually those that form a comparatively high 'pedestal'. Thus the Ban Kao potter confused unrelated functional devices derived from two entirely different vessel-types. His method of attaching the hollow bulbous legs to the vessel body, moreover, is an aspect of ceramic practice alien to China — whether it was a locally developed technique, or one introduced from some other cultural area is a problem requiring further investigation.* One thing is clear, no one would 'invent' a vessel like the Ban Kao Type 1 for a practical purpose. Studying the vessel from a functional viewpoint and taking into consideration limitations attending pottery design for vessels of the *li*-cauldron type, one may thus discover further evidence along these lines supporting Per Sørensen's arguments for Lung-shan Culture influences reaching Ban Kao in the early second millennium B.C. Perhaps it may be considered excusable to turn one's attention far across the Pacific to the Americas and to speculate upon the close identity and the possibility of similar misapprehension that might be claimed to attend the origin of pre-Classic Guatemalan, Chupicuaro, and other vessels with hollow tetrapods and flattened teat-nubbin bases — the tetrapods often perforated as in the Ban Kao examples.

In the study of décor a similar technical line of enquiry may be pursued. Take, for instance, the *t'ao-t'ieh* motif which extends far back into antiquity in China but *not* — and this observation is a key-point in the discussion — prior to the emergence of metallurgy in China. Ch'en Ch'i-lu lists four forms of its occurrences throughout the Pacific and in the Americas stating to the effect that in its earliest manifestation the motif simply comprised two profiles of an animal placed face-to-face with the result that a third entity can be envisaged. In China we may, however, point to quite early art motifs that appear to have relevant associations with the concept of 'bilateral splitting of an animal', 'simultaneous image', *t'ao-t'ieh*, etc. as the feature is variously termed in these volumes. Perhaps of highest antiquity is the *jen-mien-yü-hsing* 人面魚形 motif in Yang-shao painted pottery (on the basis of the Lung-shan date discussion above, datable

---

* It will be noted in the recently published Report that a further method of leg attachment occurs amongst the pseudo *li*-cauldrons (*cf.* Pl. 34, 10) — no inner sleeve-like attachment device being employed as in the case of the example Type 1 (Sorensen, below, Volume 2) which is representative of the majority of the pseudo *li*-cauldrons from this site. Interestingly, few of the Ban Kao pedestalled bowls have perforations (*cf.* Pls. 34, 1; 47, 12) while none of the pseudo *li*-cauldrons lack this feature.

long before the second millennium B. C.). This is not, however, a true *t'ao-t'ieh* but rather an example of the second type listed by Ch'en Ch'i-lu. Possibly this second type — two antithetic fish profiles with a human head between — may be considered to be the earlier version in China. So far as I have observed there is no instance of the 'simultaneous image' (or true *t'ao-t'ieh*) in Yang-shao painted pottery — it is not until the Early Shang phase of the Bronze Age that the *t'ao-t'ieh* appears in the 'nuclear area'.

Chinese bronze casting was a sectional mould method, and without going into details either in respect of the casting technique or of the manner in which décor was incorporated in the clay models and moulds, it will simply be stated here that technical considerations to a very large extent influenced the choice and placement of décor. Because of the equal division of mould-pieces containing a band of decoration around a vessel, the contents of the décor were likewise equally apportioned and thus formed repeating patterns. However, it became customary to place the rather stylised representations of birds and animals face-to-face and on either side of a mould join — in the majority of cases, the true join rather than a pre-assembly join. Now, because of the technical need to incorporate a flange along the true join, the two head-to-head animals then appeared to form simultaneously the third entity — the *t'ao-t'ieh*. The flange functioned more or less as a nose, the one eye of one animal and the one eye of the other formed concurrently the pair of eyes of the *t'ao-t'ieh*. Each of the antithetically placed animals lent thus a horn, an ear, a trunk-like nose, and an eye towards the *t'ao-t'ieh* face. These contributing elements were insufficient, however, to provide a lower jaw for this third entity; consequently, the *t'ao-t'ieh* presents the curious appearance of a jawless creature. The phenomenon which has been given various kinds of fanciful explanations may be demonstrated thus to be actually no more than the outcome of technical aspects of mould preparation and casting practice. Without the flange — a necessary means of raising the line of mould join above the immediately adjacent areas of décor so as to allow easy tooling away of inter-mould metal spicules after the release of the casting — the nose-like effect would be lost, and, accordingly, the idea of placing animal profiles face-to-face with the flange between, thus forming simultaneously the third entity, would probably not have evolved.

If these preceding points are correct in principle (there are a few minor matters that require elaboration and will receive attention elsewhere later) it will be further obvious that to gain a better appreciation of art motifs extensively spread around the Pacific and which appear in the Chinese scene archaeologically attested far earlier than anywhere else, a great deal of inter-disciplinary communication and cooperation will be needed. It is not merely a matter for our colleagues working throughout the Pacific area to seek to break through the language barrier; it is just as essential that those of us in the sinological side who are concentrating on pre-Han studies should endeavour to explore our materials with far wider perspectives in mind than we normally do. The extensive range of subject matter in these volumes should serve well to give those of us specializing in the Chinese and Japanese side a pretty thorough background so as to enable us to see our materials in an even more fascinating light.*

2. Chinese Chronology

Because certain influences from the Chinese sphere into Southeast Asia and the Pacific seem obviously to have taken place well within historical times (i.e. Shang, Chou, and Han) a brief note on aspects of the early chronology of China is called for and also provision of

* The arrangement of the papers differs slightly from the order in which they were read at the Symposium. Because of the interconnections of many of them a number of possible ways of presentation order might be proposed. The one chosen tends to bring together papers of related subject and area interest. Purposely the decision was made to place Clinton Edward's survey last. The reader, having considered the evidence for diffusion, will certainly wish to know more regarding the 'mechanics' of cultural contacts. It is most fortunate, therefore, that we have here assessments made by one who is so fully familiar with practical aspects of ships and navigation. This important phase of the overall problem of accounting for diffusion routes is one that most of us who are not 'blue-water sailors' simply seek to discuss with the data available in atlases and pilot charts alongside us. Perhaps even more significant is Clinton Edwards' final sentence reminding us that the possible motivations for undertaking lengthy sea voyages must be determined before a complete theory of trans-Pacific raft voyaging can be expressed.

a Table for convenient reference. Prior to 841 B.C. chronologies based upon data recorded since Han times show little agreement and the available solar eclipses in both archaeological and literary documents — less than a dozen items — are so imperfect in respect of crucial data that far from offering a basis of control they serve only to add to the general confusion. Since Wang Kuo-wei published his reconstruction of the original form of the *Chu-shu chi-nien* 竹書紀年 (the 'Bamboo Annals') in 1917, a host of studies on the question of Shang and Chou chronology has appeared. The basic problem has been to establish the date of the Chou conquest of Shang — upon this hinges the general framework of whatever scheme may be offered and, in particular, the lengths of individual reigns where disagreement prevails. Table 1 indicates something of complexities and uncertainties underlying the various chronologies which have been advocated. At present two chronological systems are accepted by one school or another: the orthodox or *san-t'ung-li* 三統曆 system which has been followed for nearly 2,000 years, and the reconstructed *Bamboo Annals* system which is based upon a single sentence containing numerals easily mis-written, an ambiguous context, and comprising merely an observation recorded in an early commentary in reference to the *Bamboo Annals* — it is not even an entry in the work itself!

For various reasons which I have propounded elsewhere the reconstructed *Bamboo Annals* system which results in the date 1028 B.C. for the fall of Shang and the commencement of Chou in the following year (1027 B.C.) — a century later than the orthodox chronology (1122 B.C.) — is highly suspect. Until an acceptable chronology can be established upon the basis of archaeological documentation, the discovery of more precise eclipse records, or even the application of radiocarbon dating techniques to appropriate Shang and Chou remains, the orthodox system should be followed if only for the very good reason that every major reference work is based upon it. Table 2 provides a highly simplified view of the orthodox chronological system and incorporates, for the most part, only the period or dynastic names appearing in these volumes. For general convenience, however, the Table is extended down to the present, but again only in simplified form.

3. Maps

In addition to specialised or distributional maps provided by individual authors, additional location maps have been compiled and are inserted amongst the various papers in places where their presence would seem to be helpful. Because of the frequent mention of several of the major States of Eastern Chou times throughout the first six or seven of our papers an historical map is shown in Figure 2 for general reference. Similarly other groups of papers later have to share mutually suitable maps in order to avoid excessive overlapping of the same geographical data. Consultation of the Index will be found helpful in locating the appropriate map.

4. Conventions and Editorial Policy

Editorial work has, not unexpectedly, developed into a task of some magnitude especially in respect of the sinological papers involving as it has amongst the more routine work a major task of translation.

TABLE 1. *A comparative outline of the numerous chronologies proposed for the Western Chou period covering the reigns of ten rulers. The data are complex and considerable explanation is required to clarify various aspects of this Table; however, the reader need merely run his eye along each horizontal column to observe the discrepancies attending individual reign lengths. Groups 3, 4 and 5 comprise chronologies proposed over the last 30 or 40 years. Group 4 illustrates the questionable mode of research involved in respect of the 1027 B.C. system—each scholar juggles the data he has selected so that it fits in a period of 186 years culminating in the date 841 B.C. whence extant chronologies agree in most respects. Every few years a new system is proposed. The two most recent are not incorporated in this Table: Chou Fa-kao (HJAS, 23: 108-13) who seeks to advance the date of the Chou conquest of Shang to 1018 B.C. and Mizuno Seiichi who has now apparently dropped the 1027 B.C. system for one which places the Chou conquest date at 1089 B.C. (Tōyō bijutsu Vol. 5, p. 19 [Asahi Shimbun, 1968])—the details of this new system have yet to be explained but it is good to see that the latest proposal is one tending in the right direction—a return to the orthodox system upon the basis of which all major reference works are compiled.*

	Ancient Bamboo Annals	Shih-chi (100 B.C.)	Yü-lan Shih-chi	Han-shu (70 A.D.)	Ti-wang shih-chi (270)	Huang-chi ching-shih (1070)	T'ung-chien wei-chi (1070)
1 WU	-	3	-	7	7	7	7
2 CHOU KUNG	-	7	7	7	7	7	7
2a CH'ENG	} 44 yrs	-	-	30	30	30	30
3 K'ANG	6th	-	-	16th	26	26	26
4 CHAO	19th	-	-	-	51	51	51
5 MU	37th [47th]	55	55	-	55	55	55
6 KUNG	-	-	-	-	20	12	10 [25]
7 YI	1st	-	25	-	[20]	25	25
8 HSIAO	7th	-	15	-	-	15	15
9 YIH	7th	-	-	-	16	16	15
10 LI	-	37	37	-	-	37	40
Up to beginning of MU WANG'S reign	100 yrs	-	-	-	121 yrs	121 yrs	121 y
Up to beginning of KUNG HO period	[197 yrs] [297 yrs]	-	-	281 yrs	-	281 yrs	281 y
CHOU DYNASTY commences	[1027 B.C.] [1138 B.C.]	-	-	[1078 B.C.] [1110 B.C.] [1122 B.C.]	[1122 B.C.] [1116 B.C.]	1122 B.C.	1122 B

BASIC DATA   GROUP 1

T'ung-chih (1150)	T'ung kao (1290)	T'ung chien ch'ien-pien (1290)	Current Bamboo Annals (1400-1600)	Shinjō Shinzō (1928)	T'ang Lan (1955)	W.P.Yetts (1957)	Wu Chi-chang (1936)
7	7	7	6	3	–	3	7
7	7	7	7	7	–	–	7
30	30	30	30	30	–	30	30
26	26	26	26	26	–	25	26
51	51	51	19	24	–	19	51
55	55	55	55	55	–	55	55
10	12	12	12	12	–	15	20
25	25	25	25	25	–	3	17
15	15	15	9	15	–	7	15
15	16	16	8	12	–	32	16
40	37	37	12	16	–	20	37
121 yrs	121 yrs	121 yrs	88 yrs	100 yrs	–	77 yrs	121 yrs
281 yrs	281 yrs	281 yrs	209 yrs	225 yrs	–	209 yrs	281 yrs
1122 B.C.	1122 B.C.	1122 B.C.	1050 B.C.	1066 B.C.	1075 B.C.	1050 B.C.	1122 B.C.

3rd – 13th CENTURIES   1050-1075 B.C. GROUP

	Lei Hai-tsung (1931)	Ting Shan (1940)	Ch'en Meng-chia (1944)	Karlgren (1945)	Tung Tso-pin (1952)	T'ang-shu li-chih (c.945)
1 WU	(−) $^{1027-}$	3 $^{1030-}_{1028}$	3 $^{1027-}_{1025}$	7 $^{1027-}_{1021}$	7	
2 CHOU KUNG	(−)	7 $^{1027-}_{1021}$	− (7) $^{1024-}_{(1018)}$	[7] $^{1020-}_{(1014)}$	7	
2a CH'ENG	(25)	12 $^{1020-}_{1009}$	20 (13) $^{(1017)}_{1005}$	(1013)	30	
3 K'ANG	(25)	26 $^{1008-}_{983}$	38 $^{1004-}_{967}$	981	26	
4 CHAO	(25)	19 $^{982-}_{964}$	19 $^{966-}_{948}$	16* $^{980-}_{965}$	18	
5 MU	(25) $_{928}$	37 $^{963-}_{927}$	20 $^{947-}_{928}$	37* $^{964-}_{928}$	41	
6 KUNG	(25) $^{927-}$	18 $^{926-}_{909}$	20 $^{927-}_{908}$	15* $^{927-}_{913}$	16	
7 YI	(25)	20 $^{908-}_{889}$	10 $^{907-}_{898}$	−* 912	12	
8 HSIAO	(25)	7 $^{888-}_{882}$	10 $^{897-}_{888}$	−*	30	
9 YIH	(25)	3 $^{881-}_{879}$	30 $^{887-}_{858}$	−* 874	46	
10 LI	(−) $_{842}$	37 $^{878-}_{842}$	16 $^{857-}_{842}$	32* $^{873-}_{842}$	37 $_{842}$	
	841	841	841	841	841	
Up to beginning of MU WANG'S reign	75 yrs	67 yrs	80 yrs	[56 yrs]	100 yrs	
Up to beginning of KUNG HO period	186 yrs	189 yrs	186 yrs	186 yrs	270 yrs	
CHOU DYNASTY commences	1027 B.C.	1030 B.C.	1027 B.C.	1027 B.C.	1111 B.C.	1111 B.C.
	1027 B.C. GROUP				1111 B.C. GROUP	

(For CH'ENG, K'ANG, CHOU KUNG — Karlgren column braced together = 40 yrs)

(For YI, HSIAO, YIH — Karlgren column braced together = 39 yrs max)

* Asterisks denote incomplete reign lengths

TABLE 2

CHINESE CHRONOLOGY

Shang		1766 - 1123 B.C.
Chou		1122 - 222 B.C.
	Western Chou	1122 - 771
	Eastern Chou	770 - 222
	Ch'un-ch'iu Period	770 - 471
	Warring States Period	470 - 222
Ch'in		221 - 207 B.C.
Han		206 - 220 A.D.
	Western Han	206 B.C. - 8 A.D.
	Wang Mang Interregnum	A.D. 9 - 24
	Eastern Han	25 - 220
Six Dynasties		221 - 589
Sui		589 - 618
T'ang		618 - 906
The Five Dynasties.		906 - 960
Northern Sung		960 - 1127
Southern Sung		1127 - 1279
Yüan		1260 - 1368
Ming		1368 - 1644
Ch'ing		1644 - 1912

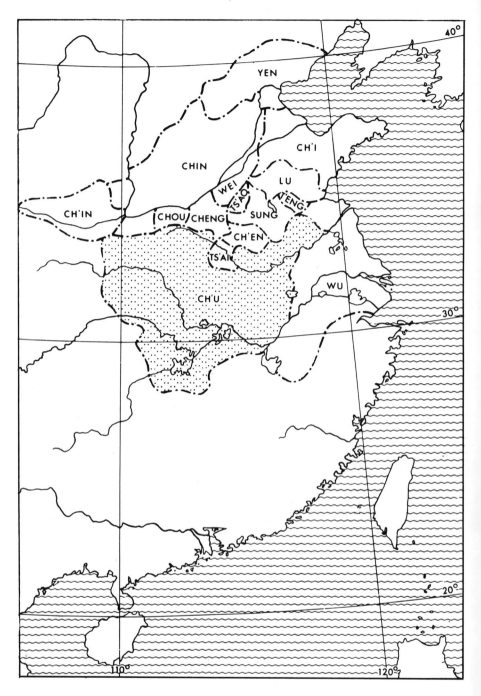

FIGURE 2. *The major States in China during the Ch'un-ch'iu period. After Albert Herrmann,* An Historical Atlas of China, *1966 ed.*

The general aim, however, has been to attain a reasonable degree of uniformity in convention amongst all the papers, but a fair amount of individuality has been purposefully preserved, for after all these volumes are not in any sense a single author work. So far as rigidity in convention is concerned, one system of Chinese romanisation has been applied throughout the papers, some standardisation of terminology has been effected, spellings have been made uniformly British, bibliographies have been re-cast into one general form of presentation and more or less the same form of reference method, with only slight irregularities, is employed throughout the papers. Chinese characters are liberally presented in the text for the convenience of sinological readers — in quite a few of the Bibliographies their presence is, of course, essential, but where too large a proportion of the same literary sources is repeated in two or more papers, characters are sometimes omitted. Diacritical marks are largely dispensed with not only in the Chinese romanisation but also in Thai place-names.

As several of the papers written in English by those of our colleagues whose natural language is not English have had to be rather extensively re-cast — altogether seven papers — some possibility of an occasional misinterpretation of the original *mss* on my part may have escaped us (the authors concerned have each checked my edited version). However, such slips that may have skipped our attention should in the majority of cases turn out to be only of minor importance.

5. Illustrations

Line-drawings have in numbers of cases been made by the authors themselves. Where executed by draughtsmen on the authors' behalf, a brief acknowledgement is made in an appropriate place in the papers concerned. Some of the submitted illustrations required re-lettering and a certain amount of 'touching-up'; other illustrations comprising originals which would not reproduce well — mainly indifferent quality photographs — have been converted into line-drawings under my supervision. The general aim has thus been to maintain a reasonably high standard of illustration in terms of accuracy and of aesthetic considerations throughout these volumes.

6. Acknowledgments

It is our great pleasure to record here on behalf of all concerned with the Symposium and this, its Proceedings, our deep appreciation to Dr. Arthur M. Sackler who has made this venture possible. It is our hope that with the publication of these volumes he will sense from the efforts behind our contributions — better than mere words can express — the full extent of our thanks.

We are indebted to the Department of Art History and Archaeology of Columbia University for its organization of the Symposium; the untiring work of Douglas Fraser with the secretarial assistance of Miyeko Murase has contributed tremendously to the success of the Symposium — in addition, Douglas Fraser organized the Photographic Exhibition *Early Chinese Art and the Pacific Basin* and edited the catalog issued to Symposium participants which has now been published with copious illustrations. Professor Emeritus L. Carrington Goodrich generously spared valuable time from the Ming Biographical Project to chair the Organizing Committee and the Symposium itself. We are grateful to Miss Phyllis Cohen for secretarial assistance, to Mr. Gene McCabe who designed and constructed the display panels of the Photographic Exhibition, to Mr. Philip Mazzola and other good friends whose valuable assistance made the Symposium so successful.

I wish to acknowledge expressly hereunder my personal gratitude to those who have helped in so many ways during the preparation of the manuscript for publication. Firstly, I should like to record the fact that the editorial task has been made much lighter and of much shorter duration than it might otherwise have been, thanks to the fine spirit of friendly and academic cooperation of all who have contributed to these volumes. Without the necessary atmosphere of team-work, prompt attention to correspondence (a major problem with contributors residing in a dozen different countries) the general enthusiasm of all towards the project right from the start, and so on — without all this the task would have been immeasurably more difficult and vastly more time-consuming. My sincere thanks to all my colleagues. The valuable assistance of two draughtsmen requires special mention in view of the considerable amount of work involved in the processing of so heavily illustrated a publication: I am especially indebted to Miss Winifred Mumford for general assistance, the compilation of the maps, re-lettering and re-touching, and her fine renderings. Mr. Erwin Feeken who has worked for me in several other publications did many of the maps, drawings and the lettering of many tables. Photographic work was done mainly by Mr. Ian Cottrell of the Visual Aids Unit of the Australian National University — I am most grateful for the high standards of reproduction he has so painstakingly maintained. Type-setting of Papers No. 1 to 6, 11, 15 and of many passages containing Chinese characters in Papers Nos. 9, 10, 12, 13, 14 and 16 was done by Nichiōsha Printing Company, Tokyo, with the supervisory assistance of the Editor and staff of Monumenta Serica Institute, Department of Oriental Languages, University of California, Los Angeles. Special type for the archaic and obsolete characters in Papers Nos. 3, 5 and 6 were prepared by Tsukiji Design Company, Tokyo, under the supervision of Mr. Matsumaru Michio, Research Officer, Department of Far Eastern History, The Australian National University. We are most grateful for the expert assistance thus received.

The Department of Art History and Archaeology graciously agreed to handle the final details concerning layout, design, and other such technical matters in order to expedite the publication of our papers. In this same connection I should like to record also my personal appreciation of the painstaking work done by Miss Mitsuko Maekawa. Last but not least my sincere thanks to Mrs. Doris Craft who tackled the tremendous task of manuscript typing.

NOEL BARNARD
25th October, 1968

CHAIRMAN'S OPENING REMARKS

L. CARRINGTON GOODRICH

It is my pleasure and privilege to welcome you to this Symposium on the art of Ch'u and its possible influences far beyond its centres in the Yangtze Valley. I do this with the greater freedom as I am not a member of the Department of Art History and Archaeology of Columbia University, nor of The Sackler Fund to Promote Central Asiatic Studies—not even any longer a member of the faculty of Columbia University. I am just a professor emeritus of Chinese who in 1937 happened to visit some of the grave sites outside the city of Ch'ang-sha where important treasures were found, then and later. All of us owe much to Dr. and Mrs. Arthur M. Sackler for their untiring interest in Asiatic art, and to Professor Douglas Fraser, Dr. Noel Barnard, and a number of others who conceived and worked long and hard to bring about this Symposium. I am sure that we shall be the richer for the exchange of ideas which is to take place today and in the days that are to follow.

Many questions will arise, as they did over a decade and a half ago, as to the nature of the art on both sides of the Pacific Basin. Perhaps with the greatly increased archaeological and anthropological data of the years since then some of them will be answered. But doubtless a few will remain to plague us. It is well to recall that an ancient poet of the State of Ch'u asked many questions himself, and hardly expected answers. Let me give you a few quotations, taken from the masterly translation of David Hawkes:

Who was there to pass down the story of the beginning of things in the remote past? What means are there to examine what it was like before heaven above and earth

1

below had taken shape? How is it possible to probe into that age when the light and darkness were still undivided? And how do we know of the chaos of insubstantial form?

What manner of things are the darkness and light? How did the yin *and* yang *commingle? How do they originate things, and how change them?*

Who planned and measured out the round shape and ninefold gates of Heaven? Whose work was this, and who first made it?

How are the Ladle's Handle and the Cord tied together? How was Heaven's Pole raised? How do the Eight Pillars of Heaven keep it up? Why is there a gap in the south-east?

Where do the nine divisions of Heaven each stretch to and where do they join? The ins and outs of their edges are very many. Who knows their number?

How does Heaven coordinate its motions? Where are the twelve Heavenly Houses divided? How are the sun and moon connected with them, and the stars spaced out over them?

The sun sets out from the Valley of Morning and goes to rest in the Vale of Darkness. From the dawn until the time of darkness, how many miles is his journey?

What is the peculiar virtue of the moon, the Brightness of the Night, which causes it to grow once more after its death? What does it advantage it to keep a frog in its belly?

How did the Mother Star get her nine children without a union? Where is Po Ch'iang, the Wind Star, and where does the warm wind live?

What is it whose closing causes the dark and whose opening causes the light? Where does the sun, the Bright God, hide before the Horn proclaims the dawning of the day?

(T'ien-wen, 1-22)*

Questions, questions! The bards of Ch'u were raised on them. It is our business here to see if some light may be thrown on the themes set for our deliberations.

---

* David Hawkes, *Ch'u Tz'u The Songs of the South*, Oxford University Press, 1959. Cited with the kind permission of the author.

MAJOR ASPECTS OF CH'U ARCHAEOLOGY[1]

CHANG KWANG-CHIH

The archaeology of the Ch'u 楚 has no traditional status or boundary, unlike such rigorously defined fields as the archaeology of the Shang, the Minoans, and even the Mayas. Scholars of early China are familiar with a State of Ch'u described in the *Shih-chi* 史記 (ch. 40) that emerged after a legendary ancestry during the reign of Ch'eng Wang 成王 of the Chou toward the end of the second millennium B. C. somewhere in central China. It grew in size and stature during the late Western Chou period, established a capital and power centre near Chiang-ling 江陵 on the Yangtze in modern Hupei in 689, expanded its rule to a vast area from the upper Huai-ho 淮河 to south of Lake Tung-t'ing 洞庭湖, and was finally subjugated by Ch'in 秦 in 223 B. C. Scholars are also well aware of the fact that during its millennium of political independence the Ch'u civilization was highly literary and sophisticated, its artistic achievement rivalling the classical Chinese of the north and culminating in the person of Ch'ü Yüan 屈原 (*circa* 340–280 B. C.) to whom are attributed the famed *Ch'u-tz'u* 楚辭 poems. The archaeological remains of this civilization, known in ancient texts, have only recently been brought to light and at only a handful of localities; thus archaeological definition of the Ch'u has yet to be attempted.

Remains may be attributed to Ch'u when they are discovered in the area known to be under the rule of the State of Ch'u and can be

---

1. Based on the section on Ch'u in the author's *The Archaeology of Ancient China* (revised and enlarged edition, 1968), this paper is a summary of the principal data of Ch'u archaeology, organized according to a programme for further research, and is not the result of such research. The preparation of the manuscript was aided by grants awarded in 1967 by the American Council of Learned Societies–Social Science Research Council and by the Concilium on International and Area Studies at Yale.

dated to the first millennium B. C. This method has greater application for the later periods than for the initial stages because the territory of the State of Ch'u was relatively small in the beginning and its exact location in modern geographical terms is uncertain. Archaeological assemblages verifiably Ch'u in space and time such as those in Ch'ang-sha 長沙 and Shou-hsien 壽縣 .where the word Ch'u is found in inscriptions clearly designating the State, can be used as type assemblages of the Ch'u against which other remains can be measured. Since the largest number of Ch'u finds have been discovered in the Ch'ang-sha area which is unquestionably within the geographic expanse of the *Ch'u-tz'u* poems (*cf.* Yu, 1955 : 64–96),we may use Ch'ang-sha as a type site of Ch'u archaeology, and it may even be appropriate to use the appellation 'Ch'ang-sha Culture' to begin with. In purely archaeo-logical terms, sites with remains substantially unlike Ch'ang-sha finds are probably not Ch'u but those closely similar to Ch'ang-sha may be considered Ch'u sites. In using such a method of identification the archaeologist must bear in mind the diversity of a civilization within itself, such as the differences of various periods and the contrast between the power and religious centres and the rural villages and that between the nucleus of the culture and its peripheries.

As will be described below archaeological sites thus identifiable are found in three main clusters : Hunan, mainly the Hsiang 湘 River Valley but also along the southern shore of Lake Tung-t'ing ; Hupei, in scattered regions in the eastern half of the province, on the Yangtze River and in the lower Han-shui 漢水 Valley ; and the Huai-ho Valley in southeastern Honan and northwestern Anhwei. This vast belt of Ch'u sites must represent the Ch'u civilization at its peak, principally during the late Ch'un-ch'iu and early Chan-kuo periods.

Thus Ch'u sites are known from an area approximately from 25° to 33° North latitude, an area currently dominated by monsoons and characterized by a warm-temperate climate and vegetation. Topograph-ically, all the known sites except those in Shou-hsien are located just above the floodplain, nowhere lower than 50 m above sea level and are strewn along a complex system of waterways that include a major lake, Tung-t'ing, and four major rivers, Yangtze, Hsiang, Han, and Huai. Archaeological and biological evidence gathered in recent years from both North China and Taiwan points to a postglacial hypsithermal interval during which a climate warmer and more moist than at the present prevailed and the coastline was at least several metres higher (and farther inland) than at the present (Chang K. C., 1963 : 35–9 ; Ch'en C. H. *et al.* 1965 ; Tsukada, 1966). By the beginning of the first millennium B. C. this climate optimum had passed its peak ; the beginning of a trend towards desiccation in climate and the accumulated effects of deforestation must have taken their combined toll in the north and effected there a drier and less vegetated landscape. But the Ch'u territory must still have been characterized by large areas of water, a heavy vegetation cover, and perhaps marshlands and very fertile floodplains along the shores of the lake and the banks of the rivers. Ancient texts mention a huge lake called Yün-meng 雲夢 at the site of the present Lake Tung-t'ing but considerably larger and most of the known Ch'u sites encircle this lake's ancient basin; it is certain that this large body of water was a decisive factor in the life of the Ch'u people. The Ch'u are described in ancient texts as rice-planters and fishermen, and archaeological sites are rich in wooden and bamboo artifacts. Life near water is vividly and symbolically described in many poems of *Ch'u-tz'u*. Knowledge of and additional data in environmental sciences will be indispensable for any interpretation in depth of the Ch'u life.

I. SITES

Several tombs attributed to Ch'u in Hunan (Jao, 1958 : 1) and Hupei (Shih, 1955 : 18) are known to have yielded several times in an early historical period, jade objects, inscribed tablets, and paintings but the whereabouts of these objects are of course unknown. In the 1920s and 1930s artifacts apparently of Ch'u type gradually appeared in the antiquarian markets; the tomb plunderers had acquired the bulk of their spoil from two regions, Ch'ang-sha in Hunan and Shou-hsien in Anhwei. Encouraged by collectors who were enamoured of the elegant bronzes, jades, and clay objects that were obviously different from the well-known artifacts from such North China sites as Hsin-cheng 新鄭 and Li-yü 李峪 and by wooden sculptures of a kind unknown in the north, professional plunderers procured during the 1930s and 1940s great numbers of unique relics that gradually found their way into private collections in China and abroad. The best known are the Shou-hsien bronzes in the collection of the Crown Prince of Sweden (Karlbeck, 1955) and the Ch'ang-sha objects of various collectors, notably John Hadley Cox* (Cox, 1939; Chiang, 1949; Shang, 1939).

None of the supposedly Ch'u objects in these well-known collections was taken from excavations supervised by scholars and the contexts of the artifacts were known only by hearsay. It was obvious, however, that the finds included remains from various periods and the initial chronological tasks were to distinguish between pre-Han materials and objects of Han date and later (Cox, 1939; Karlgren, 1941). On the basis of tomb construction, artifact style, type of coinage, geographic location, and the nature of the religion reflected in the artifacts, Ch'en Meng-chia 陳夢家 (Preface in Shang, 1939) concluded that the Ch'ang-sha objects are remains of the late Chan-kuo period. It was generally agreed that the objects from Shou-hsien are dated to the period of 241-223 B.C. when Shou was the last Ch'u capital (e.g. Li C.T., 1936).

Beginning in 1951, archaeological excavations carried out for the most part under professional supervision have been taking place in Ch'ang-sha and sites yielding similar remains have been located in other parts of Hunan, in Hupei, and in southeastern Honan. Ch'u archaeology thus began in earnest. Advances have been made in the last sixteen years in at least the following respects: (1) sites have been excavated by archaeologists and the context and provenance of many

* These items have recently been acquired for The Sackler Collections [Ed].

8

objects are recorded and published; (2) habitation sites as well as tombs have been brought to light; (3) the range of artifacts has widened and the large number of inscribed tablets and bronzes is especially noteworthy; (4) the number of sites has vastly increased and the area of distribution of Ch'u sites is better defined; (5) the large number of sites has enabled the construction of a notable chronological sequence and inscribed objects point to a Ch'un-ch'iu dating of some sites. In other words, even though the recent work has produced more potentials and promises than results, archaeological data have accumulated to such an extent that a characterization of Ch'u civilization by means of archaeology, a temporal-spatial delineation of Ch'u sites, and a study of both the antecedent cultures of Ch'u and its contemporary relationships with other spheres of cultural activities has now become possible. A description of the known Ch'u sites follows (*cf.* also Figure 1):

1. HUNAN

As of 1960 (Kao, 1960), Ch'u sites were known from Hsiang-yin 湘陰 (Chou S. J., 1958b), P'ing-chiang 平江 (Chou S. J., 1958c), Ch'ang-sha, Chu-chou 株州, Hsiang-t'an 湘潭, Hsiang-hsiang 湘鄉, Li-ling 醴陵, Heng-yang 衡陽, Lei-yang 耒陽, and Ch'en-hsien 郴縣 in the Hsiang River valley and Ch'ang-teh 常德 in the Yüan 沅 River valley. Subsequent work further extends the distribution to Shih-men 石門 of the Li 澧 River valley farther to the north (Chou S. J., 1964). More than 1,200 tombs were known by 1960 from Ch'ang-sha alone and about 100 tombs each were recorded for Heng-yang and Ch'ang-teh. These tombs have been arranged into a relatively long sequence of development, as will be described below, and the beginning of the Ch'u civilization in this area south of Lake Tung-t'ing is now pushed back to the middle of the Ch'un-ch'iu period at the latest (about 600 B. C.). Ch'ang-sha, however, remains the best known of the Hunan sites.

9

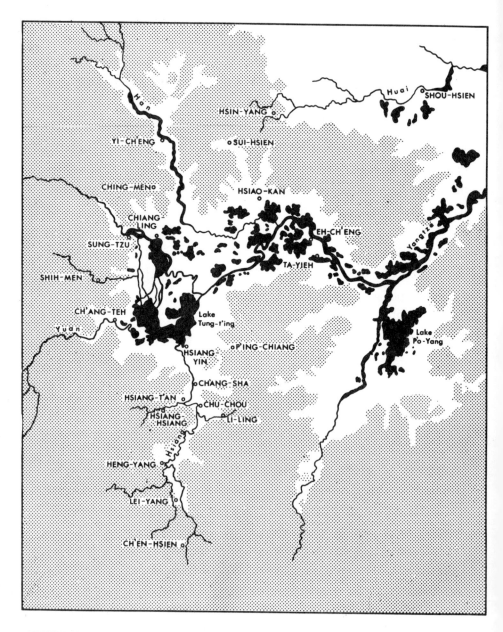

FIGURE 1. Location of Ch'u sites described in the paper. Dotted areas over 50 m in elevation. Solid spots on the Yangtze are areas of water, probably remnants of the ancient Lake Yün-meng.

Ch'ang-sha 長沙

The city of Ch'ang-sha is on the east bank of the Hsiang River at the northern border of the 50 m contour line and at the maximum of the ancient Lake Yün-meng. Ch'ang-sha was probably located at the river mouth and was referred to in contemporary texts as a city of considerable magnitude under the State of Ch'u. Aside from a very small number of storage pits suggestive of habitation areas most of the Ch'u sites are burials; these are found on the ridges and slopes of the low hills in the northern, eastern, and southern suburbs and vicinities of Ch'ang-sha within a radius of some 5 km from the centre of the city. The Ch'u city of Ch'ang-sha, possibly located at the city's present site, remains to be archaeologically identified.

Although the bulk of the known artifacts of Ch'u have come from this region, all their provenances have not been determined. Table 1, on the following two pages, lists all the sites in the area that have been described in the literature.

Other Hsiang River Sites

Hundreds of Ch'u sites are said to have been found in the Hsiang River valley outside Ch'ang-sha but only a few have been described. An ancient town dated to late Chou period is reported from Hsiang-yin, north of Ch'ang-sha (Chou S. J., 1958b) and a habitation site of the Chan-kuo period is known from P'ing-ching 平江, east of Hsiang-yin 湘陰 (Chou S. J., 1958c). Tombs of Ch'ang-sha types are reported from Heng-yang 衡陽 (Li C. K., 1956) and Chu-chou 株州 (Kao, 1959) south of and upstream from Ch'ang-sha. The brief descriptions that are available are inadequate for full information pertaining to these sites but they indicate that Ch'ang-sha-type remains are distributed throughout the Hsiang River valley, south to the southernmost portions of Hunan. Also, these include habitation sites that supplement our knowledge of the Ch'u derived in Ch'ang-sha mainly from burials.

11

Name of site	Location relative to city	Nature of site	Number
Wu-chia-ling 伍家嶺	2 km N	tomb	25
Yang-chia-wan 楊家灣	N	"	1
Sha-hu-ch'iao 沙湖橋	2.5 km N	"	35
Shang-ta-lung 上大壠	"	"	3
Kan-chia-ts'un 甘家村	"	"	7
Hei-shih-tu 黑石渡	"	"	6
Chiao-kung-miao 焦公廟	"	"	9
Wang-chia-lung 王家壠	"	"	2
Ch'en-chia-ta-shan 陳家大山	1 km NE	"	13
		"	4
		"	21
Lieh-shih-kung-yuan 烈士公園	.5 km NE	"	1
		"	1
		"	3
Hsin-ma-t'ou (?) 新碼頭	NE	"	1
Tzu-tan-k'u 子彈庫	E	"	1
		"	35
Liu-chia-ta-shan 柳家大山	E	"	32
Wu-li-p'ai 五里牌	2.25 km E	"	1
		"	3
Yang-chia-shan 楊家山	2.25 km E	"	1
Shih-tzu-ling 識字嶺	.25 km SE	"	34
		"	8
Tso-chia-t'ang 左家塘	SE	"	1
Hsiao-lin-tzu-ch'ung 小林子冲	1 km SE	"	14
Yang-t'ien-hu 仰天湖	.5 km S	"	1
Sao-pa-t'ang 掃把塘	.5 km S	"	1
Tso-chia-kung-shan 左家公山	S	"	31
T'ai-tzu-ch'ung 太子冲	5 km S	storage pits	5
?(tzu) 子	S	tomb	1
Huang-ni-k'eng 黃泥坑	?	"	53
Yüeh-liang-shan 月亮山	?	"	52
Liao-chia-wan 廖家灣	?	"	22
Ma-yüan-ling 麻園嶺	?	"	8
Tzu-t'an-p'u 紫檀舖	?	"	1
?	N & E	storage pits	9

TABLE 1. List of Ch'u sites.

Range of remains	Excavated by	During	References
usual*	IA**	1951–52	Hsia 1952; Hsia, Ch'en, & Wang, 1957
72 inscribed bamboo tablets	CPCO***	1954	Yang, 1954; Wu & Tai, 1957
usual	CPCO	1956	Li & P'eng, 1957
"	"	"	"
"	"	"	"
"	"	"	"
"	"	"	"
"	"	"	"
"	IA	1951–52	Hsia, 1952; Hsia, Ch'en & Wang. 1957
"	CPCO	1956	Chou S. J., 1959
"	CPCO	1957	Chang C. Y., 1958
"	CPCO	1952	Ku, 1954
"	CPCO(?)	1956	Lo T. C., 1958
"	Provincial Bureau of Culture	1957	Chou S. J., 1958a
"	Provincial Museum	1958	Kao & Liu, 1959
silk manuscript	Plundered	1942	Shang, 1964
usual	CPCO	1952–56	Wen, 1959a
"	Provincial Museum	1959	Hunan Museum, 1960
37 inscribed bamboo tablets	IA	1951–52	Hsia, 1952; Hsia, Ch'en & Wang, 1957
usual	Provincial Museum	1959	Lo C., 1960
"	"	1958	Kao & Liu, 1959
"	IA	1951–52	Hsia, 1952; Hsia, Ch'en & Wang, 1957
"	CPCO	1952–56	Wen, 1959a
crossbow mechanism	CPCO	1957	Kao, 1964
usual	"	1957	Chang H. J., 1958
42 inscribed bamboo tablets	"	1952	Anonymous, 1954; Lo F. Y., 1954; Shih, 1955; Tai, 1957; Wu & Tai, 1957
crossbow mechanism	"	1952	Kao, 1964
writing brush	"	1952–56	Wu, 1954; Wu & Tai, 1957; Wen, 1959a
	CPCO(?)	1958	Chou C. J., 1960
	CPCO	1957	Chou & Wen, 1960
usual	"	1952–56	Wen, 1959a
"	"	"	"
"	"	"	"
"	"	"	"
"	"	1956	Wu, 1957
Ch'un-ch'iu	Provincial Museum	1958	Kao & Liu, 1959

*   The usual categories of Ch'u artifacts: stone, pottery, wooden, bamboo, lacquer, bronze, iron, etc.

**   Institute of Archaeology, Academia Sinica (Peiping)

*** Commission for the Preservation of Cultural Objects (of Hunan Province)

Ch'ang-teh 常德

Forty-four tombs of Eastern Chou date were discovered in 1956 on the hills and on hill slopes near ·Teh-shan-chen 德山鎮, a small town on the southern bank of the Yüan 沅 River about 5 km east of Ch'ang-teh city on the northern bank (Wen, 1959b). Eighty-four additional tombs were excavated in the same region during 1958–9 (Yang, 1959 ; 1963). Ch'ang-teh is about 150 km northwest of Ch'ang-sha on the western shore of the Great Lake and both the topography of the burials and their remains are similar to Ch'ang-sha finds. Additional sites are known from farther north along the western shore of the lake ; it is certain that the discovery of Ch'u sites from the hills and river valleys surrounding the Great Lake Yün-meng is only just beginning.

Shih-men 石門

A walled town site was investigated in 1960 in the area of the Wei-hsin 維新 Commune, in Shih-men-hsien near the mouth of River Li 澧, north of Ch'ang-teh (Chou S. J., 1964). The potsherds found here are said to resemble the ones from other Ch'u habitation sites.

2. HUPEI

At this time Hunan is the leading site of Ch'u archaeology because of the prolific remains found in Ch'ang-sha but there is little question that Hupei will eventually be the centre of Ch'u finds, for the major activities recorded in ancient texts of the Ch'u took place north of the Great Lake and the most important Ch'u capitals were situated in central Hupei. Ching Mountain 荊山, said to be the region where the early Ch'u lords rose to eminence and from which Ching 荊, another name of the Ch'u people, was derived, is located at the centre of the province. Tan-yang 丹陽, the first capital, dating back to the end of the second millennium B. C. is sometimes said to be in this area (Hsü, 1960 : 167–70 ; Ch'en P., 1964) and Ying 郢, in the modern city of Chiang-ling or Ching-chou 荊州 on the Yangtze

River at the centre of Hupei, was the State capital of the Ch'u from 689 until 278 B.C.

Archaeological sites in Hupei dated to the Eastern Chou period, however, are yet few and far between. Many Ch'u tombs have apparently been excavated in the province in recent years but much of the data remains unpublished. A brief summary of the known sites, from west to east, follows.

Sung-tzu 松滋

Twenty-seven pit-graves of the Ch'u type were excavated in 1960 on a small knoll near the village of Ta-yen-tsui 大岩嘴 on the southeast bank of the Wei-shui 洈水, a small tributary of the Yangtze, south of Sung-tzu-hsien in southern Hupei, only 75 km north of Shihmen (Ch'eng and Wang, 1966). These are all rectangular graves, either narrow or broad types, in which wooden chambers were built which held wooden coffins. Pottery, bronzes, wooden artifacts, lacquer ware, and jade objects similar to Hunan types were discovered.

Chiang-ling 江陵

Chiang-ling, or Ching-chou, on the Yangtze River in central Hupei has been a pivotal city throughout Chinese history as the gate into the rich southwestern province of Szechwan and the Ch'u capital of Ying is known to be near Chiang-ling, probably at the site of Chinan-ch'eng 紀南城 north of the modern city. Several hundred burial mounds surrounding the Chi-nan-ch'eng site are believed to be the burial places of the Ch'u and fourteen burial areas were excavated between 1961 and 1966. Spectacular finds rivalling or even surpassing those of Ch'ang-sha may very well be expected in this area in the near future to judge from the little that has been published so far (Kuo T.W., 1962; Kuo and Liu, 1964; Hupei Bureau of Culture, 1966; Shih, 1963).

Three tombs — Wang-shan 望山 no. 1, Wang-shan no. 2, and Sha-chung 沙塚 no. 1 — about 7 km northwest of Chi-nan-ch'eng on a low, flat hill were excavated in 1965–6. They are all large and rectangular (9–16 m long, 4–7 wide, 7–8 deep) pit-graves with wooden chambers. Wang-shan 1 has a double chamber and a single coffin;

Wang-shan 2 has two chamber layers and two coffins; and Sha-chung 1 has a single chamber but two coffins. A huge number of artifacts was found in the graves — including 23 inscribed bamboo slips in Wang-shan 1 and 13 in Wang-shan 2. Bronzes, pottery, wooden and bamboo objects, lacquered wooden artifacts and sculptures, and jade objects are many and well-preserved. Of particular interest are a bronze rapier with the inscription, 越王鳩淺 [= 句踐] 自用寶劍 'A valued sword for the personal use of Kou-chien, King of Yüeh' [497-65 B.C.]; a lacquered wooden screen in bas-relief with 51 animal images; a wooden double-headed monster similar to the Ch'ang-sha type; a tool-box full of tools and implements; a bronze lamp base featuring a man riding on a camel; and remains of chestnuts, fresh ginger, and sweet fennel; cherry, apple, and plum pits; melon seeds; and bones of fish, chicken, and animals (Hupei Bureau of Culture, 1966).

Other Hupei Sites

A bronze *ko* 戈 and a bronze sword of late Chou type were found in Ching-men 荊門, some 90 km north of Chiang-ling (Wang Y. P., 1963a); a walled town site attributed to the Ch'u in the local lore was investigated in Yi-ch'eng 宜城 in the middle Han-shui Valley (Wang S. T., 1965); several habitation sites probably of Eastern Chou period have been described in Sui-hsien 隨縣 in northeastern Hupei (Mao and Li, 1959); a large number of Ch'u-type coins was unearthed in Hsiao-kan 孝感 on the lower Han-shui (Ch'eng, 1964; 1965); and tombs of Chan-kuo types were discovered in E-ch'eng 鄂城 and Ta-yeh 大冶 counties in eastern Hupei on the northeastern corner of the Great Lake (Hsiung, 1958; Kuo C., 1959).

The locations of these sites suggest that the distribution of the Ch'u civilization in Hupei is along the shores of the Great Lake Yün-meng in the Yangtze Valley and also along the Han-shui Valley almost as far upstream as the Hupei-Honan border. Whether or not Ch'u sites will be found farther upstream into Honan or even into southern Shensi will bear upon the problem of the origins of the civilization but we must leave this to future explorations.

3. HUAI RIVER VALLEY

The sites described above can be referred to as the Great Lake sites, for these sites in Hunan and Hupei border on the southern, western, and northern shores of the Great Lake. In northeastern Hupei and southeastern Honan the Ta-pieh Mountains 大別山 served as the divide between the Han-shui Valley to the southwest and the Huai River valley to the northeast. The mountain chain decreases in altitude toward the northwest and the Han and the Huai Rivers merge in southern Honan at the source of some of their tributaries. The Chou period sites in this area should be studied with interest, for it is presumably in this area that one will find the link between the Great Lake Ch'u and the Huai River Ch'u.

Thus far, only two sites are known from the Upper Huai that have been attributed to the Ch'u civilization; these are the tombs in Hsin-yang, southeastern Honan, and finds in Shou-hsien, north-western Anhwei.

Hsin-yang 信陽

Two large tombs with wooden chambers were unearthed in 1957 and 1958 on a low hill about 4 km northwest of the town of Ch'ang-t'ai-kuan 長臺關 of Hsin-yang county on the northern bank of the Huai-ho, in southeastern Honan (Pei *et al.* 1957; Ho and Huang, 1958; Honan CPCO, 1959). The tomb construction and the grave goods — including well-preserved wooden sculptures and lacquer ware (Ch'en and Chia, 1958) and bronzes (Ku, 1958) — are closely similar to the Ch'ang-sha finds and the culture represented here has been identified as that of the Ch'u although Kuo Mo-jo 郭沫若 (1958) believes that an inscription on a bronze bell indicates otherwise. Kuo also believes that the tombs can be dated to the late Ch'un-ch'iu period, earlier than the date attributed to the Ch'ang-sha finds. This, as well as the fact that the Hsin-yang tombs are between Ch'ang-sha and Shou-hsien, two regions where Ch'u sites definitely were known, confers unusual importance on the Hsin-yang site in Ch'u archaeology.

17

Shou-hsien 壽 縣

The scattered but highly significant collections of bronzes from Shou-hsien have been mentioned above. There is no question about their being of Ch'u affiliation, for 'quite a number of bronzes are inscribed and refer to the last Ch'u Kings, one of them being Yu Wang 幽王 (237–228 B.C.); the objects must have been deposited between 228 and 222 when Ch'u was annihilated by Ts'in [i. e. Ch'in]' (Karlgren, 1941 : 8; see also Liu, 1935; Chu, 1954). Most of the important finds were traced to a low hill near Chu-chia-chi 朱家集 and in 1934 Li Ching-tan 李景聃 of the Academia Sinica conducted an investigation and obtained some data on the provenance of the artifacts (Li C. T., 1936).

During the last decade a large number of ancient tombs has been unearthed in the area of Shou-hsien and for many of them an Eastern Chou dating has been suggested (e. g. Anhwei CPCO and Anhwei Museum, 1956; Hsiu and Pai, 1959; Ma T. K., 1960; 1963). This area, however, did not come under Ch'u rule until the end of the Chan-kuo period and, unless inscriptions give a definite dating to the finds as in the case of the tomb of the Marquis of Ts'ai 蔡侯, the State affiliation of the finds is difficult to determine. The Chu-chia-chi tomb, therefore, must serve as the stylistic criterion for the study of the other Shou-hsien tombs in terms of Ch'u archaeology.

II.   CHARACTERISTICS OF THE CH'U CULTURE

The archaeological sites enumerated above are either habitation or burial relics. The remains of habitations are few and the sites have not been thoroughly excavated. Their temporal-spatial relationships and their connection with the burial complexes are not clear. The situation in Chiang-ling where clusters of burials are distributed around the walled city site of Chi-nan-ch'eng, is highly suggestive and more information from this area may become available before very long.

Three habitation sites with earthen walls have been located, one in Hupei and two in Hunan, as described above. They have been dated to either Eastern Chou or the period spanning Eastern Chou and early Han. Their physical descriptions can be summarized as follows:

Site	Shape	Orientation	Hang-t'u	N-S length	E-W length	Wall width
Yi-ch'eng 宜城	rect.	N-S, E-W	yes	2000 m	1500 m	24–28 m
Shih-men 石門	rect.	N-S, E-W	?	300 m	600 m	8 m
Lo-ch'eng 羅城	rect.	N-S, E-W	yes	490 m	400 m	14 m

In all three cases apparently no more than a brief reconnaissance was made at the sites and very few details are available. Remains found within and near the walls can be dated to Eastern Chou or Eastern Chou – Han periods and it may be proper to refer to these sites as walled-town sites of the Ch'u. Their rectangular shape and orientation in four cardinal directions place them in the Chinese tradition of town building, as does the construction of the earth walls. The site near Yi-ch'eng, about 7.5 km south-southeast of the modern town, is the largest. There are two openings in each wall and a third opening is found at the southern end of the east wall. At the southeastern corner is an oval earthen platform about 5 m high, described as a lookout tower. At the northeastern part within the walled area is an earthen platform with a flat top, a little over 1 m high and a large burial-like mound is located about 1 km to the south. If this earthen platform was the site of an ancient Ch'u *t'ai*-platform 臺, described in such ancient texts as the *Kuo-yü* 國語, it would again resemble the practice of North China during the Eastern Chou period. Northwest of the town, about 250 m away, is a small hill with scattered potsherds on top. This may or may not have been an adjacent hamlet at the time of the town's occupation. Ancient remains are scattered throughout the town; many of them can be dated to the Han Dynasty such as *pan-liang* 半兩 coins and bronze mirrors of Han style but other items are apparently Eastern Chou, such as cord-marked *li*-tripods 鬲, *yi-pi* 蟻鼻 coins, and sherds of *tou* 豆. Local inhabitants refer to the site as 楚皇城 'Ch'u-huang-ch'eng' (Royal City of the Ch'u) and historical geographers agree that it was probably occupied continuously during the Ch'u and the Han periods although the exact identification with Ch'u cities in the texts is not possible (Wang S.T., 1965).

The walled-town sites at Shih-men and Lo-ch'eng in Hunan are smaller but they can be more reliably dated to the Eastern Chou period on the basis of the cord-marked *li*-tripods and narrow-stemmed *tou* sherds. Judged according to the chronological sequence of artifact types from the Ch'u tombs in Ch'ang-sha (see below) these sites can perhaps be dated to an earlier period within the Eastern Chou range. No other information pertaining to these sites in matters of architectural detail is available. Paintings of houses in lacquer ware (Peking Historical Museum, 1954; Shang, 1955) give some idea about the kind of shelters that were constructed (Figure 2) and an incised scene on a bronze vessel of unknown provenance but possibly of the Ch'u culture according to a special kind of musical instrument it contains (see below) illustrates the kind of superstructures on the earthen platform that could have been built by the Ch'u (Ma C. Y., 1961).

Other habitation sites, possibly of a village-hamlet nature and without remaining earthen walls, are known from Sui-hsien in Hupei (Mao and Li, 1959) and Ch'ang-sha (Chou S. J., 1958a) and P'ing-chiang (Chou S. J., 1958c) in Hunan. Two Sui-hsien sites have been reported; remains are scattered in areas 1,500 × 500 and 1,300 × 800m, on the surface and in pocket-shaped storage pits. Cord-marked reddish and grayish *li*-tripod sherds are the most common finds at the sites. Both the Hunan sites consist of oval or near-oval storage pits. The T'ai-tzu-ch'ung 太子冲 site in Ch'ang-sha has yielded stone knives, grinding stones, and sherds of *li* and *tou*. In the Wung-chiang 瓮江 site on a small hill near P'ing-chiang were found thick ashy layers, sherds, an iron axe, some bronze vessels, two decorated bronze bells, two bronze spades, and a piece of bronze slag. The finds at these sites give a general idea about the nature of the peasant habitations, possible locus of handicrafts, and a use of materials for purposes slightly different from that shown in the tombs.

FIGURE 2. Three painted scenes, spread out, on lacquered wooden boxes. After Peking Historical Museum, 1954.

21

These discoveries of habitation sites are, needless to say, insufficient to represent the kind of urbanism and civic and public structures that can surely be assumed to have existed in the State of Ch'u. But tombs are plentiful and from them are derived the bulk of our knowledge concerning this civilization.[2] The finds show that the Ch'u people built elaborate graves for their dead. The tombs in the entire area were all earthen pits, rectangular in shape, with or without passage ramps. Some pits were narrower than others and may have been earlier in date. The orientation of the tombs was somewhat irregular but north and east headings were relatively more common. The bottom of the pit was often plastered with a layer of limy white clay; chemical analysis undertaken with samples from Ch'ang-sha (Wen, 1959a : 43) has shown that the main components of the clay are SiO_2 (approx. 60%), Al_2O_3 (approx. 20%), and NaOH (approx. 10%). This coating of the floor appears in many cases to have helped preserve the organic remains in the grave. Around the walls of the pit a platform was sometimes built corresponding to the so-called 二層臺 erh-ts'eng-t'ai, or second-level platform, found in northern Chinese Bronze Age tombs. Niches or cavities were excavated in the walls for storing grave goods. At the centre of the tomb a wooden chamber was built, inside which a wooden coffin was placed (Figure 3). Occasionally there is an inner wooden chamber. The coffin was often wrapped with cloths probably a measure against moisture. Grave goods were placed inside the coffin or outside in the chamber and the whole pit was then filled with earth, sometimes compacted by pounding. Both the Shou-hsien and the Hsin-yang tombs were built in a similar manner but the latter had a far more complicated wooden chamber structure, divided into several sections.

Such elaborate burials indicate a highly opulent society and an advanced technology and economy but direct evidence of farming techniques is limited to the occasional discovery of farming implements, including iron hoes and spades. There is no evidence of the use of

2. A summary of the new finds of Ch'u can be found in Cheng, 1963. Illustrated catalogues of Ch'u remains found in recent years include *Ch'u wen-wu chan-lan-huei*, 1954; Tai *et al.* 1958.

22

FIGURE 3. *Wooden coffin and its outer chambers from a Ch'u tomb in Ch'ang-sha. After Kadokawa, 1963: Vol. 12, Fig. 123.*

the plough which had begun both in contemporary North China and in the territory of Yüeh to the east. According to historical records, however, it is fairly certain that in the State of Ch'u as well as Yüeh, rice was cultivated and irrigated by both artificial and natural means. To the northerners of the Eastern Chou period as well as those of subsequent historical periods, the rich natural resources in and south of the Yangtze Valley had been objects of constant envy. Ssu-ma Ch'ien 司馬遷 says in the 'Ho-chih lieh-chuan' 貨殖列傳, *Shih-chi*, that the 'territory of the Ch'u and the Yüeh is vast but the population is sparse. Rice is the staple food and fish the main dish. The people 耕 *keng* with fire and 耨 *ju* with water'. There are various interpretations of the last sentence but whatever the interpretation the use of irrigation for the cultivation of rice can be inferred. The *Shih-chi* also mentions the collecting of molluscan shells for food, a practice substantiated by the finding of shell-tempered pottery at one of the Sui-hsien sites mentioned above. The remains of fish, chicken, and animal bones and of fruits and spices found in Chiang-ling, Hupei, described above, are important in this connection.

In addition to agricultural implements, iron was employed to make axes, adzes, knives, weapons (swords, *chi* halberds 戟, and arrow-heads), and even ornaments (rings and belt hooks) (Huang, 1957). Lead was also melted by the Ch'u smiths who fashioned it into mortuary money and covers for wooden handles. But as far as the archaeological data quantitatively show bronze was still the basic raw material for artifact making. In the tombs, bronze vessels (*ting* tripods 鼎, *tui* tripods 敦, *hu*-vases 壺, and dippers), weapons (swords, *ko*

23

halberds, and spears), horse and chariot fittings, belt-hooks, mirrors, musical instruments (such as bells and possibly kettledrums) and even seals have been found in great numbers. According to an actual count of bronze and iron artifacts uncovered from 209 tombs in the Ch'ang-sha area (Wen, 1959a) their relative frequency of occurrence is as follows :

Bronzes		267
Vessels	24	
Ornaments	58	
Weapons	143	
Musical instruments	3	
Balance and weight sets	16	
Seals	2	
Miscellaneous	13+	
Iron Artifacts		30
Weapons	10+	
Tools-implements	18+	
Miscellaneous	2	

The proportion of bronze and iron objects as shown by grave finds is not necessarily identical with one derived from habitation sites and in habitation sites stone continued to play an important rôle in implement manufacture. A chemical analysis of some specimens of bronze (Wen, 1959a : 48) shows that the ratio of copper, tin, and various other components was completely controlled. A large *ting* tripod unearthed from the Shou-hsien tomb (Liu, 1935) is said to weigh nearly 900 pounds, indicating an advanced level of bronze casting. The large number of bronze artifacts and their distinctive local features rule out the possibility that these bronze artifacts were imports from North China and the possible bronze foundary site in P'ing-chiang-hsien, mentioned above, gives this credence.

In addition to metallurgy of both bronze and iron, the Ch'u civilization was apparently highly developed in handicrafts including ceramics, wood carving, carpentry, bamboo crafts, leatherwork, lacquer work, silk and hemp weaving, and stone and jade crafts. The pottery is predominantly grayish or brownish in colour, either of fine texture or tempered with sand, depending upon the kind of vessel and its use. Glaze was applied in some cases. The basic technique of manufacture was by wheel although hand-made and moulded pieces occur frequently. Most of the pots are plain, but there is also decorated pottery which is corded, stringed, incised, or painted in red, yellow, blue, white, or black in spirals and geometric designs. *Ting* and *li* tripods, *hu* vases, *tou*, bowls, cups, stoves, urns, and so forth are all represented and the occurrence of particular shapes seems to have some chronological significance (Figure 4). Bamboo mats, bows,

FIGURE 4. *Important types of pottery vessels found in Ch'u tombs of Ch'ang-sha A:* li, *B:* ting, *C:* tou, *D:* tui, *E:* hu . *After Hsia, Ch'en, and Wang, 1959.*

suitcases, wooden combs, spears, and leather remains are among the extraordinary discoveries made in recent years. Bamboo was also cut into elongated slips to be written on; dozens of these inscribed slips have been found in tombs along with remains of a writing brush and its container. Wood carving is another noted craft of the Ch'u and wooden human and animal figurines, drums, animal statues with antler horns, and carved boards and screens have been found. Remains of wooden bases for the musical instruments called 瑟 *se* occur in the tombs at Hsin-yang and Chiang-ling. These relics vividly testify that industrial specialization had developed to a considerable extent in this part of China during the Eastern Chou period, a fact which is confirmed by the many handicraft products listed on the bamboo slips – probably tallies of grave goods many of which have since perished.[3]

3.   Of great interest is a toolbox found in Wang-shan Tomb 2 of Chiang-ling (Hupei Bureau of Culture, 1966) : 'Rectangular; height 21 cm, length 84 cm, width 16 cm, thickness 1.5 cm. Has a lid, 1.5 cm thick. In the box were placed 2 wooden-handled bronze engravers, 1 bronze adze, a coarse-grain grinding stone, and a fine-grain grinding stone'.

Supported by agriculture and industry of such high levels of complexity, the political and social organization of the Ch'u was presumably also complex and no doubt deserves the designation of 'State'; and the titles of King and Earl must have been accompanied by corresponding political institutions. Archaeological evidence is lacking in this regard but the remains of bronze coins (*yi-pi-ch'ien*) and bronze scales and weights show considerable social and economic sophistication. Moreover, the Ch'u was certainly a literary civilization; its writing is still to be seen on bamboo tablets, weapons, bronze vessels, and on a piece of silk fabric.

Regarded by their northern Chinese contemporaries as an 'especially religious-minded people', the Ch'u have left an enormous amount of religious-ritual remains. The elaborate burial customs indicate highly complicated rites of ancestor worship. In the ' T'ienwen' 天問, Ch'ü Yüan asks a series of questions concerning the creation of the cosmos and of man, the various deities, and the legendary history of the Ch'u Kings. It has been suggested that this poem was probably composed in the ancestral temple of the Ch'u ruler, on the interior walls of which pictures depicting the various myths and legends were painted and that Ch'ü Yüan asked questions on various topics as he looked at these pictures. Ancestral temples of this nature have yet to be found. But among the Ch'u people there must have been beliefs concerning various spirits and deities, as indicated by the text and illustrations of the Ch'u Silk Manuscript and by the remains of wooden animal statues, wooden human figurines, and wooden anthropomorphic statues with protruding tongues and with antlers. Serpents, phoenix, and dragons were favourite decorative motifs and musical instruments (wooden and bronze drums, bells, various kinds of wooden and bamboo wind and string instruments, and pottery whistles) must have had some ceremonial use.

III. THE CH'U STYLE

The classification of cultures can be carried out at various levels of contrast, and the same archaeological entity can be given a number of labels. Is this civilization, described above according to archaeological evidence, Ch'u? Or is it Chinese? Or is it Chou? Although these labels do not represent mutually exclusive concepts the question is worth asking, for in endeavouring to answer it one must place the Ch'u sites and remains in a series of appropriate temporal, spatial, and classificatory contexts that are yet to be formulated in such a new field of study as Ch'u archaeology.

The traditional view, that by the time of Eastern Chou much of China proper was culturally unified to prepare the road for the Ch'in political unification, has been increasingly borne out by recent archaeological evidence (Cheng, 1963 : 293). Chinese civilization of the Shang and Chou periods needs no definition in the present context and the Chinese identity — in terms of material culture, form of society and government, basic components of the arts, and mythology — of the Ch'u requires no argument. Was Ch'u, however, merely a regional segment of the Chinese civilization of the Eastern Chou period and in substance and form indistinguishable from the rest of Chinese civilization of the time? Or did it have its own distinctive style contrasting with other styles? At first glance the question may appear superfluous, for of course everyone knows that Ch'u civilization is different from the more 'classical' civilization in the north. But in concrete and specific archaeological terms a *Ch'u style* has yet to be characterized. Michael Sullivan (1961) speaks of Ch'u art as 'a quite different style' (p. 69) that is characterized by 'elegance, refinement, and verve', (p. 72); and William Watson (1962 : 60–7) identifies the Huai style as the art style of the Ch'u State and characterizes the Huai style on the basis of the Shou-hsien bronzes (see also Watson, 1961 : 167–80). If these are inadequate — if accurate — descriptions of what the Ch'u style really is, it is only partially because the data are scanty and recent. It may seem curious that the effort to characterize the civilizational style of a State with an areal expanse greater than a third of civilized China during the Eastern Chou period has yet to be undertaken but it is largely because the issues are confusing and questions are difficult to formulate.

An analysis of the Ch'u civilization, contrasted with the classical civilization in the north, can be undertaken in at least the following directions: ethnic identity, government, cultural ecology, and cultural style. To· discuss these different but overlapping dimensions of the Ch'u civilization one cannot avoid taking textual information into account but we shall confine ourselves below to the archaeological evidence and use textual information only minimally and with reference to the archaeological data.

The Ch'u Kings trace their ancestry to Chu Jung 祝融 Minister of Fire, in the legendary court of Ti K'u 帝嚳 and ultimately to Huang Ti 黃帝, the Yellow Emperor, Ultimate Ancestor of all ancient Chinese rulers. Despite efforts to derive the Ch'u ancestry from an eastern group (e. g. Hu Hou-hsüen 胡厚宣) most historians are convinced that the Ch'u emanated from the region of Shensi and the area of the Chou in the northwest (Ch'en P., 1964; Ch'in, 1958). The expansion of the Ch'u State, to judge from the general locations of the various capitals, appears to have been from northwest to southeast. In other words, the Ch'u rulers seem to have descended from an ancestor in common with the Chou. This is essentially a historic problem and the archaeological significance of it will be discussed later. But for the sake of argument it can be stated as an accepted fact that the Ch'u rulers were Chinese.

However, the Ch'u rulers apparently were less Chinese than the rulers of most northern States. In both the ' Ch'u-yü ' 楚語 of the Kuo-yü and the Shih-chi the Ch'u themselves make the statement that ' we are Man Yi 蠻夷 barbarians '. The Ch'u royalty married into northern Chinese States (e. g., Ch'in 秦, Ts'ai 蔡) but Hsi Fu 析父 in the ' Ch'u-shih-chia ' 楚世家 of the Shih-chi made it clear that the Ch'u did not enjoy the same privileges from the Chou royalty as did such other States as Ch'i 齊, Chin 晋, Lu 魯, and Wei 衞. If, as Ling Shun-sheng 凌純聲 says (1954 : 407 ; 1960 : 416) there were diverse ethnic elements in Ch'u, and rulers and ruled belonged to different ethnic groups, it is possible that the " we " in the statement ' we are Man Yi ' referred to the Ch'u people rather than the Ch'u court. In archaeological terms we have not yet isolated a single

Ch'u group, let alone several different strains and unless and until a number of different styles can be isolated from the remains in the future, our discussions must assume a single Ch'u culture. This culture is based upon the same legendary foundation as the civilization in the north and it appears to use the same language. Two principal texts written in the Ch'u language are known : the *Ch'u-tz'u* and the Ch'u Silk Manuscript found in Ch'ang-sha. In grammar and lexical composition these texts are as Chinese as any Chou texts found in the north. Inscriptions found on the bronzes and on bamboo slips are apparently of the identical language. It may be said that this merely proves that the Ch'u people were assimilated by the northern Chinese linguistically but until the evidence of a previous language is found, there is no basis for arguing its existence. It is true, as Mencius stated, that the language spoken in Ch'u was different from that of Ch'i and that some Ch'u words recorded in the *Tso-chuan* 左傳 (Hsüan Kung 宣公, fourth year) and in the *Ch'u-tz'u* apparently differed from comparable words in the north but such differences are relatively trivial, they can be dialectical and do not point to a different and separate language. The inscriptions found on Ch'u remains are stylistically identical with inscriptions elsewhere in China at the time and only the prevalence of characters with exaggerated bird compounds (鳥篆 *niao-chuan* ' bird-script ') is a Ch'u character (Wen, 1959a : 58). In short, there is no credible archaeological evidence that the Ch'u people were of a different ethnic group from the contemporary Chinese in the north.

But the Ch'u culture differs from the contemporary northern Chinese civilization in significant ways. First, Ch'u was a separate State and its governmental form could not help having certain idiosyncracies. *Tso-chuan* (Wen Kung 文公 First Year) and the *Shih-chi* mention that succession in Ch'u often goes to junior sons. This may mean an earlier departure of sons from the parental residence and a more mobile and flexible type of family structure. The basic components of settlements and the pattern of urbanization and State rule seem to be identical with those of the north, to judge from the little information that there is from archaeology but it is significant that the Ch'u currency, 郢爰 *ying-yuan* and *yi-pi-ch'ien*, is radically different in form from the northern coins. Possibly the Ch'u had a self-contained and independent economic network.

Perhaps the natural environment accounts for much of the difference in economic and subsistence patterns between Ch'u and the north. The *Shih-chi* (vol. 129) says that the Ch'u and Yüeh area was vast and abundant in rice, fish, and shellfish, that the population was sparse, food was adequate without trade, and starvation was unheard of. Because of this, however, Ssu-ma Ch'ien claims that life was easy without the necessity of accumulating wealth and 'south of the Yangtze and the Huai-ho no one is either dead from starvation or extremely rich'. Archaeology will help on the latter point when more data from habitation sites become available but there is variation in the elaboration of tomb construction and the amounts of grave goods do indicate a life of considerable abundance. Today, most of South China receives more than fifty inches of rainfall annually but north of the Tsin-ling there is a sharp drop to twenty inches or less. In the Yangtze Valley the growing season continues for 250 days of the year but in the Huang-ho delta it is 225 days and even less west of the delta (Cressey, 1955 : 66, 69). Two thousand years ago these figures may have been different but the north-south difference must have been the same. With its abundance of water, the shores of the Great Lake were able to support a powerful State whose territorial expansion eventually reached imperial proportions. The 'elegance, refinement, and verve' of its art and the complexity of its industries and handicrafts testify to the advanced state of Ch'u techniculture and also to a considerable specialization of status and rôle of its people.

There is little question that the variety and sophistication of Ch'u handicrafts surpassed the contemporary north in many areas. Actual remains of silk clothing and the abundance of characters with a 'silk' radical (Wen, 1959a : 58) indicate the importance of the silk industry. Although lacquerware was found widely in China during the Chan-kuo period and had centres of production probably in central Honan or Szechwan or both, 'no site has yielded so many lacquers of late Eastern Chou and Han as did Ch'ang-sha in Hunan' (Loehr, 1965 : 72). Manufacture of lacquerware requires special wood materials and technical skill of the highest sophistication (T'an, 1953) and it alone tells much about the state of Ch'u industry. In form, the lacquered winged cups, or 羽觴 *yü-shang* mentioned in the *Ch'u-tz'u* is particularly distinctive. On the bottom of the winged cups are often incised characters specifying the locale of the manufacturer (Shang, 1939 : 24-5); quite possibly the techniques for their making were the treasured possession of families, clans, or guilds.

In most items of material culture other than the above the Ch'u shared identical forms and styles with their northern contemporaries but there are certainly areas of distinction. Many wooden figurines of humans show tattooed faces (Figure 5); these were not necessarily absent in the north but were apparently rare. Ch'u sites have yielded the largest number of bronze mirrors (Li C. K., 1957) and the earliest archaeological remains of crossbows were found in this area (Kao, 1964). Some scholars regard the crossbow as a Ch'u invention (T'ang, 1958; Chou C. C., 1961).

But it is the area of religion and art that contrasts the Ch'u most sharply with the northern Chinese. To the northern Chinese the Ch'u appeared to be particularly 'possessed by a belief in shamanism and ghosts and of elaborate rituals' (*Han-shu* 漢書, 'Ti-li-chih' 地理志). From the *Ch'u-tz'u* itself one gathers that 'in Ch'u the function and status of the witch or 'shaman' (巫 *wu*), who could draw down the gods of mountains, rivers, and stars, or the spirits of the sick or the dead by means of dancing or incantations, seem to have been more important than elsewhere' (Hawkes, 1959 : 9). There is much vivid and realistic description in the *Ch'u-tz'u* of ritual scenes and divination undertaken by the local inhabitants (Waley, 1955; Yu, 1955 : 268-9) and a world view in which nature, the other world, and fantasy are prominently featured throughout the entire piece of work (Yu, 1955 : 9). Archaeologically this is borne

31

FIGURE 5. Dresses and facial tattoo of wooden human figurines found in Ch'u tombs of Ch'ang-sha (A: after Hsia, Ch'en, and Wang. 1959; B-E: after Chiang. 1949).

out by the elaborate wooden burial constructions, the abundant goods in the graves, the great variety of elaborate musical instruments (Wang S. H., 1958), the many fantastic animals and mythical figures in the decorative art of Ch'u remains (Figure 6) and the Ch'u Silk Manuscript itself. Much of this is also in evidence in burials in the north but in Ch'u sites it is carried to an even greater degree, and the different combination of pottery vessels (*li* + 缽 *po* + *hu*, *li* + *po* + *hu* + *tou*, or *ting* + *tui* + *hu* in Ch'u as against *li* + *tou* + 罍 *lei*, *li* + *tou* + 盂 *yu* + 尊 *tsun*, or *li* + *tou* + *hu* in North China tombs of the same period) must suggest difference in ritual attitude toward burial and toward the dead (Wen, 1959a : 57).

In the area of visual art one may enumerate the following significant components.

Wooden human figures Realistic carved figures of men and women are often found in tombs (Figure 7). The *Shih-chi* (Meng-ch'ang-chün chüan 孟嘗君傳) mentions wooden and clay human figurines in the north and tombs from the Chan-kuo period in northern China have yielded figures of clay. In Ch'u sites usually only wooden figures are found. These may represent retainers to be buried with the dead, or they may be ancestral images.

Images of monsters Fantastic images, apparently of mythological derivation, are frequently found and are highly distinctive. In some cases their identity cannot be deciphered. Sometimes they are tiger-like monsters with antlers, or animals in human postures. Tongues are often protruding — to show contempt, frighten, or serve some unknown purpose (Figure 8). Ling Shun-sheng (1956) has shown that the protruding tongue motif is common in the southern Pacific; he thinks it indicates historical connections of the Ch'u with the Pacific peoples but he has not looked into its symbolic meaning. In the Ch'u Silk Manuscript there is also a monster figure with three heads. The *Shan-hai-ching* 山海經 mentions peoples in the south with split tongues and double heads. and also 'deities' with horns. The meaning of these monsters in Ch'u art requires further study but there appears to be little doubt that they suggest a distinctive Ch'u religious and mythological feature. No representations of faces with

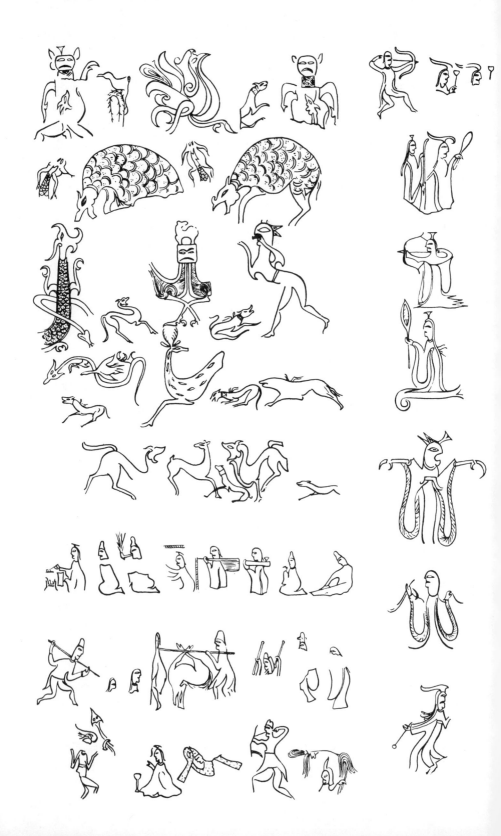

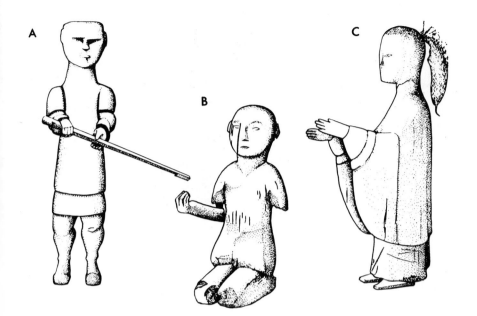

FIGURE 7. *Wooden human figurines from Ch'u tombs (A: Ch'ang-sha after Chiang, 1949; B, C: Hsin-yang, after P'ei, Chang, and Chia, 1957).*

protruding tongues are known in North China until the Han Dynasty (Yin, 1960) and no archaeological remains of fantastic animals with two horns have come to light. Horned human figures appear in the north in Eastern Chou bronze art but these and the Ch'u horned fantastic animals are not necessarily comparable.

Birds   In decorative art there is no other single element more prevailing than the bird: solitary and dominant, or in pairs, or gracefully stylized (often in spiral shapes) into repetitive components of band or area décors (Figure 9). Most of the birds have a plume on the head and long feathers hanging below; the term 鳳 *feng* (phoenix) may be justified. Sullivan (1961 : 71) says ' the bird motif is one of many indications of Changsha's connections with South China and Tonkin', and it gives some credence to the view of some that the Ch'u and the Shang were closely related.

Combination of birds and other (fantastic and realistic) animals   Birds in Ch'u art are often combined with other animals — with a pair of serpents in a wooden sculpture in the collection of the Cleveland

FIGURE 6.   *Painted human and animal figures on a lacquered wooden se found in a Ch'u tomb of Hsin-yang. After Ch'en and Chia, 1958.*

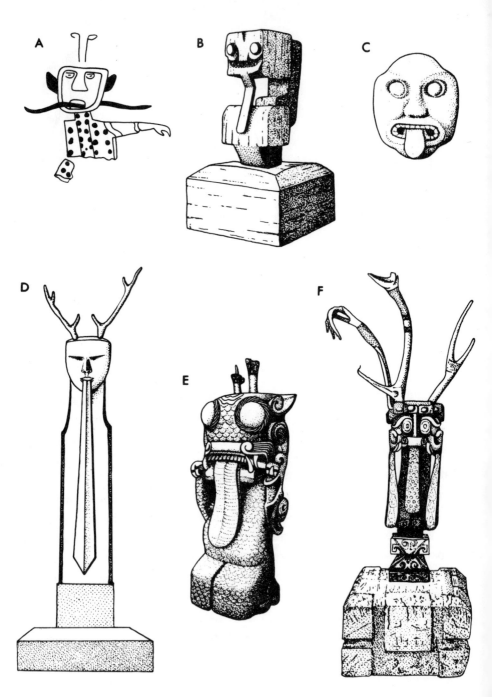

FIGURE 8. *Human and monster images with protruding tongues found in Ch'u tombs* A: Ch'ang
sha, Ch'u Silk Manuscript, after Shang, 1964; B-D, F: Ch'ang-Sha, after Chiang, 1949; E: Hsin
yang, after P'ei, Chang, and Chia, 1957. C is of soap-stone, the remainder are of wood.

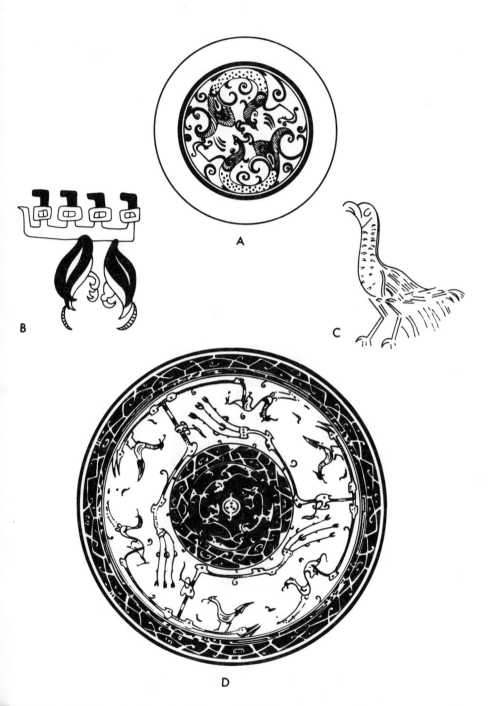

FIGURE 9. Birds in various forms in Ch'u art · A, D: Ch'ang-sha, painted lacquer dishes, after Peking Historical Museum, 1954; B: Ch'ang-sha, Ch'u Silk Manuscript, after Shang, 1964; C: Interior decoration of a winged cup, Singer Collection, after Loehr, 1965.

Museum of Fine Arts; a *lung* 龍 image in a silk painting uncovered
from the site at Ch'en-chia-ta-shan 陳家大山 near Ch'ang-sha
(Figure 10 after *Ch'u wen-wu chan-lan-huei*, 1954); a pair of tigers

FIGURE 10. *Silk painting of lady, dragon, and bird found
in a Ch'u tomb at Ch'en-chia-ta-shan, Ch'ang-sha. After* Ch'u
wen-wu chan-lan-huei, *1954.*

in the wooden drum-frames found in Ch'ang-sha, Chiang-ling, and
Hsin-yang (Figure 11 after Yüan, 1963; Chia, 1964; Kuo and Liu,
1964; Hupei Bureau of Culture, 1966).

Elements of Ch'u art are certainly not confined to the above, for
geometric patterns of many sorts, a decorative style of inscriptions

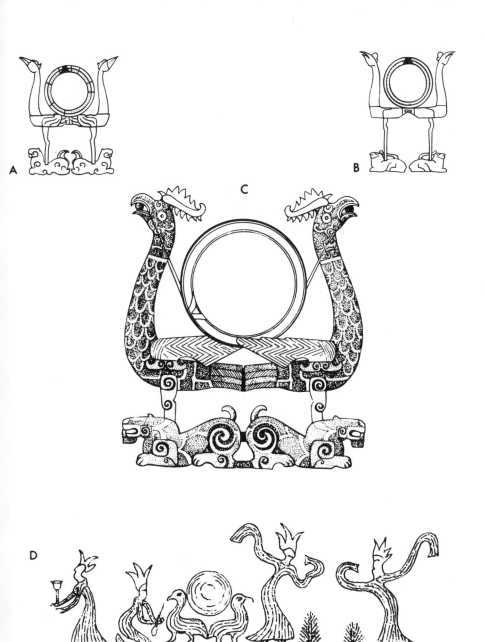

FIGURE 11. Wooden sculptures of tigers and birds, probably used as drum supports in the manner shown in the dancing scene at bottom, found in Ch'u tombs A: Ch'u tomb No. 4 at P'ai-ma-shan, Chiang-ling, Hupei, after Kuo and Liu, 1964; B: Ch'u tomb No. 34 at Keh-p'i-ssu, Chiang-ling, after Kuo and Liu, 1964; C: Ch'u tomb No. 1 at Hsin-yang, Honan, after Chia, 1964 and Ho and Huang, 1958; D: enlarged from a segment of a long scene illustrated in Ma C. Y., 1961.

39

for weapons, incised or painted scenes on bronzes and lacquerware, and other features are also present. In these, however, distinctively Ch'u patterns have yet to be isolated.

IV. CHRONOLOGY AND HISTORY OF DEVELOPMENT

The civilization characterized above according to archaeological evidence was located in the middle Yangtze on the shores of the Great Lake, in the valleys of the major Yangtze tributaries in Hunan and Hupei and in the upper Huai-ho northeast of the Ta-pieh Mountains. In time, there is meagre stratigraphic evidence in Ch'ang-sha (Hsia, Ch'en and Wang, 1957 : 69) that the Ch'u tombs post-date the local Neolithic culture characterized by polished stone implements and geometric-stamped pottery. No such scientific and independent evidence as radiocarbon dates is available to place the archaeological Ch'u civilization within an absolute time-scale to show throughout the area exactly at what point or points the Neolithic culture ended and the Ch'u civilization began. The question at what time Ch'u gave way to Han is relatively straight-forward – though by no means simple – and we can begin the chronological discussion at the lower end.

The last Ch'u capital at Shou-ch'un 壽 春 fell to the imperial army of the Ch'in Dynasty in 223 B. C., and a few decades later the entire Ch'u area came under the rule of the Han Empire. The Ch'u civilization was not, however, terminated or wiped out and replaced by a different Ch'in or Han civilization. In the Ch'ang-sha area the archaeological Ch'u civilization has been shown to continue in the same sequence of cultural development without appreciable interruption (Hsia, Ch'en and Wang, 1957 : 163). To be sure, the State of Ch'u gave way to. the Ch'in and Han Empires and two archaeological phenomena are indicative of this changeover of government : the appearance in the graves of large numbers of mortuary *pan-liang* coins of clay ; and the drastic reduction and, in many cases, total disappearance of weapons of bronze and iron of all kinds in the archaeological inventory. Other changes are noticeable in the kind of artifacts found in the tombs (such as the replacement of pottery *tui* by square jars, minor changes in the attributes of *ting* tripods, and new stylistic developments in mirror typology) but these are minor in the beginning and do not constitute any drastic break from the Ch'u base (Kao, 1960 : 34–5). It would not be accurate to say that around 200 B. C. in the area of Ch'u the Ch'u civilization suddenly came to an end. It is possible, however, to use 200 B. C. as a chronological boundary to delineate the lower limits of an archaeological Ch'u civilization that flowered under the Ch'u State.

How far back in time can we trace the archaeological Ch'u civilization as characterized above? As we said in the beginning, reliable historical records place the initial establishment of the State of Ch'u at Tan-yang at the time of Ch'eng Wang of Chou, or about 1100 B. C. During the reign of Yi Wang 夷 王 of Chou or of Hsiung-ch'ü 熊 渠 of Ch'u, Ch'u power appears to have reached most of central Hupei in the valleys of the Yangtze and Han rivers. Ying, on the middle Yangtze, became a capital in 689 B. C. and the further expansion of Ch'u to the east culminated in 606 the year when Ch'u had the imprudence and audacity to express explicit curiosity and interest in the ceremonial *ting* treasures of the Royal Chou. Thus it appears that the period of Western Chou witnessed the gradual expansion of the Ch'u power from central Hupei outward and that by the time of the Ch'un-ch'iu period at the latest all of Hupei, much of Hunan, southern Honan, and northeastern Anhwei came under Ch'u rule.

The Ch'u remains in the area of maximal distribution as described above, therefore, are in all likelihood confined to the period of Eastern Chou. In the early years of the study of Ch'ang-sha finds all the Ch'u remains in the region were dated to the Chan-kuo period, i. e. between about 450 and 200 B. C. (Ch'en's Preface in Shang, 1939). Recent work at Ch'ang-sha shows, however, that a long sequence of cultural development apparently took place in this area prior to 200 B. C. — a sequence not likely to have been entirely restricted to this short period of 250 years. The most recent summary of. the typological development of the Ch'ang-sha finds is given below in full (Kao, 1960 : 33-4) :

> Ch'u tombs of Ch'ang-sha can be grouped into three chronological periods : Early, Middle, and Late.
>
> *Early Period*
>
> Corresponding in time to the Ch'un-ch'iu or to early Chan-kuo. About 100 tombs, located close to the city. Usually small in size, the tombs are vertical pit-graves. Most of the wall niches are at the head end but a few have side-niches and waist-pits. A few have stairs and passage ramps. The fill of the graves is usually reddish and rarely was it pounded. Most of the pottery is soft, decorated with cord-marks and circumferential string-marks (弦 紋 *hsüan wen*) but there are a few hard-pottery and thin brown-glazed pots decorated with check- and *-marks. The following associations of vessel forms are usual : *li + po + hu + tou + kuan; lei + po + tou;* and *hu + po + tou + kuan.* The most typical forms are *li*-tripods, *lei*-pots, and cord-marked, round-bottomed *hu*-pots. *Tou* (pedestalled bowls) are also common. Bronze mirrors are plain or at most decorated with single ring or simple feather patterns and four T-pattern designs. Bronze swords include the following types : yellow, short daggers ; rapiers with hollow handles ; rapiers with solid handles with two hoops ; swords cast in two different colours ; and swords with turquoise inlaid patterns. Bronze spear-heads, axes, and belt-hooks are also found. Iron implements include spades, hoes, and knives, all found near the bottom of graves, probably buried intentionally. Iron knives and pottery *li* go together, and iron hoe-tips and *lei* go together. *Li* and *lei* are sometimes found together, but as a rule *li* is earlier.
>
> *Middle Period*
>
> Largely corresponding to the early Chan-kuo period, tombs of this period number over six hundred. Small

pit-graves are still the main type of tombs but larger, wider graves and graves with passage ramps grew in number. Niches are often placed at the sides. Pottery *ting*, *tui*, and *hu* occur in association; each tomb has from one to four sets of such pottery combination. *Li* is completely replaced by *ting*. Other pottery artifacts include dippers, *tou*, bowls, *kuan-* 錇 *p'ou-*, and 盂 *yü-* pots, and spindle whorls. In addition to the plain and the T-pattern types, bronze mirrors are decorated in the following patterns: sheer background designs; four-leaf designs; compound lozenges; and complicated T-pattern designs. Iron implements increased in number and variety. Hoe, spade, pounder, adze, knife, and other implements are found and weapons include bronze *ko*-halberds, spearheads, swords, arrow-heads, and others. Also brought to light from tombs of this period are scale weights, seals, bells, containers, rings, and other bronze objects; boxes, cases, winged cups, and other lacquerware objects; and ornaments of stone, jade, agate, and glass.

Late Period

More than four hundred tombs of this Late Period have been excavated; these correspond in time to late Chan-kuo period. There is further decrease of narrow rectangular tombs and increase of broader ones. (The proportion is about one quarter of the former type and three quarters of the latter). White *kaoling* clay was used to seal the wooden chambers; more than forty tombs still have their wooden chambers intact. Head-niches are fewer and side-niches increase. A few cave-chamber graves and multiple burials also occur. The wooden chamber and coffin were made of planks of cypress and cedar (*nanmu*) attached together by means of elaborate and well-made tenons and mortices. Cases of pivotable covers are known. Some coffins are wrapped in silk belts and mats cover a few outer coffins or chambers.

In pottery the association of *ting* + *tui* + *hu* continues and a new set (*ting* + 盉 *ho* + *hu*) appears. New pottery forms appear, such as square vessels, incense burners, shallow dishes, and other types. Bronze mirror decorations grew more complicated and elaborate : compound arcs, animal figures, dragon designs, and phoenix designs. Many bronze weapons such as *ko*-halberds, swords, and spear-heads are elaborately decorated and many have incised and cast inscriptions, including bird-style characters. *Ko*-halberds with long and four-perforation necks, bronze *chi*-halberds, and bronze cross-bow mechanisms appear at this time. Bronze vessels include *ting*, *hu*, flat *hu*, and various types of shallow dishes ; the decorative designs on *hu* and flat *hu* are fine and elaborate. Other bronze objects include scales, weights, seals, and belt-hooks. Iron implements include hoes, saws, knives, picks, pounders, and other types, and iron swords, *chi*-halberds, and arrow-heads begin to prevail. Iron was even used for such utilitarian objects as *ting*, cup, and iron-footed bronze *ting* tripods. Lacquerware was at its peak : shield, bow, winged cup, shallow dish, box, case, small table, drum, sword-sheath ; both the lacquerware technology and its decoration are at their heights. Many wooden objects are found : human figures, monster animals, combs, axes, swords, sword-boxes, arrow-containers and other types all showing a high level of sculpture art. There is a wide variety of silk textiles, and embroidery in various geometric and realistic designs was prevailing. Leather objects include belts, saddle-like objects and other types. In addition, there are writing brushes of hair, inscribed bamboo tablets, pasteglass, and jade carvings.

The above chronological sequence is a relative one apparently based primarily upon typological grounds (see also Kao, 1962; Wen, 1959a: 55-6). It is nevertheless useful for dating specific tombs and objects contained in tombs on a relative basis; for instance, the Ch'u Silk Manuscript of Ch'ang-sha is allegedly found in association with a pottery set of *ting* + *tui* + *hu* and on these grounds the tomb from which it was found could be dated to either the Middle Period or an early part of the Late Period (An and Ch'en, 1963: 59-60; Shang, 1964: 19). The reference of such a relative sequence to an absolute time scale, however, is uncertain. The Early Period of Ch'ang-sha has been tentatively dated to the Ch'un-ch'iu period. *Li*-tripods, one of its diagnostic features, appeared in the area as early as the Neolithic period and the shapes of *li* from Ch'ang-sha tombs are identical with the cord-marked *li*-tripods found at the town site of Lo, traditionally attributed to the site of the Lo of the Ch'un-ch'iu period. A few iron implements were found at the bottom of the graves, apparently intentional grave goods, as against iron implements of later periods that were found in the fill of the tombs. Iron may have begun in North China around 600 B.C. or slightly earlier (van der Merwe, 1966: 132) but in the beginning because of its rarity was probably regarded as more precious and valuable than in later periods when it was used widely and manufactured more cheaply.

The possibility of a Ch'un-ch'iu dating of the Ch'u remains at Ch'ang-sha known at present is strengthened by the finding at Hsin-yang. Here an iron belt hook was brought to light indicating an early stage of iron use. One of the bronze bells found at Tomb No. 1 in 1957 has the following inscription: 佳劉篙屈柰晋人，救戎于楚竟 *Wei Hsing-Yi ch'ü-ti Chin-jen, chiu Jung yü Ch'u-ching* ('Hsing Yi stopped the Chin's attack and rescued the Jung in the Ch'u territory'). Kuo Mo-jo (1958) believes this refers to the same event recorded in *Tso-chuan* under the entry of 525 B.C. indicating that the bell was cast toward the end of the Ch'un-ch'iu period but earlier than Chan-kuo. Kuo believes that for this reason, ' we should not regard all Ch'u tombs at Ch'ang-sha as being of the Chan-kuo

45

period. Therefore, we should not date the Hsin-yang tomb according to the Ch'ang-sha scale but rather should use the Hsin-yang tomb to date some Ch'ang-sha tombs '.

Typological sequences of Ch'u remains similar to Ch'ang-sha can be formulated from Ch'ang-teh also (Kao, 1960 : 34) and it appears certain that the archaeological Ch'u civilization as it is now known spanned the period from about 600 B. C. through about 200 B. C. in the wide area from the Hsiang-chiang to the Huai-ho. This is in broad agreement with the historical information.

The nature and spatial locus of the antecedent culture to the archaeological Ch'u described above are far from clear. In the area of Ch'u distribution the earliest prehistoric culture is the rice-growing, painted pottery-making Ch'ü-chia-ling 屈家嶺 Culture that centred in the lower Han-shui Valley of eastern Hupei but extended westward into the middle Yangtze of central Hupei. Its influence is seen in eastern Szechwan (Chang Y. P., *et al.* 1965 : 75). This was followed by a Lungshan 龍山 Culture characterized by the black pottery (Chou S. J., 1962 ; Chang Y. P., 1962a ; 1962b) which in turn was replaced, at least in the southern part of the area, by the Geometric Ware (Hsia, Ch'en and Wang, 1957 : 69). In other words, the Great Lake area had a long Neolithic sequence of Lungshanoid (Ch'ü-chia-ling) — Lungshan — Geometric sequence, the same sequence as that of the southeastern coast (Chang K. C., 1959 ; 1964).

Beginning around 1500 B. C. at the latest, the bronze cultures of North China extended their influence into the Han-shui and the Yangtze Valleys and bronze assemblages of Shang and Western Chou (Chang K. C., 1963 ; Li C., 1963 ; Wang Y. P., 1963b ; Kuo M. J., 1963 ; Chou S. J., 1962) types have been found in the Han-shui Valley and farther up the Yangtze in Szechwan (Chang K. C., 1963: 276). The mechanisms of the bronze culture influence in the middle Yangtze are not yet clear nor are the consequences in the local cultural history known but apparently a Bronze Age civilization gradually began to take root in a basically Neolithic context. Until greater numbers of sites are known and thoroughly investigated, the crucial period of Western Chou will remain unknown in the Hupei sequence, and the origin of the Ch'u civilization will not be revealed in archaeological terms.

BIBLIOGRAPHY

Anonymous
  1954 'Ch'ang-sha Yang-t'ien-hu Chan-kuo-mu fa-hsien ta-p'i chu-chien chi ts'ai-hui mu-yung tiao-k'o hua-pan' 長沙仰天湖戰國墓大批竹簡及彩繪木俑雕刻花板, *WW* 1954.3 : 53-9.
An Chih-min and Ch'en Kung-jou 安志敏・陳公柔
  1963 'Ch'ang-sha Chan-kuo tseng-shu chi ch'i yu-kuan wen-t'i' 長沙戰國繒書及其有關問題, *WW* 1963.9 : 48-60.
An-hwei CPCO and An-hwei Museum
  1956 Shou-hsien Ts'ai-hou-mu ch'u-t'u yi-wu 壽縣蔡侯墓出土遺物, 考古學專刊, 乙種第五號. Peking.
Chang Chung-yi 張中一
  1958 'Hu-nan Ch'ang-sha Ch'en-chia-ta-shan Chan-kuo mu-tsang ch'ing-li chien-pao' 湖南長沙陳家大山戰國墓葬清理簡報, *KK* 1958.9 : 57-61.
Chang Hsin-ju 張鑫如
  1958 'Hu-nan Ch'ang-sha Hsiao-lin-tzu-ch'ung-kung-ti Chan-kuo-Tung-Han-T'ang-mu ch'ing-li chien-pao' 湖南長沙小林子冲工地戰國東漢唐墓清理簡報, *KK* 1958.12 : 28-34.
Chang Kwang-chih 張光直
  1959 'Hua-nan shih-ch'ien min-tsu wen-hua-shih t'i-kang' 華南史前民族文化史提綱, 中央研究院民族學研究所集刊, *BAS* 7 : 43-103. Taipei.
  1963 *The Archaeology of Ancient China*, Yale University Press, New Haven and London.
  1964 'Prehistoric and early historic culture horizons and traditions in South China', *Current Anthropology*, 5 : 359, 368-75, 399-400.
Chang Yün-p'eng 張雲鵬
  1962a 'Hu-pei Ch'i-ch'un Mao-chia-tsui Hsi-Chou mu-kou chien-chu' 湖北蘄春毛家嘴西周木構建築, *KK* 1962.1 : 1-9.
  1962b 'Hu-pei Huang-kang Lo-ssu-shan yi-chih ti t'an-chüeh' 湖北黃岡螺螄山遺址的探掘, *KK* 1962.7 : 339-44.
  1965 *Ching-shan Chü-chia-ling* 京山屈家嶺, 中國田野考古報告集, 考古學專刊, 丁種第十七號, Peking.
Ch'en Ch'eng-huei, Ch'en Sho-min and Chou K'un-shu 陳承惠・陳碩民・周昆叔
  1965 'Liao-tung-pan-tao P'u-lan-tien fu-chin han ku lien tzu ti ch'üan hsin-shih ch'en-chi-wu ti pao-fen fen-hsi' 遼東半島普蘭店附近含古蓮子的全新世沈積物的孢粉分析, *Quaternaria Sinica*, 4 (2) : 167-73.
Ch'en P'an 陳槃
  1964 'Ch'u-tu Tan-yang k'ao' 楚都丹陽考, *Proceedings of the Asian Historians Conference*, Hong Kong (Pre-print)..
Ch'en Ta-chang and Chia Eh 陳大章・賈峨
  1958 'Fu-chih Hsin-yang Ch'u-mu ch'u-t'u mu-ch'i-ch'i mo-hsing ti t'i-hui' 複製信陽楚墓出土木漆器模型的體會, *WW* 1958.1 : 24-8.

Cheng Te-k'un 鄭德坤
   1963   *Chou China* (*Archaeology in China*, Vol. III), W. Heffer and Sons, Cambridge.
Ch'eng Hsin-jen 程欣人
   1964   'Hu-pei Hsiao-kan Yeh-chu-hu chung fa-hsien ta-p'i Ch'u-kuo t'ung-pei' 湖北孝感
          野猪湖中發現大批楚國銅貝, *KK* 1964.7 : 369.
   1965   'Hsiao-kan-hsien fa-hsien ti Ch'u-pei cheng-li wan-pi' 孝感縣發現的楚貝整理完
          畢, *WW* 1965.12 : 62-3.
Ch'eng Hsin-jen and Wang Fu-kuo 王富國
   1966   'Hu-pei Sung-tzu-hsien Ta-yen-tsui Tung-Chou t'u-k'eng-mu ti ch'ing-li' 湖北松
          滋縣大岩嘴東周土坑墓的清理, *KK* 1966.3 : 122-32.
Chia Eh 賈峨
   1964   'Tsai-t'an Hsin-yang Ch'u-mu hsüan-ku chi ku-chü ti fu-yüan wen-t'i' 再談信
          陽楚墓懸皷及皷簴的復原問題, *WW* 1964.9 : 23-6.
Chiang Hsüan-yi 蔣玄怡
   1949   *Ch'ang-sha: Ch'u-min-tsu chi ch'i yi-shu* 長沙：楚民族及其藝術, 2 vols. 美術攷
          古學社, Shanghai. Vol. 1, 1949; Vol. 2, 1950.
Ch'in Chung-mien 岑仲勉
   1958   *Liang-Chou wen-shih lun-ts'ung* 兩周文史論叢 商務印書館, Shanghai.
Chou Ch'ing-chi 周慶基
   1961   'Kuan-yü nu ti ch'i-yüan' 關於弩的起源, *KK* 1961.11 : 608.
Chou Shih-jung 周世榮
   1958a 'Ch'ang-sha Lieh-shih-kung-yüan ch'ing-li ti Chan-kuo mu-tsang' 長沙烈士公園
          清理的戰國墓葬, *KK* 1958.6 : 47-9.
   1958b 'Hu-nan Hsiang-yin Ku-lo-ch'eng ti tiao-ch'a chi shih-chüeh' 湖南湘陰古羅城
          的調查及試掘, *KK* 1958.2 : 10-14.
   1958c 'Hu-nan-sheng shou-tz'u fa-hsien chan-kuo shih-tai ti wen-hua yi-ts'un 湖南省首
          次發現戰國時代的文化遺存, *WW* 1958.1 : 39-41.
   1959   'Ch'ang-sha Ch'en-chia-ta-shan Chan-kuo Hsi-Han T'ang Sung mu ch'ing-li' 長
          沙陳家大山戰國西漢唐宋墓清理, *KK* 1959.4 : 206-7.
   1960   'Chang-sha T'ai-tzu-chung wen-hua yi-ts'un' 長沙太子冲文化遺存, *WW* 1960.3 :
          64-6.
   1962   'Hu-nan Shih-men-hsien Tsao-shih fa-hsien Shang-Yin yi-chih' 湖南石門縣皂市
          發現商殷遺址, *KK* 1962.3 : 144-6.
   1964   'Hu-nan Shih-men-hsien Ku-ch'eng-t'i ch'eng-chih shih-chüeh' 湖南石門縣古城
          堤城址試掘, *KK* 1964.2 : 104-5.
Chou Shih-jung and Wen Tao-yi 文道義
   1960   '57 ch'ang-tzu. 17 hao mu ch'ing-li chien-pao' 57 長子 17 號墓清理簡報, *WW*
          1960.1 : 63-4.
Chu Teh-hsi 朱德熙
   1954   'Shou-hsien ch'u-t'u Ch'u-ch'i ming-wen yen-chiu' 壽縣出土楚器銘文研究, *Li-
          shih yen-chiu* 歷史研究, 1954.1 : 99-118.
Ch'u wen-wu chan-lan huei 楚文物展覽會
   1954   *Ch'u wen-wu chan-lan t'u-lu* 楚文物展覽圖錄, 北京歷史博物館出版, Peking.
Cox, John H.
   1939   *An Exhibition of Chinese Antiquities from Ch'ang-sha, Lent by John Hadley Cox,
          March 26 to May 7, 1939*, Gallery of Fine Arts, Yale. New Haven.
Cressey, George B.
   1955   *Land of the 500 Million*, McGraw-Hill. New York.
Hawkes, David
   1959   *Ch'u Tz'u, the Songs of the South*, Clarendon Press. Oxford.

o Kuan-pao and Huang Shih-pin 賀官保・黃士斌
1958   'Hsin-yang Ch'ang-t'ai-kuan ti-erh-hao Ch'u mu ti fa-chüeh 信陽長台關第二號
        楚墓的發掘, KK 1958.11 : 79–80.
onan CPCO
1959   'Ho-nan Hsin-yang Ch'u-mu ch'u-t'u wen-wu t'u-lu' 河南信陽楚墓出土文物圖
        錄, 河南人民出版社.
sia Nai 夏鼐
1952   'Ch'ang-sha chin-chiao ku-mu fa-chüeh chi-lüeh' 長沙近郊古墓發掘記畧, WW
        1952.2 : 68–77.
sia Nai, Ch'en Kung-jou and Wang Chung-shu 陳公柔・王仲殊
1957   Ch'ang-sha fa-chüeh pao-kao 長沙發掘報告. 中國田野考古報告集, 考古學專
        刊, 丁種第二號, Peking.
siu Yen-shan and Pai Hsia 修燕山・白俠
1959   'An-hui Shou-hsien Niu-wei-kang ti ku-mu ho Wu-ho-hao-ch'eng-chen hsin-shih-
        ch'i shih-tai yi-chih' 安徽壽縣牛尾崗的古墓和五河濠城鎮新石器時代遺址,
        KK 1959.7 : 371–2.
siung Ya-yün 熊亞雲
1958   'Hu-pei Eh-ch'eng Ch'i-li-chieh Chan-kuo mu-kuo-mu ch'ing-li' 湖北鄂城七里
        界戰國木槨墓清理, KK 1958.8 : 50–1.
sü Hsün-sheng 徐旭生
1960   Chung-kuo ku-shih ti ch'uan-shuo shih-tai 中國古史的傳說時代, Science Press
        (enlarged edition). Peking.
uang Chan-yüeh 黃展岳
1957   'Chin-nien ch'u-t'u ti Chan-kuo Liang-Han t'ieh-ch'i' 近年出土的戰國兩漢鐵
        器, KK 1957.3 : 97–8.
Iu-nan Museum
1960   'Ch'ang-sha Liu-chia-ta-shan ku-mu-tsang ch'ing-li chien-pao' 長沙柳家大山古
        墓葬清理簡報, WW 1960.3 : 51–5.
Iu-pei Bureau of Culture 湖北省文化局文化工作隊
1966   'Hu-pei Chiang-ling san-tso Ch'u-mu ch'u-t'u ta-p'i chung-yao wen-wu' 湖北江
        陵三座楚墓出土大批重要文物, WW 1966.5 : 33–55.
ao Tsung-yi 饒宗頤
1958   Ch'ang-sha ch'u-t'u Chan-kuo tseng-shu hsin-shih 長沙出土戰國繒書新釋, Hong
        Kong (privately printed).
ao Chih-hsi 高至喜
1959   'Hu-nan Chu-chou Chan-kuo-mu ch'ing-li' 湖南株州戰國墓清理, KK 1959.12 :
        686–7.
1960   'Hu-nan ku-tai mu-tsang kai-k'uang' 湖南古代墓葬概況, WW 1960.3 : 33–4.
1962   'P'ing Ch'ang-sha fa-chüeh pao-kao' 評長沙發掘報告, KK 1962.1 : 46–9.
1964   'Chi Ch'ang-sha Ch'ang-te ch'u-t'u nu-chi ti Chan-kuo-mu·chien t'an yu-kuan nu-
        chi kung-shih ti chi-ko wen-t'i' 記長沙常德出土弩機的戰國墓—兼談有關弩
        機弓矢的幾個問題, WW 1964.6 : 33–45.
ao Chih-hsi and Liu Lien-yin 劉廉銀
1959   'Ch'ang-sha-shih tung-pei-chiao ku-mu-tsang fa-chüeh chien-pao' 長沙市東北郊
        古墓葬發掘簡報, KK 1959.12 : 649–54.
arlbeck, Orvar
1955   'Selected objects from ancient Shou-chou', Bulletin of the Museum of Far Eastern
        Antiquities, Vol. 27 (pp. 41–130).
arlgren, Bernhard
1941   'Huai and Han', Bulletin of the Museum of Far Eastern Antiquities, Vol. 13.

49

Ku T'ieh-fu 顧鐵符
1954   'Chang-sha 52.826 hao mu tsai k'ao-ku-hsüeh shang chu wen-t'i' 長沙 52.826 號
        墓在考古學上諸問題, *WW* 1954.10 : 68-70.
1958   'Yu-kuan Hsin-yang Ch'u-mu t'ung-ch'i ti chi-ko wen-t'i' 有關信陽楚墓銅器的
        幾個問題, *WW* 1958.1 : 6-8.
Kuo Chia 郭佳
1959   'Hu-pei ti-ch'ü ku-mu-tsang ti chu-yao t'e-tien' 湖北地區古墓葬的主要特點,
        KK 1959.11 : 622.
Kuo Mo-jo 郭沫若
1958   'Hsin-yang-mu ti nien-tai yü kuo-pieh' 信陽墓的年代與國別, *WW* 1958.1 : 5.
1963   'Pa Chiang-ling yü Shou-hsien ch'u-t'u t'ung-ch'i ch'ün' 跋江陵與壽縣出土銅
        器群, *KK* 1963.4 : 181.
Kuo Teh-wei 郭德維
1962   'Sheng-k'ao-ku-tui tsui-chin ch'ing-li-le yi-hsieh Chan-kuo Gh'u-mu' 省考古隊最
        近清理了一些戰國楚墓, *WW* 1962.2 : 56.
Kuo Teh-wei and Liu Pin-huei 劉彬徽
1964   'Hu-pei-sheng Chiang-ling ch'u-t'u hu-tso-niao-chia-ku liang-tso Ch'u-mu ti ch'ing-
        li chien-pao' 湖北省江陵出土虎座鳥架鼓兩座楚墓的清理簡報, *WW* 1964.9 :
        27-32.
Li Cheng-kuang 李正光
1956   'Ch'ang-sha Heng-yang ch'u-t'u Chan-kuo shih-tai ti t'ieh-ch'i' 長沙衡陽出土戰
        國時代的鐵器, *KK* 1956.1 : 77-9.
1957   'Lüeh-t'an Ch'ang-sha ch'u-t'u ti Chan-kuo shih-tai t'ung-ching' 畧談長沙出土
        的戰國時代銅鏡, *KK* 1957.1 : 96-106.
Li Cheng-kuang and P'eng Ch'ing-yeh 彭青野
1957   'Ch'ang-sha Sha-hu-ch'iao yi-tai ku-mu fa-chüeh pao-kao' 長沙沙湖橋一帶古墓
        發掘報告, *KK* 1957.4 : 33-67.
Li Chien 李健
1963   'Hu-pei Chiang-ling Wan-ch'eng ch'u-t'u Hsi-Chou t'ung-ch'i' 湖北江陵萬城出
        土西周銅器, *KK* 1963.4 : 224-5.
Li Ching-tan 李景聃
1936   'Shou-hsien Ch'u-mu tiao-ch'a pao-kao' 壽縣楚墓調查報告, 田野考古報告,
        KKHP 1936.1 : 213-79.
Ling Shun-sheng 凌純聲
1954   'T'ung-ku t'u-wen yü Ch'u-tz'u Chiu-ko' 銅鼓圖文與楚辭九歌, *Annals o,
        Academia Sinica*, Vol. 1 (pp. 403-17).
1956   'T'ai-tung ti t'u-shih-jen-hsiang chi ch'i tsai T'ai-p'ing-yang ch'ü ti lei-yüan' 臺束
        的吐舌人像及其在太平洋區的類緣, 民族學研究所集刊, 2 : 137-52. Taipei.
1960   'Kuo-shang-li-hun yü kuo-shou chi-hsiao' 國殤禮魂與馘首祭梟, 民族學研究
        所集刊, 9 : 411-49.
Liu Chieh 劉節
1935   *Ch'u-ch'i t'u-shih* 楚器圖釋, 國立北平圖書館出版. Peiping.
Lo Chang 羅張
1960   'Ch'ang-sha Wu-li-p'ai ku-mu-tsang ch'ing-li chien-pao' 長沙五里牌古墓葬清理
        簡報, *WW* 1960.3 : 38-49.
Lo Fu-yi 羅福頤
1954   'T'an Ch'ang-sha fa-hsien ti Chan-kuo chu-chien' 談長沙發現的戰國竹簡, *WV*
        1954.9 : 87-90.
Lo Tun-ching 羅敦靜
1958   'Hu-nan Ch'ang-sha fa-hsien Chan-kuo ho Liu-ch'ao ti tung-shih-mu' 湖南長?
        發現戰國和六朝的洞室墓, *KK* 1958.2 : 41.

Loehr, Max
    1965   *Relics of Ancient China*, The Asia Society. New York.
Ma Ch'eng-yüan 馬承源
    1961   'Man-t'an Chan-kuo ch'ing-t'ung-ch'i shang ti t'u-hsiang' 漫談戰國青銅器上的
            圖像, *WW* 1961.10 : 26-30.
Ma Tao-k'uo 馬道闊
    1960   'Huai-nan-shih Pa-kung-shan-ch'ü fa-hsien chung-yao ku-mu' 淮南市八公山區
            發現重要古墓, *WW* 1960.7 : 71-2.
    1963   'An-hui Huai-nan-shih Ts'ai-chia-kang Chao-chia ku-tui Chan-kuo mu' 安徽淮南
            市蔡家崗趙家孤堆戰國墓, *KK* 1963.4 : 204-12.
Mao Tsai-shan and Li Yüan-k'uei 毛在善 · 李元魁
    1959   'Hu-pei Sui-hsien Tung-chou yi-chih ti fa-hsien' 湖北隨縣東周遺址的發現, *KK*
            1959.11 : 635-6.
P'ei Ming-hsiang, Chang Chien-chung and Chia Eh 裴明相 · 張建中 · 賈峨.
    1957   'Wo kuo k'ao-ku-shih shang ti k'ung-ch'ien fa-hsien — Hsin-yang Ch'ang-t'ai-kuan
            fa-chüeh yi-tso Chan-kuo ta mu' 我國考古史上的空前發現一信陽長臺關發
            掘一座戰國大墓, *WW* 1957.9 : 21-2.
Pei-ching li-shih po-wu-kan (Peking Historical Museum) 北京歷史博物舘編
    1954   *Ch'ang-sha ch'u-t'u ku-tai ch'i-ch'i t'u-an hsüan-chi* 長沙出土古代漆器圖案選集
            人民美術出版社出版. Peking.
Shang Ch'eng-tso 商承祚
    1939   *Ch'ang-sha ku-wu wen-chien chi* 長沙古物見聞記, 金陵大學中國文化研究所叢
            刊甲種. Nanking.
    1955   *Ch'ang-sha ch'u-t'u Ch'u ch'i-ch'i t'u-lu* 長沙出土楚漆器圖錄, 上海出版公司.
            Shanghai.
    1964   'Chan-kuo Ch'u-po-shu shu-lüeh' 戰國楚帛書述畧, *WW* 1964.9 : 8-20.
Shih Shu-ch'ing 史樹青
    1955   *Ch'ang-sha Yang-t'ien-hu ch'u-t'u Ch'u-chien yen-chiu* 長沙仰天湖出土楚簡研究羣
            聯出版社. Shanghai.
Shih Chih-lien 石志廉
    1963   'Ch'u Wang-sun Yü t'ung-ko' 楚王孫魚銅戈, *WW* 1963.3 : 46-7.
Sullivan, Michael
    1961   *An Introduction to Chinese Art*, University of California Press.
Tai Ya-tung, *et al*. 戴亞東
    1958   *Ch'u wen-wu t'u-p'ien chi* 楚文物圖片集, 河南人民出版社.
Tai Ya-tung
    1957   'Ch'ang-sha Yang-t'ien-hu ti-25-hao mu-kuo-mu' 長沙仰天湖第25號木槨墓, *KK*
            1957.2 : 85-94.
T'an Tan-chüng 譚旦冏
    1953   'Ch'u ch'i-ch'i' 楚漆器, *Ta-lu tsa-chih* 大陸雜誌, 6(1) : 13-17.
T'ang Mei-chün 唐美君
    1958   'Tai-wan t'u-chu-min-tsu chih nu chi nu chih fen-pu yü ch'i-yüan' 臺灣土著民
            族之弩及弩之分布與起源, 考古人類學刊, 11 : 5-34.
Tsukada Matsuo 塚田松雄
    1966   'Late Pleistocene vegetation and climate in Taiwan (Formosa), *Proceedings of the
            National Academy of Sciences*, 55 : 543-8.
van der Merwe, Nikolaas J.
    1966   *The Metallurgical History and Carbon-14 Dating of Iron*. Unpublished Ph. D. Dis-
            sertation, Yale University.
Waley, Arthur
    1955   *The Nine Songs: A Study of Shamanism in Ancient China*, George Allen & Unwin.
            London.

Wang Shan-ts'ai 王善才
  1965   'Hu-pei Yi-ch'eng "Ch'u-huang-ch'eng" yi-chih tiao-ch'a' 湖北宜城「楚皇城」遺址
          調查, *KK* 1965.8 : 377–82.
Wang Shih-hsiang 王世襄
  1958   'Hsin-yang Chan-kuo Ch'u-mu ch'u-t'u yueh-ch'i ch'u-pu tiao-ch'a-chi' 信陽戰國
          楚墓出土樂器初步調查記, *WW* 1958.1 : 15–23.
Wang Yü-t'ung 王毓彤
  1963a   'Ching-men ch'u-t'u ti yi-chien t'ung-kuo' 荊門出土的一件銅器, *WW* 1963.1 :
          64–5.
  1963b   'Chiang-ling fa-hsien Hsi-Chou t'ung-ch'i' 江陵發現西周銅器, *WW* 1963.2 : 53–
          5.
Watson, William
  1961   *China*, F. A. Praeger. New York.
  1962   *Ancient Chinese Bronzes*, Charles E. Tuttle. Rutland Vt.
Wen Tao-yi 文道義
  1959a   'Ch'ang-sha ch'u-mu' 長沙楚墓, *KKHP* 1959.1 : 41-58.
  1959b   'Hu-nan Ch'ang-te Te-shan Chan-kuo mu-tsang' 湖南常德德山戰國墓葬, *KK*
          1959.12 : 658–62.
Wu Ming-sheng 吳銘生
  1954   'Ch'ang-sha Tso-chia-kung-shan ti Chan-kuo mu-kuo-mu' 長沙左家公山的戰國
          木槨墓, *WW* 1954.12 : 3–19.
  1957   'Hu-nan Ch'ang-sha Tzu-t'an-p'u Chan-kuo-mu ch'ing-li chien-pao' 湖南長沙紫
          檀舖戰國墓清理簡報, *KK* 1957.1 : 19–22.
Wu Ming-sheng and Tai Ya-tung 戴亞東
  1957   'Ch'ang-sha ch'u-t'u ti san-tso ta-hsing mu-kuo-mu' 長沙出土的三座大型木槨墓
          KK 1957.1 : 93–101.
Yang Hua 楊譁
  1954   'Ch'ang-sha Yang-chia-wan MOO6-hao mu ch'ing-li chien-pao' 長沙楊家灣MOO
          號墓清理簡報, *WW* 1954.12 : 20–46.
  1959   'Hu-nan Te-shan ch'u-t'u Ch'u wen-wu' 湖南德山出土楚文物, *KK* 1959.4 : 207-
          8.
  1963   'Hu-nan Ch'ang-te Te-shan Ch'u-mu fa-chüeh pao-kao' 湖南常德德山楚墓發掘
          報告, *KK* 1963.9 : 461–73, 479.
Yin Ju-chang 殷汝章
  1960   'Shan-tung An-ch'iu Mao-shan shui-k'u fa-hsien ta-hsing shih-k'o Han-mu' 山東
          安邱牟山水庫發現大型石刻漢墓, *WW* 1960.5 : 59.
Yu Kuo-en 游國恩
  1955   *Ch'u-tz'u lun-wen chi* 楚辭論文集, 文藝聯合出版社. Shanghai.
Yuan Ch'üan-yu 袁荃猷
  1963   'Kuan-yü Hsin-yang ch'u-mu hu-tso-ku ti fu-yüan wen-t'i' 關於信陽楚墓虎座鼓
          的復原問題, *WW* 1963.2 : 10–12.

TRADITIONS OF MATERIAL CULTURE
IN THE TERRITORY OF CH'U

WILLIAM WATSON

The concept of a 'Ch'u Culture' has gained currency in the last decade in recognition of the existence in the Ch'u region of (a) a tradition of metallurgy in some respects distinct from that of metropolitan China, (b) an individual iconic tradition manifested in strange effigies, (c) a characteristic art expressed in wooden sculpture and lacquer work. The term 'Ch'u Culture' has not, however, been used hitherto in any strict sense of archaeological classification but only to denote aberrant cultural manifestations within the boundaries of the historical Ch'u State. The diversity of traditions in this area both in the pre-metal period and the Bronze Age produced a notably complex cultural development. We may expect the archaeological record to be complicated by the contact of cultural traditions differing in geographical affinity and in social and technological levels to a degree hardly reached in other parts of China.

Ch'u Culture as an entity more or less clearly definable thus far by surviving material remains hardly goes back before the fifth century B.C. and extends into the first century B.C. It thus covers only the latter part of the duration of the historical Ch'u State and the first century of the Han dynasty; but some factors which determine its individuality reach farther into the past. To what degree traits of material culture relate to a distinct ethnic group (constituting perhaps the bulk of the Ch'u population) it is not yet possible to determine in detail and there must still be an arbitrary element in the archaeologist's attempt to define a Ch'u Culture on the lines of the conventional classification. In the late fourth and the third centuries B.C. a most individual ·product is seen in the elaborate wooden cult figures and other carvings recovered from timbered tombs. Here the suggestion of ethnic identity is strongest of all and we may be fully justified in regarding these carvings and other associated material as remains of a 'Ch'u Culture' in a strict sense. In this paper, however, 'Ch'u Culture' is taken in the wider meaning and under it is consigned all archaeological material from the Ch'u region which does not directly derive from the Central Plain and is not an extension of normal metropolitan Chou Culture (Chiang K. C., 1963; Cheng T. K., 1963; Watson, 1961, 1963; Chiang H. Y., 1949; Ch'ang-sha Report, 1957). At the outset we note that the Ch'u territory was situated astride one of the most important cultural boundaries in East Asia : the course of the Yangtze. Our purpose here is to analyse the archaeological factors briefly, distinguishing (1) the earliest pre-metal traditions which may be regarded for the present purpose as autochthonous, (b) the direct influence of the metropolitan culture of Central China, (c) the characteristic Ch'u civilisation of the late Chou period in which elements of diverse origin are blended or associated.

I. PHYSICAL BOUNDARIES

Ch'u first appears in history when Ch'eng Wang at the end of the eleventh century B. C.* admitted into the Chou confederacy a prince of Ch'u whose city is said to have been at Tan-yang 丹陽, west of the modern Yi-ch'ang 宜昌, on the Yangtze northwest of Lake Tung-t'ing. This was the territory of Ching 荆, a name also given to the region of Ch'u in general. Ching designates one of the Nine Provinces (九州) of Yü 禹 corresponding to the modern provinces of Hupei and Hunan. Under the rule of the descendants of this prince the Ch'u State came to comprise peoples occupying the whole lakeland of the middle Yangtze. Its southern limit was recognized as extending only a little south of Lake Tung-t'ing. Northward, the valley of the Han-shui was early brought under Ch'u rule but political expansion into the Huai-ho Basin, to the northeast was partly barred until the middle of the fifth century B. C. when the collapse of Ts'ai 蔡 and

---

* According to the orthodox chronology (see p. XL) this dating would be nearly a century earlier but the later date is one followed by a majority of scholars. [Ed.]

Ch'en 陳 gave Ch'u control of the tributaries of the left bank as well as the main course of the river. The early frontier with Chin 晋, Chou 周 and Cheng 鄭 (Han) remained firm. It was in the Huai-ho Valley that cultural traditions of north and south most freely mingled, no less in the Neolithic period than in the Bronze Age. It is in this area, where attribution of cultural phenomena specifically to independent Ch'u tradition is most hazardous, that are found the bronze ritual vessels of modified design and the introduction of a new style of decoration on which the recognition of a 'bronze art of Ch'u' has rested.

To the east we hear from the sixth century B. C. of the States of Wu 吳 and Yüeh 越, on whose tribal relation to the inhabitants of the Ch'u territories historical records have little clear to say. Before the conquest of Wu by Yüeh in 473 B. C. the constant hostilities between these two States may provide one reason why influences from the Central Plain, measured in the spread of bronze types, proceeded southwards into Ch'u territory rather than to the east and southeast coast. It remains uncertain how far inland the Yüeh tribes and political control extended from the east coast. It is variously speculated (a) that the peoples of Yüeh and Ch'u, distinct ethnically, moved from the west and from the east along the Yangtze towards the low lying lakelands of the middle course, the Ch'u eventually occupying this middle course exclusively, or (b) that the Wu and Ch'u tribes were akin, and indigenous on the middle Yangtze, the Wu eventually advancing farther to the east. Apart from a lingering sentiment of the distinctness of these tribes from the Han people, the historical tradition has little to offer. Some transcriptions of Ch'u words survive and suffice to show that the language was at least not closely related to that of the inhabitants of the Huang-ho Valley. Ssu-man Ch'ien describes the easy life of the Ch'u-Yüeh population with the northerner's contempt for soft southern men. (*Shih-chi,* ch. 129; Franke, 1930: 57-8, 141-2).

The political boundaries of Ch'u to the west, south, and east approximate to physical features, the limits of a low lying and well-watered terrain. The geographical and cultural boundary in the west follows the edge of the Kweichou Plateau and the highlands of Szechwan ;

in the south the line of the Nan-ling 南嶺 Range cuts off Kwangsi and Kwangtung; in the east the Wu-yi 武夷 Range cuts off Fukien. To the north there is no physical barrier and the boundary of the Ch'u sphere is only cultural and political although its approximation to the southern edge of the loess points to an economic frontier established in an earlier age and perhaps still effective to a degree. The political boundary in the feudal period was relatively stable but by 377 B.C. seems to have moved south to the vicinity of Sung-tzu 松滋 a little north of the Yangtze (Ch'eng H.J., 1966). The site of Tan-yang, the capital of the first prince of Ching, is at the extreme west of what became the territory of the Ch'u State. As also in the Chou and Ch'in 秦 political expansions, the agglomeration of peoples that came to constitute the Ch'u State proceeded eastward at first.

II. CULTURAL BOUNDARIES: NEOLITHIC

In the southeast the Wu-yi Range is the western limit of the Neolithic and early Bronze Age cultures characterized by pottery with impressed ornament. This was one of the most conservative areas of ancient China and the observed cleavage between it and the earliest cultures of the Ch'u region must recede into the remotest past. Northward this tradition is traced only a short distance beyond the Yangtze mouth and does not reach to the Huai-ho Basin. In the Yangtze delta region it is strong around Lake T'ai 太湖 and outlying sites nearly all on low hillocks near otherwise flat ground, extend well into the lakeland region of Ch'u. Nevertheless the cultures with geometric impressed pottery as their most striking feature belong essentially to the lower course of the Yangtze and not the middle course. In the west of the Chou region, the western part of Hupei and Hunan, occurrences of the impressed pottery are very rare indeed. (Chikamori, 1963 : 72–3 ; Chiang, 1959 ; Hu Y.C., 1957).

The cultural boundary of Ch'u to the north, following the edge of the loess, is formed by the southern limit of the primary Yang-shao 仰韶 region. The effectiveness of this boundary in the late Neolithic period is very striking: painted pottery Neolithic culture advanced some distance to the southeast down the rivers of the Huai-ho system but not southwards into Ch'u. The resistance of the Ch'u region to the penetration of the northern Neolithic traditions is underlined by the well developed and characteristic facies of this Neolithic along the northern boundary. In Honan this is the classical Yang-shao/Lung-shan succession. On the lower Yangtze the Ch'ing-lien-kang 青蓮崗 culture in north Kiangsu and the Lung-shan 龍山 phase at Shou-hsien in Anhwei equally represent the limit of the advance of developed farming culture (Chang K.C., 1963: 107). Two sites in the foothills on the upper Han-shui at Yün-hsien 鄖縣 and Chün-hsien 均縣 in the extreme northwest of the Ch'u area reveal an undisturbed succession from Yang-shao (a deep deposit with earlier and later phases) through a more localized variety of Yang-shao (Ch'u-chia-ling 屈家嶺 Culture) to a latest phase with Lung-shan features. (*K'ao-ku* 1961, 10: 519–30). From these sites the *li* 鬲 is absent: the Lung-shan pottery is quite individual, with a large proportion of beater-made and mat-marked pottery and none of the thin burnished black ware. This is far from suggesting a simple migration from a northern or northeastern centre. The southern cultural boundary runs east and west along the northern foothills of the Nan-ling in south Hunan and Kiangsi but on our present knowledge the effectiveness of this boundary is more apparent in the Bronze Age.

Varieties of stone tools show geographical distributions which overlap to varying extent in the Ch'u territory while differing widely in their farther extension (Figure 1). Examples of nearly all the leading types of axes are found along the middle Yangtze. The rectangular type of Lung-shan occurs there though the more strongly attributable trapezoid form seems to be confined to the lower course. Of the two types characteristic of the southeastern area of geometric pottery, the segmented axe reaches generally as far as the Yangtze basin but the shouldered axe common in the southeast and thence showing a westerly distribution touches only the south of the Ch'u area, if it may be said to be present there at all. The sub-cylindrical axe is present on the

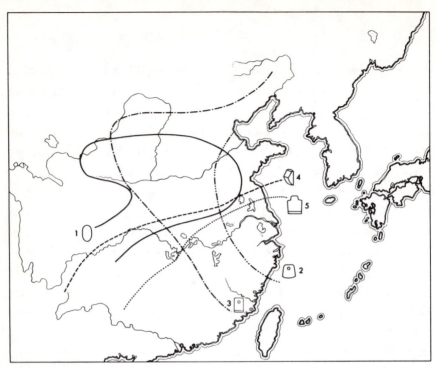

FIGURE 1.   General distribution of stone axe types, the boundaries indicating approximate
western and northern limits. 1: Walzenbeil (axe of oval section); 2: Flat trapezoid axe: 3: Flat
oblong axe; 4: Segmented axe; 5: Shouldered axe.

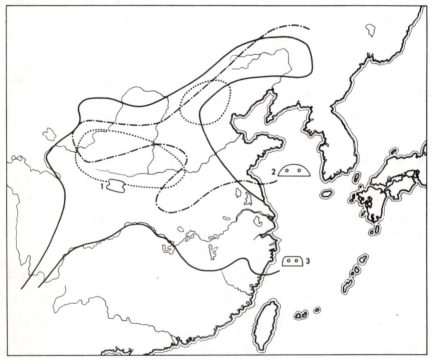

FIGURE 2.   General distribution of stone knives. 1: Primitive type with notched sides; 2:
Crescentic type; 3: Trapezoid type. After An Chih-min, 1955: Pl. 8.

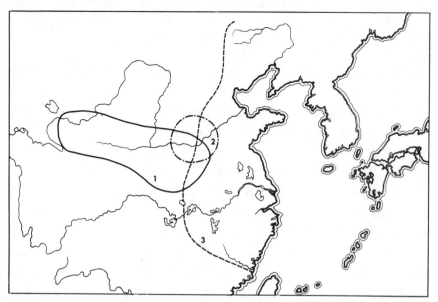

FIGURE 3. Burial rites in early China, 1: Area with tendency to orientate the burial head to west or northwest in the Neolithic Period; 2: Area of prone burials in the early Bronze Age; 3: Eastern limit of area with tendency to orientate burial head to east or northeast in the Neolithic Period.

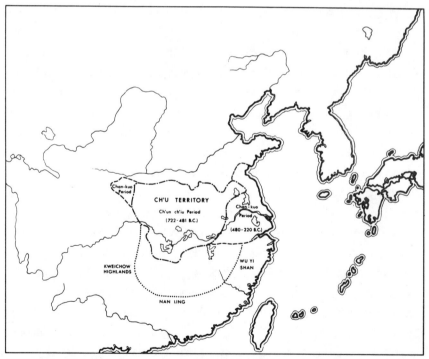

FIGURE 4. Historical and archaeological boundaries of Ch'u with which data in the preceding Figures (1 - 3) may be compared (after Herrmann). The heavy broken lines show the extent of the State of Ch'u. The northern boundary running along the southern edge of the primary loess coincides with a persistent cultural boundary. The area to the south annexed within the thin dotted line and bounded by the mountains indicated extends the Ch'u region to the approximate archaeological limits considered in this paper and in Hayashi's paper below.

middle Yangtze, in the Ch'u region generally, and spreads from there to the middle course of the Huang-ho. Thus the earliest archaeological record shows the commingling in Ch'u of northern and southern traditions, the broad line of division between the two being the Yangtze Valley. It is interesting to note also the distribution of stone knives (Figure 2). On the whole these belong to China north of the Yangtze but the crescentic and rectangular notched varieties do not reach into the Ch'u region. The neatly rectangular or trapezoid knife with single or double perforation does, however, include the whole of the middle and lower Yangtze in its distribution which is perhaps sufficient evidence of its broadly later date (An C. M., 1955). We know nothing yet about the Neolithic burial rite in Ch'u ; one would not expect it to conform necessarily to any of the spheres definable on the middle and upper Huang-ho or on the northeastern seaboard (Figure 3).

III. CULTURAL BOUNDARIES: BRONZE AGE

The earliest elements of higher culture traceable in Ch'u are certainly intrusive — the bronze age penetration from the north beginning already in the Shang period. The most natural Shang movement and influence was southeastwards, across the low-lying land of the left-bank Huai-ho tributaries into Kiangsu. In the Ch'u area proper reliable evidence of a Shang presence, in bronze form, is rare and sporadic and the finds are poorly documented. The bronzes are vessels : a rectangular *ting*, with human faces, a *yu* of the most refined late-Shang quality, a rectangular *tsun* with rams, five large *nao*-bells. All these are reported from a comparatively small area about 25 miles northwest of Ch'ang-sha. Some bronze arrow-heads of the large Shang type were found at T'an-mu-ch'iao 檀木橋 in this district (Kao C. H., 1963). In Anhwei bronzes of early Shang type occur and in typical grave groups : here the spread of Shang civilization was earlier and more consistent than in the rest of Ch'u. (*cf.* Ko C. K., 1965). Bronze vessels of Western Chou type come from Chiang-ling-hsien 江陵縣 on the middle Yangtze. They show some individuality in the shapes

60

of *ting* and *kuei* and in the treatment of the *lei-wen* ground-pattern but the variation is within the normal limits found on Western Chou bronzes of the Central States.   Pieces from Kiangsi are even closer to the Royal Chou style.   These and similar sporadic finds in Ch'u hardly indicate local manufacture.   They are confined to ritual vessels.   No chariot pieces or typical Western Chou weapons have been found in Ch'u.

There is, however, evidence of a local bronze tradition implanted in Ch'u by the end of the eighth century B.C.   For example a *ko*-halberd collected in Hunan, inscribed with the name (on Kuo Mo-jo's interpretation) of Jo Ao 若敖, the fourteenth King of Ch'u who died in 790 B.C., is hardly later than the sixth century, even if we accept the doubt thrown on the contemporaneity of inscription with manufacture.   At either extreme of the possible dating the *ko* marks an archaism *vis-à-vis* the contemporary metropolitan shape (Kao C.H., 1959; Shang C.T., 1962).   Similar formal archaism in the design of *ko* lasted until the first century B.C. in Yünnan where the tradition was not interrupted by the influx of the weapon types characteristic of the Chan-kuo period (*Shih-chai-shan Report*, Plates 15, 16).   For contrast with the archaic tradition which leads back to the opening of the Chou period we can point to bronze vessels found at Shu-ch'eng-hsien 舒城縣, Anhwei whose ornament represents a contemporary or recent derivation from the mid-Chou style.   These pieces are to be compared with vessels found at Hsin-cheng in Honan, in a context judged to descend to 675 B.C. at the latest (Yin T.F., 1964).

It is not possible to relate this early independent metallurgy in Ch'u directly to the genesis of the Dong-son culture farther south. From the sixth to the second century B.C., the period in which at some point the Dong-son metallurgical tradition began to take characteristic shape, we find in Ch'u territory only weapons of the classical metropolitan types, although in some instances decorated in an aberrant manner (Figure 5).   These weapons were not communicated from Ch'u to the Dong-son southern sphere, any more than the bronze vessels and mirrors of the late Chou period which embody Ch'u peculiarities of shape and ornament.   Non-metropolitan forms of bronze weapons (swords

FIGURE 5. Bronze sword of classical form with variegated surface and inlaid inscription from Tomb No. 1 at Wang-shan, Chiang-ling, Hupei. After Wen-wu *1966.5, Pl. 1.*

with fully cast hilt, individual types of splayed socketed axes, and long-barbed arrow-heads) were, however, made in the southern coastal region and probably continued in use there until the arrival of the standard Han products (Mo Chih, 1964; Yang, 1961) and these have Dong-son affinities (Figure 6).

Chikamori argues that the southern tradition of bronze metallurgy derives from an influence advancing around the east coast. He points to the fact that in the southeastern and southern coastal regions the earliest bronze which has a local aspect is associated with the later phase of the impressed pottery with hard body (e.g. Ch'in K.C., 1962, Figures 4, 6; Chikamori, 1963). This view remains debatable, since the earliest south-coast bronze weapons may have arisen from the imitation of metropolitan forms which were standard in Ch'u in the Chan-kuo period, or they may have come from southwest China, Szechwan/Yünnan. But it does not appear that any independent provincial developments in Ch'u contributed directly to the differentiation of the Dong-son bronze culture. When the Dong-son bronze tradition was forming, towards the end of the Chan-kuo period, the Ch'u region, as far as concerns bronze production, was already absorbed completely into a metropolitan tradition. The Nan-ling Range effectively separates the Ch'u from the Dong-son sphere, whether the latter is mapped in terms of bronze weapons or bronze drums. A few isolated drums are recorded in southern

Hunan but they barely encroach on Ch'u territory and there is no evidence that these records are of drums of the early type (Ho C. S., 1965).

The bronze tradition of Yünnan as attested at Shih-chai-shan is no more directly dependent on an independent development in Ch'u than is the Dong-son culture. On the other hand some bronzes present in Szechwan, distinct from both Dong-son and metropolitan types, belong to a group which may extend eastwards into the upper Yangtze valley, the northern part of the Ch'u area (Figure 7). The type sites are at Pao-lun-yüan 寶輪院 and Tung-sun-pa 冬筍霸, the characteristic bronzes being tanged swords with the snake-and-hand and other emblems, a stumpy halberd blade without the lateral *hu* projection, and a narrow socketed spear-head of more archaic appearance than the mid-Chou metropolitan pattern. The coffins found in some tombs are canoe-like, carved from single trunks. This 'boat-coffin culture' as such is not known to extend into Ch'u territory but the occurrence of the characteristic halberd and sword in Ching-men-hsien 荊門縣 in central Hupei, 75 km north of Chiang-ling 江陵, suggests a community of weapon types and metallurgy. They probably represent a tradition confined to the upper Yangtze and not spread through the whole of the Ch'u territory (Feng H. C., 1958; Yü W. C., 1963; 1964).

In the production of bronze weapons an original feature contributed in the Ch'u-Yüeh area of the south was the addition of ornament of kinds unknown in the main tradition. An early sign of this predilection in Ch'u territory is seen in the halberd of King Jo Ao which is covered with oval inlays of what is thought to be silver. With the advent of swords and halberds of Chan-kuo type the ornament consists principally of (a) abstract and geometric ornament (including a dragon head) cast in incised line on the *nei* (tang) and *hu* of halberds (Chou S. J., 1958, Plate 5, no. 1; *Ch'ang-sha Report*, Plate 16); (b) variegation of the colour of the bronze surface of sword and halberd blades, usually in neat geometric diaper (Hupei Cultural Office, 1966: Plate 1, Wang T. K., 1955 Figure 6).[1] The occurrence of weapons decorated in

---

1. The method used to produce this ornament is not understood. Chinese writers refer to it as inlay.

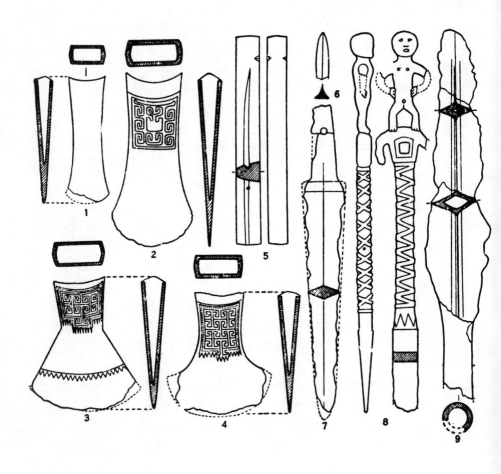

FIGURE 6. *Above: bronze socketed axes, daggers, and spear-head found in Kwangtung, fifth to thir*
centuries B.C. After K'ao-ku *1964.3, P. 141.*

Opposite page: bronze sword, socketed axes, and arrow-head excavated near Canton. After K'ao
ku *1961.11, p. 599.*

64

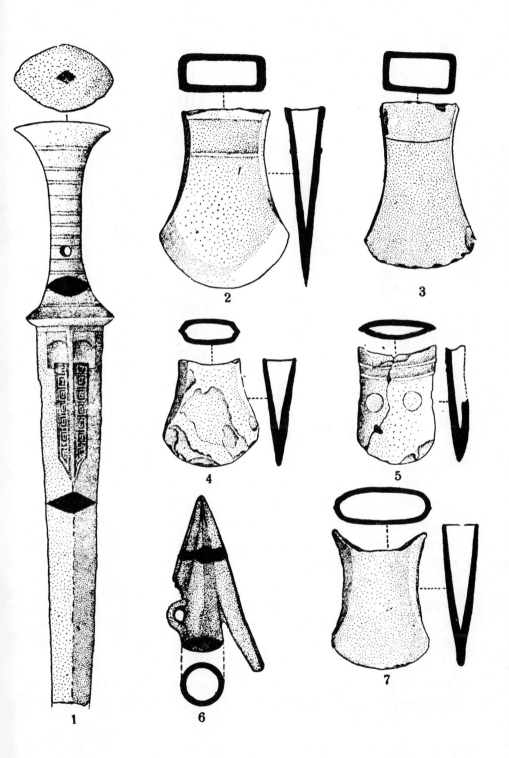

1   2   3   4   5   6   7

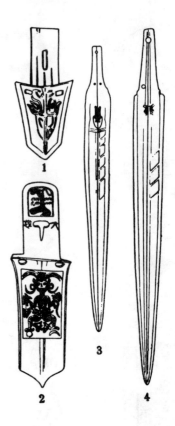

FIGURE 7. Bronze swords and halberds from Szechwan and the northwest of ancient Ch'u (1, 3: excavated at Tung-sun-pa, Szechwan; 2, 4: excavated at Ching-men-hsien, Hupei—sixth to fifth centuries B.C.). After K'ao-ku *19641, p. 54.*

these manners appears to be confined to the Ch'u area proper (Ch'ang-sha, Chiang-ling). They have not been found in the great Ch'u tombs near Shou-hsien. Some halberd blades found in Ch'u have cast linear ornament on the *nei* quite similar to that found on several halberds of the boat-coffin graves in Szechwan. The elaborate variegation of the blades of bronze swords and spearheads (it seems to be rarer on halberds) is in many cases – the majority being collectors' pieces – associated with gold-inlaid inscriptions in 'bird-script' calling them weapons of the King of Yüeh. It is not clear in how particular a sense this attribution is to be taken: perhaps all that is meant is a richly decorated sword etc. of the kind tradition associates with Yüeh Kings. If the meaning is particular we should have to say that the sword found in the Chiang-ling tomb was a gift from a latter-day Yüeh King to the person buried here with it. In spite of the inscriptions it remains uncertain whether the taste for variegated bronze and the skill to produce it are to be sought in the first place in Ch'u or Yüeh.

IV. STRATIGRAPHY

From excavations at the larger sites the cultural succession of characteristic Ch'u types can be divided into three phases (*Ch'ang-sha Report*, 1957 ; Hupei Cultural Office, 1966 ; Yang Hua, 1963 ; Chou S. J., 1958 ; Wen T. Y., 1959 ; Wu M. S., 1957 ; Ch'eng H. J., 1966). The beginning of the early phase is to be dated before, but possibly not much before 500 B. C.

Early Phase

The tombs are rectangular shafts with recess at the head. Iron digging tools but not iron swords are found. At Ch'ang-sha and Ch'ang-te 長 德 this phase is already furnished with bronze swords of classical type : with plain guard and plain ribs on the grip or with the tubular grip. The bronze mirrors are plain (or in one instance at Ch'ang-sha with an open-work dragon in the archaic style). The pottery is coarse, with *li* of the Ch'u type, a lesser number of *tou* (tazza) but no *ting* (tripod). The Ku-lo-ch'eng 古 羅 城 site in Hsiang-yin-hsien 湘 陰 縣 belongs to the early phase and there is a historical record of the occupation of this region by Ch'u in 537 B.C. The *li* is distinct from that of the Yang-shao region and is not likely to have reached the Ch'u area under Yang-shao or Lung-shan influence. More probably it spread to the south in Shang/Early Chou times in which case it would have travelled separately from the advance of metallurgy.

Middle Phase

This must occupy the fourth century B. C. The *li* has disappeared and the *tou* is the commonest pottery form. It is joined by the *tui* (egg-shaped) and *ting*. The bronze swords are as before but some guards have cast ornament and occasionally linear inlay of gold. The mirrors include the three types: quatrefoil, rhombus, and T-patterns. The tombs have recesses at head and/or at one side. The first bronze halberds with decoration appear in this phase.

Late Phase

This begins not much before 300 B.C. and extends into the Western Han period, although the *floruit* of all that is most characteristic of Ch'u art is largely pre-Han. The late phase has elaborate timber-built shaft tombs with inner coffin and outer chamber. To this phase also belongs the production of lacquer and the ambitious wooden sculpture of the shamanistic idolatry peculiar to Ch'u (Watson, 1952). The mirrors are now of the T-pattern, animal procession, and dragon scroll (*k'uei-lung* 夔龍) types. Swords may now have decorated guards and variegated surface (called by the excavators 'two-colour inlays'). One of the variegated swords is of a distinctive design with broad flat midrib and plain hafting spike of rectangular section. The distinctive pots of the third phase are *hu* and *ting* with painted scrolled ornament.

While the validity of this sequence can be questioned in detail it seems very improbable that, for example, the lacquerwork and wood carvings assigned to the late phase should prove to be much earlier in the sequence. Therefore when comparable lacquerwork and wood carving found at Hsin-yang 信陽 in Honan, on the northern boundary of the Ch'u region, was assigned to an earlier date on the strength of an inscription on a bell as interpreted by Kuo Mo-jo, it was concluded that the northern Ch'u material as a whole ante-dated that from the Ch'ang-sha/Chang-te region (Pei M.H., 1957; Wang S.H., 1958; Chia O., 1964; Kuo T.W., 1964; Kuo M.J., 1958). From this dating a north - south movement of the most characteristic element of Ch'u culture might be inferred. In fact the assumption of an earlier date for the Hsin-yang tombs as compared with the similar ones in central Ch'u is open to criticism. The historical citation made by Kuo is apt but need not tie the inscribed bronze bell closely to the date of the

Tso-chuan text, i.e. 525 B. C. Even if the inscription commemorates the reception of the prince of Lu-hun 陸渾 in Ch'u, it may still have been cast on the bell at a date after the event, even after the beginning of the Chan-kuo period, when Chin, the State that put the prince to flight, no longer existed.

The reasons for dating the Hsin-yang material later than 525 B. C. are as follows:

(a) The bronze bells at Hsin-yang are decorated with a more evolved form of the spiral-diaper motif than that from the Ts'ai Hou tomb at Shou-hsien: the latter being dated either to 519 or 457 B. C. on historical arguments, the Hsin-yang material would seem to belong to the fifth century B. C. and probably to its latter half at the earliest.

(b) The comparison of bronze *ting* and *tui* found at the two sites reinforces this view. The *tui* are of the near-spherical kind which at Ch'ang-sha may be assigned to the middle of the Chan-kuo period, i.e. the fourth century B. C.

(c) The timber-built tomb chambers at Hsin-yang correspond to the late phase at Ch'ang-sha. In the Ts'ai Hou tomb at Shou-hsien there is no wooden structure.

(d) Painted pottery and an iron belt-hook were found at Hsin-yang.

V. THE HUAI STYLE

The bronze art of Ch'u is best exemplified by the finds made in two great tombs near Shou-hsien in Anhwei and its features are very familiar to students of Chinese art. It is epitomized by the terms 'Huai style' and the 'hook and volute' motif. This art begins with the adoption and adaptation of forms and decorative schemes invented in Honan and other northern territories. Among the vessels the *ting*, *kuei*, and *fu* are briefly re-designed and the *tui* is cast in bronze for the first time. These 'Ch'u vessels' have been found at Ch'ang-sha, Chiang-ling, and other central Ch'u sites but nowhere in such abundance as in the new Ch'u territories on the upper Huai-ho. It was here that practical contact with the artisan centres of the north must have been most easily made and techniques most fruitfully borrowed. In the apprehension of form the Ch'u vessels mark some advance on the etiolating Chou tradition of the previous three centuries but they could not re-capture the elusive qualities of the best Shang and Western Chou designs. They in no wise share in the spirit which animates the wooden sculptures. If this bronze art, eventually joining with the more varied metal work of the Han period, is the mirror of patrician taste, the animal and iconic art of the Ch'u wood sculptures is no less certainly rooted in a more local tradition and has a different social connotation.

Although the 'hook and volute' theme is so pervasive and so successfully varied in Ch'u bronze art, it is questionable whether the motif was invented in Ch'u. Bells decorated with a most elaborate and presumed early version of the 'hook and volute' motif have been excavated at Chi-hsien 淇縣 in north Honan and a mould for the handle of a similar bell was found at the foundry sites of Hou-ma 侯馬 in south Shansi; there is no good reason for believing that this most characteristic Chan-kuo motif was invented in the Huai-ho Valley (Watson, 1965). That it was adopted in Ch'u foundries is evident from the large number of bronze vessels and smaller pieces found at Shou-hsien and from the mirrors of the 'Shou-hsien type' found both in tombs in the Huai-ho region and at Ch'ang-sha. The mirrors are the most original Ch'u creation in bronze.

Bronzes with 'hook and volute' decoration appear in the middle phase of the Ch'u sequence; lacquer work with scrolled and geometric ornament belong to the late phase (Figure 8). How far the accident of preservation in damp soil accounts for the concentration of finds of lacquer in the central Ch'u region it is not possible to estimate but the quantity and variety of this material emphatically suggest that this craft was a native development of Ch'u. The use of lacquer and the formal designs painted on it are inseparable from the most individual branch of Ch'u art: the elaborate wood carvings of cult figures and all manner of decorative objects. In these the Ch'u tradition achieved perhaps its fullest

FIGURE 8. Details of carved wooden screen painted in various colours from Tomb No. 1 at
Wang-shan, Chiang-ling-hsien, Hupei, circa third century B.C. After Wen-wu 1966.5: Pls. 1, 2, 3,
and 19. Owing to lack of clarity in these reproductions most of the faint vestiges of coloured
designs have been omitted.

71

expression. It is significant that this art is located in the central Ch'u region and not in the Huai-ho Valley area of contact and fusion with the civilization of the northern States. Apart from the horned and tongue-protruding images, whose apostropaeic rôle is clear, there is in the sculpture an insistence on birds and snakes. Snakes are beneath the birds' feet as they are beneath the feet of animals and men on the Shih-chai-shan bronze plaques. The birds attack the snakes and in one instance a bird intent on snakes is charged by deer. A snake seizes a frog (Anonymous, 1966). The carving is fluent, akin to modelling, not assertive by formalization and distortion, unlike any manner seen in the patrician bronzes. Still it lacks some of the astonishing force found in the near-contemporary art of Yünnan, itself no less independent of the main Chinese current; and the influence which popularized the theme of the animal combat at Shih-chai-shan did not reach into Ch'u. The use of a snake as an emblem for the Yüeh tribes neighbouring Ch'u on the east is explained by Chao Hua 趙曄 (later Han dynasty) as a reference to their situation in the southeast in the sixth zodiacal position which is symbolised by a snake. But the association goes deeper than that and is shared with the populations of Ch'u and Yünnan in the south and southwest (Lo H. L., 1955: 1–2).

CONCLUSIONS

1. The Ch'u area proper (i.e. excluding the southern Huai-ho Valley) does not show a unified Neolithic tradition but its resistance to encroachment by neighbouring ceramic traditions is an argument for a measure of cultural coherence in the pre-metal period.

2. In Shang and Western Chou times there is no reliable evidence for the penetration of metallurgy into the Ch'u region though a few bronzes of northern manufacture reached the Yangtze.

3. There is a slight evidence for an independent Ch'u style in bronze-casting from the beginning of the Eastern Chou period but local bronze manufacture cannot have been common before the Chan-kuo period when weapons and vessels of the metropolitan tradition were

made in great quantity and decorated to please a local taste. It was now possible for artistic motifs originating in Ch'u (a local version of the 'hook and volute' motif, the later scrolled and geometric designs, the ornament of mirrors) to join the metropolitan tradition and travel widely in China.

4. The branch of Ch'u art represented by the cult figures and associated sculptural themes stood apart, being related, one must assume, to a body of beliefs peculiar to the Ch'u populations.

BIBLIOGRAPHY

nonymous
 1966   'Hu-pei Chiang-ling san-tso Ch'u-mu ch'u-t'u ta-p'i chung-yao wen-wu', *WW* 1966.5 : 33–5.

ı Chih-min 安志敏
 1955   'Chung-kuo ku-tai ti shih-tao' 中國古代的石刀, *KKHP* 1955.10 : 27–52.

ang Chung-yi
 1958   'Hu-nan Ch'ang-sha Ch'en-chia-ta-shan Chan-kuo mu-tsang ch'ing-li chien-pao', *KK* 1958.9 : 57–61.

ang Hsin-ju
 1958   'Hu-nan Ch'ang-sha Hsiao-lin-tzu chung-kung-ti Tung-Han-T'ang-mu ch'ing-li chien-pao', *KK* 1958.12 : 28–34.

ang Kwang-chih 張光直
 1963   *The Archaeology of Ancient China*, Yale University Press. New Haven and London.

ı'ang-sha Report
 1957   *Ch'ang-sha fa-chüeh pao-kao*, Peking.

ıeng Te-k'un 鄭德坤
 1963   *Chou China (Archaeology in China*, Vol. III), W. Heffer and Sons, Cambridge.

ı'eng Hsin-jen and Wang Fu-kuo
 1966   'Hu-pei Sung-tzu-hsien Ta-yen-tsui Tung-Chou t'u-k'eng-mu ti ch'ing-li', *KK* 1966.3 : 122–32.

ıia Eh
 1964   'Tsai-t'an Hsin-yang Ch'u-mu hsüan-ku ch'i ku-chü ti fu-yüan wen-t'i', *WW* 1964.9 : 23–6.

ıiang Tsuan-ch'u 蔣纘初
 1959   'Kuan-yü Chiang-su ti yüan-ch'i wen-hua yi-chih' 關於江蘇的原始文化遺址, *KKHP* 1959. 4 : 35–45.

ıikamori Tadashi
 1963   A tentative theory on the origin of the Dong Son bronze culture : *Shigaku* Vol. 35, No. 1, pp. 65–96. (In Japanese)

ıin Hsüeh-shan 金學生
 1961   '1958 chih 1961 nien Hu-pei Yün-hsien ho chün-hsien fa-chüeh chien-pao' 一九 六一年湖北鄖縣和均縣發掘簡報, *KK* 1961.10 : 519–30.

h'in Kuang chih 秦光杰
 1962   'Chiang-hsi Hsiu-shui Shan-pei-ti-ch'ü k'ao-ku t'iao-ch'a yü shih-chüeh' 江西修 水山背地區考古調查與試掘, *KK* 1962.7 : 353–67.

Chou Shih-jung
1958　'Hu-nan Hsiang-yin Ku-lo-ch'eng ti t'iao-ch'a ch'i shih-chüeh', *KK* 1958.2 : 10-14
Feng Han-chi 馮漢驥
1958　'Ssu-ch'uan ku-tai ti ch'uan-kuan-tsang' 四川古代的船棺葬, *KKHP* 1958.2 : 77-9!
Franke, O
1930　*Geschichte des chinesischen Reiches,* Berlin and Leipzig.
Ho Chi-sheng 何紀生
1965　'Lüeh-shu Chung-kuo ku-tai t'ung-ku ti fen-pu ti-yü' 畧述中國古代銅鼓的分和
　　　地域, *KK* 1965.1 : 31-9.
Hu Yüeh-ch'ien 胡悅謙
1957　'An-hui hsin-shih-ch'i shih-tai yi-chih' 安徽新石器時代遺址的調查, *KKH*
　　　1957.1 : 21-30.
Jao Tsung-yi
1958　*Ch'ang-sha ch'u-t'u Chan-kuo tseng-shu hsin-shih,* Hong Kong (privately printed
Kao Chih-hsi 高至喜
1963　'Hu-nan Ning-hsiang Huang-ts'ai fa-hsien Shang-tai t'ung-ch'i ho yi-chih' 湖南¹
　　　鄉黃材發現商代銅器和遺址, *KK* 1963.12 : 646-58.
1959　'Hu-nan Chu-chou Chan-kuo-mu ch'ing-li', *KK* 1959.12 : 686-7. [See Chang, ┇
　　　00, 21]
Ko Chih-kung 葛治功
1965　'An-hui Chia-shan-hsien Po-kang-yin-ho ch'u-t'u ti ssu-chien Shang-tai t'ung-ch┇
　　　安徽嘉山縣泊崗引河出土的四件商代銅器, *WW* 1965.7 : 23-6.
Kuo Mo-jo
1958　'Hsin-hang-mu ti nien-tai yü kuo-pieh', *WW* 1958.1 : 5.　[See Chang, p. 00 : 57]
Kuo Teh-wei and Liu Pin-huei
1964　'Hu-pei-shang Chiang-ling ch'u-t'u hu-tso-niao-chia-ku liang-tso Ch'u-mu ti ch'in┇
　　　li chien-pao', *WW* 1964.9 : 27-32.
Lo Hsiang-lin 羅香林
1955　*Pai-Yüeh yüan-liu yü wen-hua* 百越源流與文化, 臺灣書店, Taipei.
Mo Chih 莫稚, etc.
1964　'Kuang-tung Ch'ing-yüan ti Tung-Chou mu-tsang　廣東清遠的東周墓葬, *K*
　　　1964.3 : 138-42.
P'ei Ming-hsiang Chang Chien-chung and Chia Eh
1957　'Wo kuo k'ao-ku-shih shang ti k'ung-ch'ien fa-hsien — Hsin-yang Ch'ang-t'ai-kua┇
　　　fa-chüeh yi-tso Chan-kuo ta mu', *WW* 1957.9 : 21-2.
Shang Ch'eng-tso
1955　*Ch'ang-sha ch'u-t'u Ch'u ch'i-ch'i t'u-lu,* Shanghai.　[See Chang, p. 00 : 81]
1962　'"Ch'u-kung Wei kuo" chen-wei ti wo-chien' "楚公豪戈"眞偽的我見, *W┇*
　　　1962.6 : 19-20.
1964　'Chan-kuo Ch'u-po-shu shu-lüeh', *WW* 1964.9 : 8-20.　[See Chang : p. 00 : 82]
Shih-chai-shan Report
1959　*Yün-nan Chin-ning Shih-chai-shan ku-mu-chün fa-chüeh pao-kao,* Peking.
Wang Shih-hsiang
1958　'Hsin-yang Chan-kuo Ch'u-mu ch'u-t'u yüeh-ch'i ch'u-pu t'iao-ch'a-chi', *W*
　　　1958.1 : 15-23.
Wang Tsun-kuo 汪遵國, etc.
1965　'Chiang-su Liu-ho Ch'eng-ch'iao Tung-Chou mu' 江蘇六合程橋東周墓, *K*
　　　1965.3 : 105-15.

Watson, William
1952   'A Grave Guardian from Ch'ang-sha', *British Museum Quarterly*, XVII (pp. 52-5)
1961   *China Before the Han Dynasty*, Thames and Hudson. London.
1963   *Handbook to the Collections of Early Chinese Antiquities*, British Museum. London.
1965   'A Chinese bronze bell of the fifth century B.C.', *British Museum Quarterly* XXX (1965) 1-2 (pp. 50-6).

Wen Tao-yi 文道義
1959   'Ch'ang-sha Ch'u-mu', *KK* 1959.1 : 41-58.

Wu Ming-sheng and Tai Ya-tung
1957   'Ch'ang-sha ch'u-t'u ti san-tso ta-hsing kuo-mu', *KK* 1957.1 : 93-101.

Yang Hao 楊豪
1961   'Chieh-shao Kuang-t'ung chin-nien fa-hsien ti chi-chien ch'ing-t'ung-ch'i' 介紹廣東近年發現的幾件青銅器, *KK* 1961.11 : 599-600.

Yang Hua
1963   'Hu-nan Ch'ang-te Te-shan Ch'u-mu fa-chüeh pao-kao', *KK* 1963.9 : 461-73, 479.

Yin Ti-fei 殷滌非
1964   'An-hui Shu-ch'eng ch'u-t'u ti t'ung-ch'i' 安徽舒城出土的銅器, *KK* 1964, 10 : 498-503.

Yü Te-chieh 喻德智, etc.
1956   'Hu-pei Ch'i-ch'un Yi-chia-shan hsin-shih-ch'i shih-tai yi-chih t'iao-ch'a chien-pao' 湖北折春易家山新石器時代遺址調查簡報, *KK* 1956.3 : 21-4.

Yü Wei-ch'ao 俞偉超
1963   '"Ta-wu X-ping" t'ung-ch'i yü Pa-jen ti "Ta-wu" wu' "大武開兵" 銅戚與巴人的 "大武" 舞, *KK* 1963.3 : 153-5.
1964   '"Ta-wu" wu ch'i hsü-chi' "大武" 舞戚續記, *KK* 1964.1 : 54-7.

THE CH'U SILK MANUSCRIPT
AND OTHER ARCHAEOLOGICAL DOCUMENTS
OF ANCIENT CHINA

NOEL BARNARD

It was during 1934 when a small team of people including a couple of 12–13 year old boys was engaged in a tomb-rifling jaunt that the Ch'u Silk Manuscript was found. This team, comprising mainly members of the one family, was not new to the often profitable aspects of excursions of this kind and like scores of other groups of tomb-robbers active in and around the Ch'ang-sha area regarded such ventures as a perfectly acceptable way to spend leisure time. As to the rights and wrongs of the matter retrospective comments seem unnecessary. However, it is a remarkably fortunate coincidence that one of the parties involved in this particular find has for some years been living outside Mainland China and I had the good fortune to be introduced to him. Careful interrogation soon manifested the fact that his description of the find and his details of the tomb contents were above suspicion. He it was who actually found the Manuscript. Some of the salient points of his descriptions may be noted here. The tomb was of wooden construction comprising a series of four rectangular wooden chambers, the inner-most being the grave-occupant's coffin (Figure 1). In most essentials the participant's account of details in the tomb construction tallys with those of several tombs excavated in the Ch'ang-sha area and fully reported in various archaeological publications.[2] In space A there was found a number

---

1.   The present paper is based upon the partly completed sections of my survey *The Ch'u Silk manuscript.*

2.   A brief outline may be noted conveniently in our first paper above (Chang Kwang-chih, 'Major Aspects of Ch'u Archaeology', *cf.* also Figure 3 therein. The most comprehensive report covering the architectural details of Ch'u tomb construction is in *Ch'ang-sha fa-chüeh pao-kao* 長沙發掘報告, 1957. For details on this and other archaeological reports on excavations of Ch'u sites, see the bibliography in Chang's paper.

of pottery bowls lying around the floor of the chamber in inverted position, under each was an earthenware figurine of a pig. There were also four wooden sculptures of human figures of a type well known amongst Ch'u funereal furnishings. There were no metal artifacts. Spaces B and C were apparently devoid of tomb furnishings except for a pile of planks of timber each about 3″ thick and approximately 4 or 5 feet in length and 12″ to 18″ wide. The pile was neatly stacked against the wall in Space B. In the coffin itself appeared only the remains of hair and teeth. All in all a most disappointing venture.

The two boys, however, were trying to lift up the heavy waterlogged planks in Space B and succeeded in raising the upper-most one. Between it and the plank below it were 'folded pieces of leather-like material'. Parts were adhering to the adjacent surfaces of the planks and as a result both of the lifting of the top plank and of the dislodging of the folded pieces of 'goatskin' – as they believed the material to be – some degree of tearing occurred. Because characters and paintings were discernible they retrieved them to examine later when unfolded and dry. At the time of the discovery the material was slimy to the touch and quite fragile. At least three individual pieces were found but as no one was really interested no one assisted the boys to lift the remaining planks. As the participant remarked, there may well remain other brush-written Manuscripts between the planks as the tomb was filled in again immediately afterwards.

This description varies in several respects from those published to date, particularly that of Shang Ch'eng-tso 商承祚 (*Wen-wu*, 1964.9 : 8–10) which is the most comprehensive. According to Shang the Manuscript was excavated in September, 1942 in an ancient cemetery area located in the Eastern Suburbs of Ch'ang-sha at a place known as Wang-chia-tsu-shan 王家祖山. This information, he asserts, is much more dependable than Ts'ai Chi-hsiang's 蔡季襄 statement in his *Wan-Chou tseng-shu k'ao-ch'eng* 晚周繒書考證 to the effect

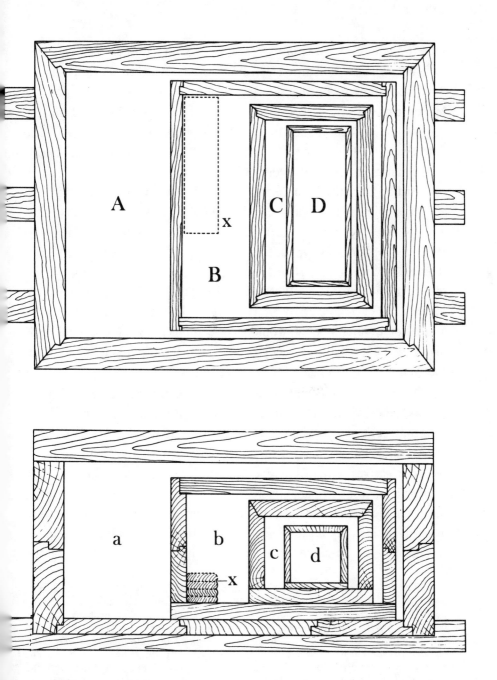

FIGURE 1.   A reconstruction of the tomb in which the Ch'u Silk Manuscript was found according to details volunteered by one of the team of tomb robbers.

that it came from T'u-chia-p'o 杜家坡. Such data has been collected
by Shang since "Liberation" from persons who were supposed to
have been present during the excavation of the tomb containing the
Manuscript. There were, he records, four persons involved in the
digging but in actual fact the team comprised 9 or 10 persons. The
date given by Shang is 8 years later than that stated by the participant
— the latter is certainly correct on this point because John Hadley
Cox had brought the Manuscript back with him to the U.S.A. in 1938
after his sojourn in Ch'ang-sha during the preceding two years (1936–
37). Shang's version of the matter is along the following lines: In
1946 the Manuscript was taken to Shanghai through the vulgar and
shameless hands of an American imperialist who by shady means had
seized it and took it to Washington. It was furtively stored in the
Library of Yale University.[3] The Freer Gallery of Art took photographs of it later on but would not let copies go abroad and thus
made it impossible for scholars in China interested in the study of
the Manuscript to engage in research on it.

The truth of the matter, however, is easily verifiable and need
not be elaborated upon here. But attention may be drawn to the
fact that contrary to Shang's last assertion above the Freer Gallery
of Art did indeed make available prints and enlargements from its
record negatives of the Ch'u Silk Manuscript to several scholars: Jao
Tsung-yi, Hayashi Minao, Umehara Sueji, and myself. Possibly others,
too. As there were certain difficulties involved these copies were
made available only on the understanding that they would be employed
specifically for research purposes and that no reproductions of the

3. The inconsistency of geographical details — his lumping together of Washington
and Yale — is no less remarkable than his confusion of chronological events. Shang
mentions the exhibition of the 'spoil' Cox 'plundered' from Ch'ang-sha which was
held in Washington (sic) the year after his return and the illustrated catalogue of
the exhibition. His reference is to the hand-book: An Exhibition of Chinese Antiquities from Ch'ang-sha, lent by John Hadley Cox, March 26 – May 7, 1939. The
exhibition was held in the Gallery of Fine Arts [hence Shang's mix-up with the
Freer Gallery of Art and Washington?] Yale University, New Haven, Connecticut.
So far as I am aware Cox did not return to China after 1939 — Shang seems to be
aware of this, too, but for polemic purposes spirits him back to the country in 1946.

photographs would be made. It is very much to the credit of the Freer Gallery of Art that such progress as has been made in studies of the Manuscript to date is largely due to its generosity and encouragement of serious study by allowing such discreet access to its files. There is an amusing side to Shang's polemics. He states in his article that he had in his own possession 'a set of natural size photographs' of the Manuscript as from 1947. His hand-copy reproduced in *Wenwu* (1964.9) was based upon these. For more than 16 years, therefore, his colleagues were similarly denied access to this even closer source of study within Mainland China itself!

According to his post-'Liberation' informant the tomb comprising a coffin and a sarcophagus both made entirely of wood was not large. The black lacquered coffin was placed against one side of the sarcophagus and the space containing the burial objects formed an 'L' shape. The Manuscript, folded in eight segments, was earlier supposed to have been found in a bamboo casket approximately 23 cms in length and 13 cms in width. Shang does not think this story is reliable and notes that the width of the Manuscript folds was greater than the width of the casket. Although he is correct in doubting the casket story the *original* folds of the Manuscript do, on the contrary, allow it to fit the casket measurements quite comfortably — Shang has mistakenly measured the folds that have occurred since the mounting of the Manuscript following excavation. The casket was supposedly discovered in the north-south aligned space at the head of the coffin while in the area to the right of the coffin were found: a lacquer *p'an*-basin; a lacquer *pei*-cup with lugs; a bronze sword enclosed in a wooden case (sheath ?); a bronze *ko*-dagger-axe; 24 round-bodied tomb-figures; an earthenware *ting*-cauldron, a *tui*-cauldron, and a *hu*-vase. Alongside the above-mentioned casket was a pile of black funereal clay tablets which were uninscribed.

In 1942 Shang received an offer of sale of 'brush-written silk pieces' from a certain T'ang Chien-ch'uan 唐 鋻 泉 known locally as 'Tailor T'ang'. Shang was informed by a friend whom he had requested to act on his behalf that when Tailor T'ang showed him the 'Manuscript' it was rolled up fragment upon fragment in white paper and this in turn was rolled in newspaper. There were not many large pieces and the piles of small fragments would, he thought, be very difficult to restore to their original positions. This was in the 'winter of 1942' but by the time Shang had replied, Ts'ai Chi-hs'iang had already completed purchase of the 'Manuscript'.4 This part of Shang's account is interesting because the Ch'u Silk Manu-script in its original (i.e. unmounted) state upon recovery could not have been the same highly fragmented collection of 'brushwritten silk pieces' as just described. It is torn, stretched and folded but for the most part still comprises a practically continuous piece of fabric except for the centre vertical folded area. From the point of view of Shang's dates, of course, the Ch'u Silk Manuscript was already in the U.S.A. 3–4 years before he received Tailor T'ang's offer of sale. Possibly all the confusion is not only due to an entirely different silk manuscript but also one from some other tomb.5

These details have been assembled here for a specific purpose. The aim is to indicate the correct significance of the find. In earlier studies of the Manuscript the opinion has been advanced that it had a magical purpose such as to 'quieten the grave' (Jao Tsung-yi), to 'protect the dead' (An Chih-min), etc. A.F.P. Hulsewé writing on

4. Chiang Hsüan-yi (Ch'ang-sha, 1950, vol. 2, p. 1) in his note on the Manuscript states, however: '... when this was excavated at Ch'ang-sha it came into the hands of a tailor who attempted to sell it to dealers' agents from various parts of our country but without success. It was not until I came to Ch'ang-sha again from Kuang-tung that I learnt he had accepted a small deposit from an American who had taken the Manuscript 'on approval' to the U.S.A. and all that was left in the owner's hands was a foreign promissory note'. Jao Tsung-yi observes that there are two stories current on this matter and that the account concerning the Manuscript coming into Ts'ai Chi-hs'iang's possession relates also that he sold it to Cox (HKJCS, 1954, vol. I. 1, p. 69).
5. It is important to keep in mind, too, that Shang had made himself unpopular amongst the 'local sages' — the t'u-fu-tsu 土夫子 as he sarcastically refers to them — and accordingly few would volunteer information to him and seldom could he gain direct access to many of the items unearthed. So, the participant informed me, and such points match well Shang's own published statements: '... if unearthed in the east, they would say: in the west...' (p, 8, note 1). Such lack of reliability amongst the accounts Shang Ch'eng-tso assembled since 'Liberation' would, of course, be of more serious proportions — obviously Shang would be told only what the 'local sages' thought safe to tell him.

these points ('Texts in Tombs', *Asiatische Studien*, XVIII/XIX. 1965, pp. 78–89) concludes that such was indeed the function of the Manuscript which 'with its pictures or [= of] the good spirits or gods fulfilled the rôle played in other cases by images of some of these spirits, like the goggle-eyed and horned creature found in another Ch'ang-sha tomb'. He suggests, too, that the *Mu t'ien-tzu chuan* 穆天子傳 may have been placed (together with the other texts) in the Wei tomb reported to have been discovered in 279 A.D. 'to serve as a guide to the Other World'. These are the only two instances of archaeological texts which might give rise to speculation on the existence of such customs attending burial practices in ancient China — the latter is a doubtful case as so many and varied are the other literary materials known to have been incorporated in the Wei tomb. As to the Ch'u Silk Manuscript, however, the situation is now perfectly clear. It was not some highly revered literary or religious work placed in a casket and set in an honoured position within the tomb. It was not the sole manuscript in the tomb — on this point we have not only the participant's recollected details to take into account but also the fact that portions of another silk document with red characters are still adhering to the surface of the Ch'u Silk Manuscript.[6] It was simply one of several brush-written documents which had been roughly folded and placed between the wooden planks described earlier. Perhaps the folded silk pieces had been inserted between the planks merely to level warped sections?

The very fact that the Manuscript and the companion silk pieces were found in a folded state is a point of major importance. Documents of this kind would invariably have been rolled into scroll form if placed in the tomb as part of the furnishings for the deceased. Because they were folded and placed between building materials,

---

6. *Cf.* details discussed by Jean Mailey below, especially p. 104; also Figures 1 and 2 accompanying her survey. It was not until some time after my interview with participant that the results of technical examination conducted in the Metropolitan Museum revealed that traces of both ink and fabric remnants of a further silk document were adhering to the surface. Hitherto, all who had studied the Manuscript simply assumed that the character remnants were the result of someone writing over the original surface — or perhaps, the characters were on the under surface of the Manuscript.

probably left as an oversight by the tomb's constructor, we may assume with some degree of confidence that materials of this kind probably meant little more to people of that period than does a newspaper or magazine to a modern artisan in a mausoleum construction company. If this interpretation is correct the implications in respect of the extent of literacy and the volume of literature that must have been current in the State of Ch'u *circa* 500–400 B.C. are obvious. One would not, of course, seek to press the point too far.7

It is not my intention to discuss in any detail the possible significance of the peripheral drawings around the two main texts of the Manuscript as this subject is covered by Hayashi Minao. Chang Kwang-chih has drawn attention to various aspects of the Ch'u cultural remains and has discussed the significance of such items as the antler-crowned, tongue-protruding tomb guardians, to which may be added the split-tongue motif; the three-headed man (trio); the single-head, double-bodied snake; etc. in the Manuscript. That the period in which this art flourished extended from the sixth to the second centuries B.C. is clear and, no doubt, a matter of especial interest to anthropologists and archaeologists working in other cultural areas of the Pacific. Because of the possibility that such art motifs may have had their origin from the State of Ch'u at a time when the literary arts were obviously well established, the non-sinologist will naturally wonder if in archaeological textual remains there occurs information of value relevant to his own lines of research. It is, accordingly, the aim in this paper to present a few brief notes on the nature of the script and of the content of inscriptions generally

---

7. There are, of course, other grounds upon which we may make assessments as to the extent of literacy amongst the merchant and artisan classes: the inscribing of coins, the stamping of pottery, the inventories of grave goods sometimes left accidentally in tombs, etc. So far as ordinary workmen are concerned, some knowledge of characters may be ascribed to them, as evidenced in the practice of numbering the individual planks of wood pre-fabricated for the tombs. In foundry remains are sometimes to be noted identifying graphs on mould-sections; iron founders often incorporated graphs which seem to comprise a name plus a sort of title. Data of this kind would certainly not only indicate literacy amongst merchants where it surely would be expected but also in workshops; it is thus evident that at least the more responsible employees had a knowledge of writing.

from the State of Ch'u and to illustrate some aspects of the problems attending transcription and translation of a long text such as that of the Ch'u Silk Manuscript.

First, let us consider some features of the script. In traditional literary sources supposedly compiled prior to the Han period (206 B.C.–220 A.D.) the view is recorded that the State of Ch'u and its people not only had different customs, speech, dress, etc. but also their culture was on a lower and notably barbarous level. Recent archaeological finds certainly do not support the baser aspects of these now obviously distorted assessments which are probably of largely Han Confucian origin. The culture was different, it is true, but the level in terms of manufacturing skills, artistic achievements, literary accomplishments, and sheer ingenuity and inventiveness was certainly no less than that of the Middle States. Upon the basis of archaeological discovery in recent years there is room for a considerable revision of thought on this matter. So far as the script is concerned the opinion has long been accepted that the writing of Ch'u differed markedly from that of the Middle States and was replete with calligraphic ornament and flourishes. However, the facts are not quite so. The script of Ch'u in the bulk of examples presently available varies little in any respect to the script of the Middle States. In weapons and in a few vessels there is employed an ornate calligraphic form of which there have been excavated to date such examples as those presented in Figure 2 — less than a dozen inscriptions all told. For the rest the script of Ch'u in the Silk Manuscript, in some 200 brush-written bamboo tablets, in the tally inscriptions of Shou-hsien, in 30 or so bronze vessels, and in a number of miscellaneous artifacts, comprises a perfectly normal, in fact 'standard' Eastern Chou style writing. Where it may appear to differ in either character structures or usage it is simply because the Ch'u archaeological vocabulary as preserved amongst the above-mentioned documents comprises by far the largest variety of characters from any geographical area of pre-Han China other than from City Shang ! From Middle States sites there are comparatively few examples of both script and text

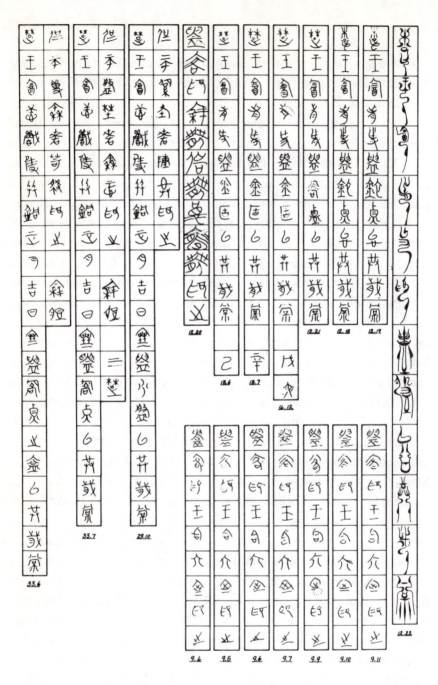

FIGURE 2. Examples of ornate script from Ch'u sites. The characters are for the most part, however, unadorned and where ornamentation is affected it is somewhat simple in scope as may be noted upon comparison with the script from more northerly sites.

86

other than the stereo-typed documents inscribed in bronze ritual vessels. Thus the calligraphic contrasts made by earlier observers are not reliably assessed at all. Recently excavated inscriptions from the State of Ts'ai 蔡 together with the well known 'bird' script of Wu 吳 and Yüeh 越 (Figure 3) show a pronounced tendency towards ornate flourishes and extraneous devices — often in the shape of birds — in which the character proper is almost dissolved. The feature here is, indeed, characteristic of the northernmost limits of Ch'u and of the two coastal States but in Ch'u itself the few available examples are less complex in ornament. The vast bulk of Ch'u script is thus unadorned and where the vocabulary and content is matched by examples amongst Middle States' inscriptions it is quite evident that in pre-Han China a remarkably standard form of script and literary language existed.

There is an important observation here which non-sinological readers should keep in mind — the universal nature of the script is but one facet of the appreciable degree of inter-communication that prevailed between States of the period over long distances and large areas of China. In assessments concerned with the passage of art motifs from the well-established cultural areas in North and Central China towards the coast and southwards, it is necessary to take into account not only the existence of a particularly virile and pulsating situation within the more civilized areas but also the outward movement of military expeditions, trade, and migration that was ever-expanding the scope of Chinese cultural influences.

Amongst the inscription texts of Ch'u there is not a great deal of information which, so far as I can judge at present, has particular bearing upon the possible diffusion of art motifs extant in China — especially from the Ch'u area — into the Southeast Asian and Pacific complex. In the inscribed Shou-hsien bronzes unearthed in 1933 the texts record briefly the names of two Kings of Ch'u (which cannot be acceptably paralleled with those in the orthodox reign-lists) and a note to the effect that the inscribed vessels were cast from captured bronze weapons — the names of the founders and the ceremonial purpose for which the vessels were cast are recorded, too. A recently excavated set of bronze bells has one inscribed with a record of an unsuccessful invasion of the Jung 戎 and of the Ch'u by the forces of Chin 晉 which were repelled on the frontiers of Ch'u. This inscription thus usefully confirms the often friendly relations between Ch'u and the surrounding tribal peoples as recorded in traditional sources. The tally inscriptions, too, refer to the defeat of the Chin army and for the most part simply detail the routes which were to be followed by the recipient of the tally. The bulk of the bamboo tablets merely list the tomb furnishings but naturally present valuable light on such matters. Some contain prose works but they are too fragmentary to allow assessments of any value. Thus we are left with the Ch'u Silk Manuscript — the only example (which is also practically complete) of a compilation likely to contain data of interest to anthropologists in, say, the fields of comparative mythology, 'religious' thought, astrological ideas, and such like.

It was originally my intention to prepare a translation of the Manuscript text for distribution at this Symposium. However, the new infrared photographs we have made of the Manuscript are so much clearer than the photographs from which several of us worked earlier that they have actually created more new problems than they have solved old ones! For some weeks I have been preparing a preliminary translation of the text and have found furthermore that even in the most up-to-date studies there is a considerable amount of revision required, even where characters, phrases, and sentences are equally clear in both the earlier and recent photographs.[8] Accordingly it has seemed to me more useful that the problems attending

8. It is interesting to note in the paper by Jao Tsung-yi that the results of a similar appraisal is evident. Before we had seen each other's contributions to this Symposium, I spent a few hours' together with Professor Jao in Hong Kong en route to New York and a few days later with Professor Hayashi Minao in Kyoto. It was not surprising to find that each of us had arrived at much the same conclusion — the whole job of interpretation has to be started afresh. Consequently Jao's paper deals with only 2 or 3 lines of text; my forthcoming 'translation' is concerned mainly with the establishment of definitive identification of the characters as a prelude to more reliable interpretation.

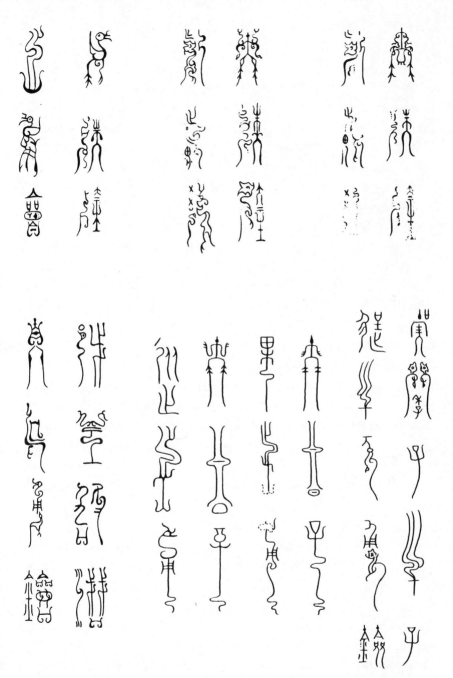

FIGURE 3.   *The ornamental script of Ts'ai, Wu, and Yüeh—States situated to the north and north-east of Ch'u. The greater degree and complexity of extraneous flourishes would seem to suggest that the origin of this type of calligraphy is to be sought here rather than in Ch'u or to the south.*

transcription of the archaic graphs into modern forms and the methods of interpretation and translation involved should be demonstrated in some detail. Not sufficient is known or appreciated of the pitfalls into which students in this field may tumble. Unfortunately, pre-Han Chinese texts cannot be read with full, let alone sufficient, understanding in the same way as most ancient Greek or Latin inscriptions — the script reform of Li Ssu 李 斯 and the effective destruction of the early literature both in Ch'in times (*circa* 220 B.C.) and in the early years of Han has resulted in the formation of fairly firm barriers with the past in respect of many points of detail and of some of crucial importance. Over and above such problems is the particularly exasperating situation attending the transmitted literary remains which being so full of Confucian thought and so obviously processed to accord with Han Confucian propaganda, that we cannot now always be certain as to what sections are reliably of pre-Ch'in origin.

The usual method of transcribing the archaic script into modern character form and to effect interpretations is that which seeks parallel forms in the *Shuo-wen* dictionary (compiled *circa* 100 A.D.) and other such epigraphic sources and thence the search for parallel phrases or similar examples of character usage in the transmitted literary sources. As a result of these approaches interpretations are often rather Han in flavour and not necessarily in accordance with pre-Han compilation. In the Ch'u Silk Manuscript (Text A, see Figure 4) therefore, it is not a matter of surprise to discover, for instance, the graph (A. 1–4) transcribed as follows : 𢒫 (original form) : 䰍 (modernised form) : 能 *neng* 'able'. The modern character 能 *neng* is then read as a loan for the character 熊 *hsiung* 'bear'. A major reason for this interpretation is that the rulers of Ch'u were supposed to have had the surname (or clan-name) 熊 *hsiung*. Han period versions of the pre-Ch'in literature often refer to this matter. Yet in the inscriptions from Ch'u we find the royal clan-name is written as 酓 which some authorities transcribe as modern 酓 *yen*. The reconstructed archaic sound of this latter character is *.iəm* (*GSR* 651) and that of 熊 *hsiung* is *gium* (*GSR* 674) — these are considered linguistically close enough to allow the one character to be phonetically used in place of the other. It will be evident thus far, therefore, that the argument relies upon the validity of 臽 = 酓 *yen* and that 䰜 = 能 *neng*. Amongst other inscriptions of Ch'u, however, we find *neng* written as 㲋 : 㺝 which is directly equivalent to modern 能.[9] It differs from the Ch'u Silk Manuscript graph in that it lacks the element 夨 : 大 *ta* 'large'. Accordingly it is quite possible, in fact almost certain, that the Manuscript character is neither *neng* nor *hsiung*!

A point of this kind requires more careful examination than has hitherto been accorded, for the literary (as against archaeological) tradition of a royal Ch'u clan-name of *hsiung* 'bear' might well gain the attention of our non-sinological colleagues working in the field of Northwest Indian art. Possibly some identity in the mythology of the two widely separated cultures might be sought.

A similar case is the graph 虘 (A. 2-1) which has been generally accepted as modern 祖 *tsu* 'ancestor', 'grandfather'. In the *Han-chien* 汗簡 — a dictionary of archaic and archaistic script — is the character 且 to which reference is made — it is an alternative form of the graph 且 *chieh* (the same graph structurally as the sound element in 祖 *tsu* 'ancestor'). It is suggested that 虘 might thus be employed as a loan for 祖 *tsu*. However, the *Han-chien* alternative form does not contain the element 虍 'tiger' but an archaic form of 尸 *shih* 'corpse'. Moreover, the simpler graph 且 when proposed

---

9.   In the Shou-hsien tally inscription the more complex graph 㺝 has been read as 能 *neng* 'able' but the context is not really sufficient to support this interpretation.

FIGURE 4A (overleaf). Hand-copy of the archaic text of the Ch'u Silk Manuscript – a preliminary reconstruction by the author based upon a trial run of infra-red photographs prepared under his supervision in the early part of 1967. The two major text sections A and B are reversed in respect of one another in the original (cf. Frontispiece); the minor sections of text surrounding A and B comprise individual 'titles' (C1, C3, C5, C7, etc.) referring to the Peripheral Figures and a longer 'caption' detailing the attributes of each (C2, C4, C6, C8, etc.). The three-character 'titles' comprise the names of the Peripheral Figures (single characters) together with a two-character indication of their main supervisory functions as explained in more detail in the longer 'captions'. In the latter the name of the Peripheral Figure is repeated in each case following the introductory particle 曰 : 曰 yüeh. Further information on these points may be studied in the papers by Jao Tsung-yi and Hayashi Minao. Figures 4B and 4C show reconstructions of the Peripheral Figures.

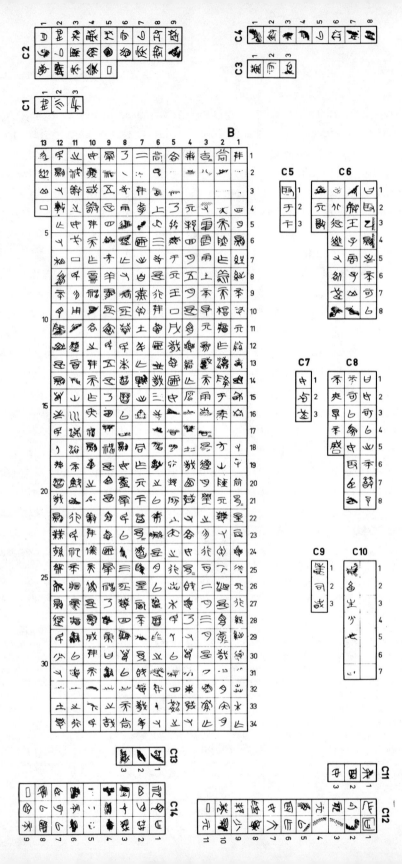

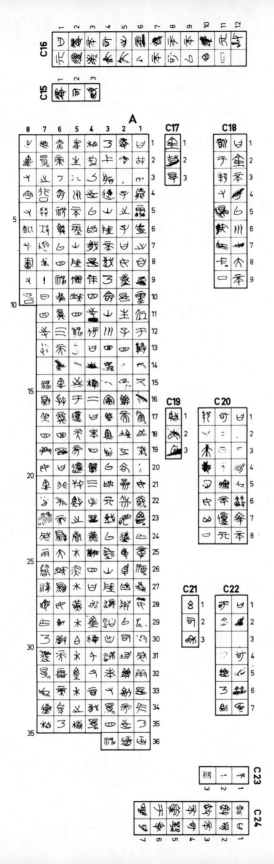

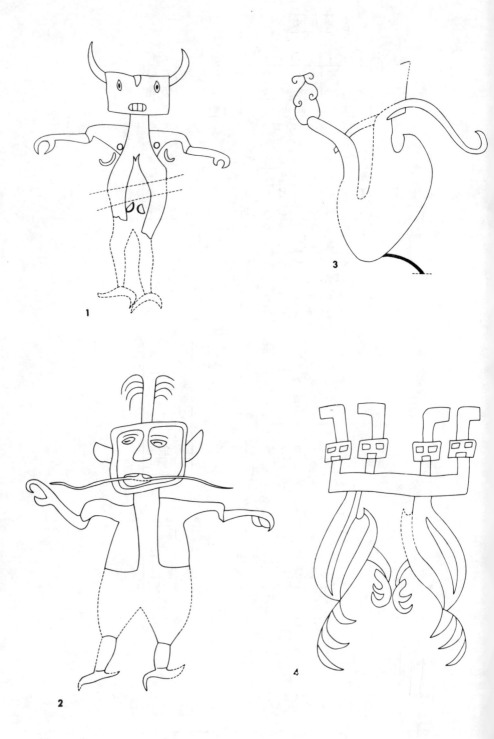

94

5

A

6

B

FIGURE 4B. Reconstructions of the Peripheral Figures in the Ch'u Silk Manuscript in outline form: Nos. 1 - 6 inclusive plus two of the four branches, a and b, which are located in each corner of the Manuscript.

7

9

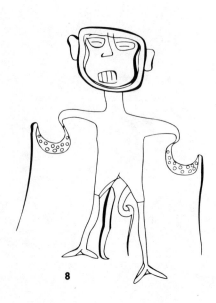

8

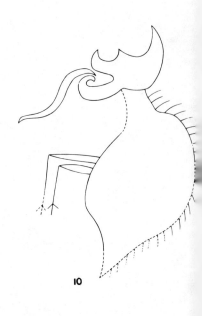

10

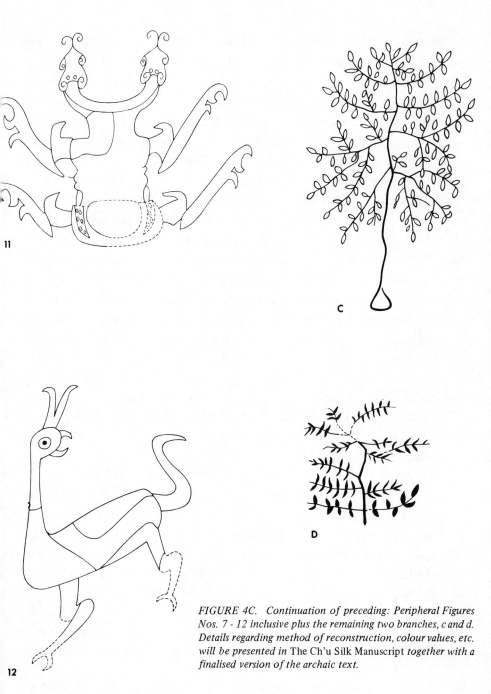

11

C

D

12

FIGURE 4C. Continuation of preceding: Peripheral Figures Nos. 7 - 12 inclusive plus the remaining two branches, c and d. Details regarding method of reconstruction, colour values, etc. will be presented in The Ch'u Silk Manuscript *together with a finalised version of the archaic text.*

97

as a loan for 祖 *tsu* may, in this case, only be a 'graphical' loan
and not a 'phonetic' loan. The thesis that 虞 is 祖 is therefore
open to doubt and this in turn brings into serious question the
remainder of the sentence wherein A. 2-13 'four' is made the final
character of the sentence, thus reading: 'Nü-huang (consort of the
mythical Emperor Yao) thence bore sons — four'. This latter interpretation is partly based upon the reading of A. 2-1 虞 as 祖 *tsu*
just discussed and also the reading of A. 1-32 as 雨 yü 'rain' which
each commentator has misread as 帝 *ti* 'emperor'. To avoid a highly
complex explanation of all this — which I have discussed in detail
elsewhere — the position may be summarised thus: the sentence with
which we have been concerned has hitherto been read with far too
pronounced a leaning towards data in traditional sources and as a
consequence the commentators have in effect had little choice but
to force their interpretations to fit the name of a mythical personage
and especially one whose consort is supposed to have had four sons.
This same graph 虞: 戲 *cha* is elsewhere clearly evident in the
Manuscript as the name of a deity associated with one of the months
of the year; as such it may be paralleled with the graph 且 *chieh*
recorded in this connection in the *Erh-ya*. To read it as *tsu* and in
the sense of 祖 *tsu* 'ancestor' in the present instance is thus even
further to be doubted.[10]

Another kind of problem arises when the reliability of certain
data in post-Han sources becomes a matter of question. The greater
clarity of detail resulting from the infrared photographs shows that
the graph A. 2-24 is written as 𢖭: 彳 comprising thus 彳 plus 止
— which combination is rendered as 辶 *ch'o* 'walk' in modern form
— with two 'feet': 𣥐 astride a curved line: 乚. It has recently been
suggested it should be read as 逃 *t'ao* 'abscond' upon the basis of
the *Han-chien* character 兆: 屰 which is stated to be a version of
the character 兆 *chao* 'omen'. Thus far there is no real quarrel
with the proposed reading, for the *Han-chien* certainly has listed this

---

10. See the comparative list in Jao's paper (p. 117) and also Hayashi's suggested
parallels with the names of Shamans from the *Shan-hai-ching*.

archaic graph which comprises two 'feet' (but no curved line) and states that it appears in the *Wang-shu-tzu pei* 王庶子碑. However, it will be noted upon further investigation, that this stele inscription is no earlier than the T'ang period — probably it is only of Sung date! All earlier recorded versions of the character 兆 *chao* (on its own or as an element in a more complex character) are written upon the same structural principles: 𣥂, 𣥞, 𣥠, 𣥎, etc. Only the *Wang-shu-tzu pei* graph has the above combination which in any case is not fully identical with our character. Further investigation in the *Han-chien* will show that many of the characters cited from this stele inscription and reproduced therein are merely archaistic creations unknown prior to the Han period. Obviously, therefore, there is a considerable risk in using such a source as a means of identifying obsolete characters employed 1500 years earlier! The point is confirmed in the commentary accompanying this graph in the *Han-chien chien-cheng* 汗簡箋正 where it is observed that the combination of 'two feet' forms the graph 步 *pu* 'step' and that this structure *is sometimes misread as* 兆!

The Manuscript graph can be transcribed directly into modern character form as: 遄 which might be equivalent to: 遄. There is, however, no character 遄 in any dictionary, thus we come to an impasse and must seek some explanation from the context and, where available, from other inscriptions with the same character in other contexts.

The aforegoing points may be taken to represent something of the difficulties which at present confront us in our attempts to establish an acceptable transcription and thence a reliable interpretation of the Manuscript text. A major reason for this situation is primarily the lack of availability to scholarship of the Manuscript since its arrival in the U.S.A. nearly 30 years ago. The earliest studies conducted were based upon hand-drawn facsimiles which are filled with errors. From about 1952 the photographs made by the Freer Gallery of Art (normal panchromatic film only) were made available to the several scholars who requested copies for research purposes. The hand-copies each of us made upon the basis of the F.G.A. photographs have been corrected and improved upon in later studies. Then with the incorporation of the Manuscript in the Sackler Collections and the sympathetic and generous interest of Dr. Arthur M. Sackler, a programme of scientific photographing of the Manuscript commenced early in 1966. This involved the preparation of infrared black-and-white as well as coloured photographs (i.e. infrared Ekta Aero Film Type 8443). The photographic reproductions together with a new reconstruction of the archaic text and detailed drawings of the peripheral figures is now practically ready for publication. In the Introduction will be incorporated a character-by-character commentary in which the individual graphs are each fully described and the various earlier proposed interpretations are reviewed. Very clear photographs (4x magnification) of each individual character arranged in an orderly list will allow future research to continue most effectively—even to the extent of calligraphic study of individual character strokes.

BIBLIOGRAPHY

Anon.
　　1959　*Ch'ang-sha fa-chüeh pao-kao* 長沙發掘報告考古學專刊, 丁種第七號, Peking.
An Chih-min and Chen Kung-jou 安志敏・陳公柔
　　1963　'Ch'ang-sha Chan-kuo tseng-shu ch'i ch'i yu-kuan wen-t'i' 長沙戰國繒書及其
　　　　有關問題, *WW* 1963.9 : 48-60.
Barnard, Noel
　　1958　'A Preliminary Study of the Ch'u Silk Manuscript — a new reconstruction of the
　　　　text', *Monumenta Serica*, Vol. XVII (pp. 1-11).
　　n. d.　The *Ch'u Silk Manuscript*, Intercultural Arts Press, New York [in press.].
Cheng Chen 鄭珍
　　1889　*Han-chien chien-cheng* 汗簡箋正〔後周郭忠恕撰, 清鄭珍箋正〕, 光緒十五年廣
　　　　雅書局刊本.
Chiang Hsüan-yi 蔣玄佁
　　1949-50　*Ch'ang-sha*: '*Ch'u min-tsu ch'i ch'i yi-shu*' 長沙 '楚民族及其藝術', 美術考
　　　　古學社, Vol. 1, 1949; Vol. 2, 1950.
Cox, John Hadley
　　1939　*An Exhibition of Chinese Antiquities from Ch'ang-sha*, lent by John Hadley Cox,
　　　　Gallery of Fine Arts, Yale University, March 26 – May 7, 1939.
Hulsewé, A.F.P.
　　　　'Texts in Tombs', *Asiatische Studien*, XVIII/XIX. 1965, pp. 78-89.

Jao Tsung-yi 饒宗頤
1954   'Ch'ang-sha Ch'u-mu shih-chan shen-wu t'u-chuan k'ao-shih' 長沙楚墓時占神
        物圖卷考釋, *Journal of Oriental Studies*, University of Hong Kong, Vol. I, No. 1
        (pp. 69–84).
Shang Ch'eng-tso 商承祚
1964   'Chan-kuo Ch'u po-shu shu-lüeh' 戰國楚帛書述畧, *Wen-wu* 1964.9 : 8–10.
Ts'ai Chi-hsiang 蔡季襄
1944   *Wan-Chou tseng-shu k'ao-ch'eng* 晚周繒書考證, 乙酉孟春付印.

SUGGESTIONS CONCERNING THE GROUND OF THE CH'U SILK MANUSCRIPT IN RELATION TO SILK-WEAVING IN PRE-HAN AND HAN CHINA

JEAN MAILEY

The fabric of the manuscript seems to have been originally a complete width of silk tabby with right and left sides determined by selvages and unfinished edges top and bottom. It is $15\frac{1}{4}''$ (387 mm) high and $18\frac{3}{4}''$ (470 mm) wide as mounted. It is woven of untwisted and apparently undyed cultivated silk (*Bombyx mori*) with approximately 57 warps and 27 wefts per square centimetre. The $\frac{1}{4}''$ selvages are of the same tabby weave as the ground with slightly higher warp count. Vertical striations caused by alternately denser and looser warp spacing are fairly regular with two more widely spaced warps, then 7 more densely spaced ones.

The manuscript seems to approximate its original state in spite of many breaks and piecings. The gridiron of fairly continuous vertical and horizontal breaks from top to bottom and from side to side probably results from the lines of intentional folding sometime during its long history. Various diagonal or random breaks and minute overlaps also occur. None of these breaks seem seriously to disturb the basic plan of the existing manuscript. The widest continuous break occurs from top to bottom in the centre. The three vertical breaks spaced on each side of this do not seem to extend unbroken from top to bottom. A few small intact stretches appear to exist along all of them so that the actual width of each half of the manuscript on either side of the vertical central break is maintained. The probably complete width may be deduced from certain other evidence to be examined below. A continuous horizontal break occurs across the approximate centre of the manuscript. Here, as in the case of all breaks but the central vertical one, the characters and the peripheral figures serve to indicate that much of the original fabric survives. Two horizontal breaks running more or less from selvage to selvage are spaced above this. On these, areas of fabric are missing in certain places but occasionally the break appears to be interrupted by small stretches of intact fabric. The upper horizontal break seems to have only one small intact area with a skilfully joined break $\frac{3}{4}''$ below it running parallel to the upper horizontal break. The three major horizontal breaks spaced below the central horizontal break seem also to have intermittent areas of unbroken fabric.

Diagonal breaks and overlaps occur especially in the right-hand half of the manuscript. Incidental piecings emphasize themselves by a difference in warp direction; they are usually pieces of the original manuscript set on the diagonal. Occasional repainting seems to occur and there are many holes. But, in general, only at the top and bottom of the manuscript are possibly significant parts of the original manuscript disturbed or missing.

Red markings of powdered cinnabar seem to be part of tabby fragments with lighter, more loosely woven, untwisted silk warps and wefts which overlay the left half of the manuscript at intervals. Actual characters on this are especially apparent in the left upper quarter of the manuscript. These fragments appear to be remains of another possibly contemporary manuscript written in red.

The plain or tabby weave in silk as a ground for painting or calligraphy is seen in a few other actual examples from this period. One is the darkened silk of variously reported dimensions and no selvages with the lady, dragon, and bird, found in Ch'ang-sha in 1949.[1] Two well-preserved silk letters from the 1st century A.D.

1. John Haskins, 'Recent Excavations in China', *Archives of the Chinese Art Society of America*, X (1956), p. 51 illustrated, and Tsien Tsuen-hsuin, *Written on Bamboo and Silk*, 1962, pp. 124-125.

FIGURE 1. A, B: examples of selvage along the extant fabric edges of the Ch'u Silk Manuscript. Vertical striations may be noted in each as well as examples of fragmentary piecing and retouching of the background colour of the fabric (e.g. A: at right-hand edge, upper half).
   In C may be noted a representative section of the central horizontal break. The manner in which this cuts through the characters indicates the small extent of the break.

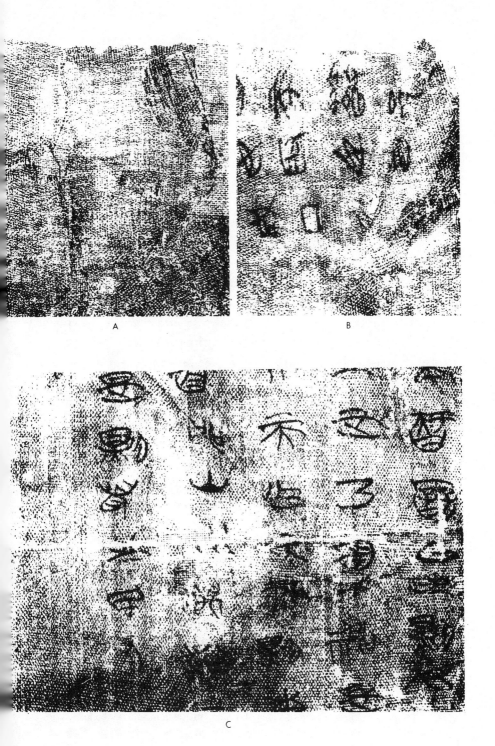

A

B

C

were uncovered by Aurel Stein's second expedition to Tun-huang.[2] A silk roll reported by Shang Ch'eng-tso 商 承 祚 in his 1939 inventory of Ch'ang-sha objects is described as a Ch'u silk roll (using the term 帛 *po* for 'silk') with a width of about $13\frac{3}{4}''$ (350 mm) on a roller about $17\frac{1}{2}''$ (440 mm) long with red lacquered ends. Because of its fragility the owner has never been able to prove his theory that it is inscribed by unrolling it.[3]

Evidence in Han and pre-Han texts for the widespread use of silk — variously named and apparently of various sorts — as a writing material is summarised by Wang Kuo-wei 王 國 維. In one section of the *Chou-li* 周 禮, he observes, it is stated that the names of meritorious subjects were written on the King's banner and in another section dealing with funerary rites appears the term 物 *wu* defined in the commentaries as 'variegated silk' upon which writing was done; when a person died they used black silk (緇 *tzu*). In the *Mo-tzu* 墨 子 it is stated that the sage-kings of high antiquity who invariably regarded the gods and the spirits as their basic guide feared that their descendants of later ages might not be able to comprehend such matters and committed these to record in writings on bamboo tablets and silk — one foot (尺 *chih*) of silk (*po*) amounted to one section of writing. In the *Yen-tzu ch'un-ch'iu* 晏 子 春 秋 it is stated that when a certain prince bestowed estates on his minister it was recorded on silk (*po*) and bamboo; in the *Lun-yü* 論 語 there is the record of Tzu Chang 子 張 writing on his silk sash (紳 *shen*); the *Yüeh-chüeh shu* 越 絕 書 describes the King of Yüeh writing in vermilion on silk (*po*); etc.[4]

Finely woven silk tabby in general is well represented among surviving late Eastern Chou and Han silks. Late Eastern Chou textiles are much rarer, however, and the examples in this group are fewer. Embroideries from Pazyrik, kurgan 5, are worked on a ground of

2.   Mark Aurel Stein, *Serindia: Detailed Report of Explorations in Central Asia and Westernmost China*, II, 1921, pp. 762–763.

3.   Shang Ch'eng-tso, *Ch'ang-sha ku-wu wen-chien chi*, 1939, A. 46a.

4.   Wang Kuo-wei, 'Chien-tu chien-shu k'ao, in the posthumous collection of his writings *Hai-ning Wang Ching-an hsien-sheng yi-shu* 2nd Series – volumes unnumbered, p. 11a.

silk tabby.5   Silk tabbies are used for the cuffs, linings, and bands of the warp-patterned silk bonnet and mitts — presumably from Ch'ang-sha — now at the Cooper Union Museum.6   Remains of Ch'u costume from a tomb at Ch'ang-sha reported by Shang Ch'eng-tso include a dress hem or border of silk (繒 tseng) with woven ornament and an inner sleeve of silk (po, op. cit., A. 44a-b). Both are ancient silk terms to be explored below, both apparently on occasion applied to tabby. Unpatterned silk tabbies form more than nine-tenths of the textiles from the Han period in the Hermitage which has one of the great collections of Han textiles in the world. The curator, E. Lubo-Lesnichenko, reports considerable variety in these tabbies. He finds 104 with equal count in warp and weft; 81 with warp count strongly predominating; and a group of 32 transitional between these in relation between warp and weft. The proportion of warp to weft per cm averages 1.5 to 1 in the group as a whole. In examples where warps predominate, the warp-density ranges from 40-49 to 130-140 per cm. One tabby has a warp count of 160 warps per cm and one, 180 (op. cit., pp. 7 - 8).

A range of widths from selvage to selvage, an especially important point in connection with this manuscript, is preserved in some of these. In the saddle-cover of embroidery on silk tabby from kurgan 5 at Pazyrik, the selvage to selvage width preserved in the ground is $19\frac{1}{2}''$ (op. cit., p. 50). The silk roll reported by Shang Ch'eng-tso to which attention has been drawn above is stated to be about $13\frac{3}{4}''$ wide with a supporting roller about $17\frac{1}{2}''$ long. This silk has been badly shrunken and distorted by immersion in alcohol. Fourteen smooth monotone silk fabrics from Noin-ula have widths varying from 18'' to 20'' (E. Lubo-Lesnichenko, op. cit., p. 19). At least, four plain silks from Lou-lan and one from Edsen-gol range from 16'' to $18\frac{4}{5}''$ in width and the inventories for these seem to indicate a few additional widths

5.   E. Lubo-Lesnichenko, Ancient Chinese Silk Weavings and Embroideries, 1961, see also pp. 13–15; Plates 26–33, 41; pp. 50, 56; Plates 49, 50.
6.   C. S. Hathaway and J. Mailey, 'A Bonnet and a Pair of Mitts from Ch'ang-sha', Chronicle of the Museum for the Arts of Decoration of the Cooper Union, Vol. 2, No. 10 (December, 1958).

of silk tabby between $18\frac{1}{4}''$ and $18\frac{1}{2}''$.[7] One from Palmyra is reportedly $21\frac{1}{5}''$ wide.[8] And a small bale of yellowish plain silk found by Stein at Lou-lan has a width of approximately $15''$. Two silk strips from the Tun-huang *limes* are $20''$ wide and just under $20''$ wide. Also found by Stein at the Tun-huang *limes* was a plain silk strip, evidently once attached to a silk roll, with the inscription translated by Chavannes as: 'Roll of silk from K'ang-fu in the Jen-cheng kingdom; width 2.2 feet, length 40 feet; weight 25 ounces; value 618 pieces of money'. Two wooden measuring sticks found at the same site show the Chinese foot to have been at that time (53 B.C.–137 A.D.) approximately $9''$. The width of this rolled silk would therefore have been $19\frac{4}{5}''$ in our terms (*op. cit.*, pp. 700–04).

These actual finds, on the whole, support the statement of the Han historian, Pan Ku 班 固, that the standard unit or length of silk in Han times called 匹 *p'i* was 2.2 Chinese feet (or $19\frac{4}{5}''$) wide and 40 Chinese feet long (Wang Kuo-wei, *op. cit.*, 'Shih pi' 釋 幣, p. 2a). Cheng Hrüan 鄭 玄 in his commentary of the same time on the *Yi-li* 儀 禮 confirms this width (*cf.* Tsien Tsuen-hsuin, *op. cit.*, pp. 120–1). Earlier use of this standard is suggested by the Pazyrik embroidery ($19\frac{1}{2}''$ wide) and by the Ch'u Silk Manuscript ($18\frac{3}{4}''$ from selvage to selvage as mounted). Wang Kuo-wei in his study of the character *pi* believes this to be true. He quotes from the Confucian classics to

7.   Vivi Sylwan, 'Investigation of Silk from Edsen-gol and Lop-nor', *Reports from the Scientific Expedition to the Northwestern Provinces of China under the leadership of Dr. Sven Hedin*, the Sino-Swedish Expedition publication 32, VII Archaeology 6, 1949, p. 94. Here Miss Sylwan states her opinion that 'The silks here reported are no evidence for the assumption that the width of silks in China was under any kind of state control'. See also Folke Bergman, 'Archaeological Researches in Sinkiang especially the Lop-nor Region', *op. cit.*, VII Archaeology 1, 1939, in same series, pp. 113–14 and p. 130 where he quotes her lists of material including three or four more widths of taffeta between $18\frac{1}{4}''$ and $18\frac{1}{2}''$ from selvage to selvage that seem to be in addition to what she summarizes above.
8.   R. Pfister, *Nouveaux Textiles de Palmyre*, 1937, p. 34.

FIGURE 2. A: vestiges of second manuscript with red (ink?) pigment, still adhering to the present manuscript. Fabric weave is particularly clear in the circular patch at extreme mid-right of photo.

*   B: Another area containing remnants of the second manuscript wherein several characters in red pigment are almost legible. Red shows up as white in these infra-red photographs.*

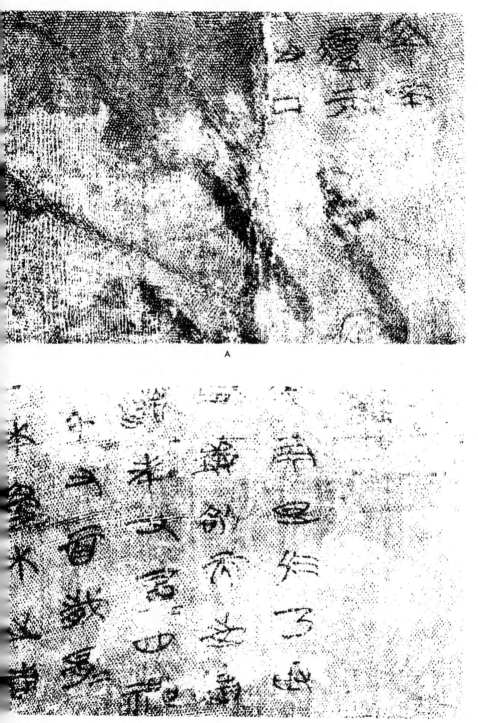

A

B

prove that standard units for fabrics existed in pre-Han days and that they were set up by the ruler assisted by an officer of domestic affairs whenever a State or City was proclaimed. The standard measurements of silk, *p'i* or *liang* (兩) — 'two' — 'double', from the custom of rolling in from each end and thus making each roll appear a double one — was usually 2.2 Chinese feet wide and 40 Chinese feet long from early Chou times on. A government proclamation in 473 A.D. recorded in the *Wei-shu* ordered the standardization of the same measurements for a *p'i* of textile 'following the old system' (*cf.* Tsien, p. 121).

The silk fabric Wang associates with this unit he calls by the Late Eastern Chou terms, 幣 *pi* or 帛 *po*, apparently used interchangeably for a silk fabric of undetermined weave. The character 繒 *tseng* is the term Chinese scholars apply to the ground of the Manuscript we are discussing today and also to the pale tabby-woven silk ground of the Ch'ang-sha painting of the lady with dragon and phoenix. Tsien describes *tseng* as 'a finely woven silk with heavy threads . . . probably made from the product of wild silkworms, and thicker, darker, and more durable than the other kinds of plain silk materials' (p. 126). The gloss for *tseng* in the *Shuo-wen* dictionary is '*po*', with the commentary by a Han scholar that '*po* is like the *pi*-coloured *tseng* of today'. *Pi* (璧) as used here refers to the ritual disk of the period, usually of pale or whitish jade, a colour suggesting that these apparently undyed tabbies probably had a green or brown tinge as if they were made of wild silk, (*cf.* Jen Ta-chung 任大椿, 'Shih tseng', *Huang-Ch'ing ching-chieh*, 65 : p. 1).[9]

These data provide a certain frame of reference for our Manuscript. Its width as mounted is close to within an inch of the $19\frac{4}{5}''$ width of the standard unit of silk measurement — the *p'i* — as recorded

---

9. Lubo-Lesnichenko in 'Some terms for Silk Fabrics in Ancient China', *Works of the State Hermitage Museum*, V, Leningrad, 1961, pp. 251-256, finds some exceptions to this equivalence of *po* and *tseng* in early definitions and translates the *Shuo-wen* commentary cited above as : 'The silk *po* now refers to the silk *tseng* which is of natural colour' presumably translating the same commentary quoted by Jen Ta-chung.
   From this commentary, Lubo-Lesnichenko also quotes the Han poet and scholar Ts'ai Yi 蔡誼 to the effect that *tseng* is expensive, thick silk with heavy dye.

in inscriptions and literature. Its width is almost in the middle of the range of selvage-to-selvage widths of surviving Late Eastern Chou and Han tabbies which is from 15" to $20\frac{7}{8}$" (with the ˙exception of the Ch'ang-sha roll). Thus the amount missing along the central break may be anything up to two and one half inches but this evidence suggests that it is only a small amount on either edge of the break — just about what appears as the piece is now mounted. Technically, there is no way of determining how much is missing from top and bottom unless we may be guided by the implications of Master Mo's statement and guess that this was once approximately a square like the ones with writings concerning the gods and the spirits.[10] In this case, the height, now $15\frac{1}{4}$" would approximate the original width which must range somewhere around $18\frac{1}{2}$" to $18\frac{3}{4}$". Thus, about $3\frac{1}{2}$" may be missing from top and bottom together.

Hazarding a venture into the endless quicksands of Chinese textile terminology,[11] one might guess the material of the Manuscript to be the *po* or *pi* of Late Eastern Chou literature and that it was cut originally from a bolt ten modern yards long (or 40 ancient Chinese feet). Its warp and weft count is comparatively low but the fabric falls within the group of tabbies where warps predominate.

Small tripod looms with two harnesses each controlled by a foot-treadle appear on several reliefs of the Han period. These are obviously tabby looms and represent the kind of loom on which the silk of the Manuscript could have been woven.[12]

10.   Professor Lu Kuang-huan who translated this text into English, feels such is the implication of this use of *ch'ih* 'foot' to a Chinese.
11.   Summarized in connection with writing materials by Tsien, pp. 125-6.
12.   The author wishes to express her gratitude to Professor Lu Kuang-huan of Columbia University for the reading of the Chinese texts and to Mr. Malcolm Delacorte of the Metropolitan Museum who identified the silk and the red colouring and gave much valuable technical advice.

BIBLIOGRAPHY

Bergman, Folke
 1939 'Archaeological Researches in Sinkiang especially the Lop-nor Region', *Reports from the Scientific Expedition to the Northwestern Provinces of China under the Leadership of Dr. Sven Hedin*, Sino-Swedish Publication 7, VII Archaeology 1.
Haskins, John
 1956 'Recent Excavations in China,' *Archives of the Chinese Art Society of America*, X
Hathaway, C. S. and Mailey, J.
 1958 'A Bonnet and a Pair of Mitts from Ch'ang-sha', *Chronicle of the Museum for the Arts of Decoration of the Cooper Union*, Vol. 2, No. 10 (December, 1958).
Jen Ta-chung 任大椿
 'Shih tseng' 釋繒, *Huang-Ch'ing ching-chieh* 皇清經解, 卷六十五 (pp. 1-5).
Lubo-Lesnichenko, E.
 1961 *Ancient Chinese Silk Weavings and Embroideries*, The Hermitage, Leningrad.
Pfister, R.
 1937 *Nouveaux Textiles de Palmyre*, Les Editions d'Art et d'Histoire. Paris.
Shang Ch'eng-tso 商承祚
 1939 *Ch'ang-sha ku-wu wen-chien chi* 長沙古物聞見記, Ch'eng-tu.
Stein, Mark Aurel
 1921 *Serindia: Detailed Report of Explorations in Central Asia and Westernmost China*, 4 Vols. Oxford, Clarendon Press.
Sylwan, Vivi
 1949 'Investigation of Silk from Edsen-gol and Lop-nor', *Reports from the Scientific Expedition to the Northwestern Provinces of China under the Leadership of Dr. Sven Hedin*, Sino-Swedish Publication 32, VII Archaeology 6.
Tsien Tsuen-hsuin
 1962 *Written on Bamboo and Silk*, The University of Chicago Press.
Wang Kuo-wei 王國維
 1936 'Chien-tu chien-shu k'ao' 簡牘檢署考, *Hai-ning Wang Ching-an hsien-sheng yi-shu* 海寧王靜安先生遺書.

112

SOME ASPECTS OF THE CALENDAR, ASTROLOGY, AND RELIGIOUS CONCEPTS OF THE CH'U PEOPLE AS REVEALED IN THE CH'U SILK MANUSCRIPT

JAO TSUNG-YI

The Ch'u Silk Manuscript is undoubtedly one of the most valuable finds in the whole history of Chinese archaeology. It contains a text of nearly one thousand characters. Unfortunately owing to the folding and wearing away of the silk, many of the characters have been obliterated and are still a matter of conjecture for the student. In the light of the bamboo tablets of Hsin-yang 信陽 and Wu-wei 武威, such details as the sign ▰ can be interpreted as a mark separating the different paragraphs for the convenience of the reader. There are, of course, characters which offer no problem of interpretation. For instance the characters 猷 雨 which appear twice (A. 1-31, 32; A. 7-24, 25) can be easily read as wind and rain.[1] But the study of the more problematic parts has been greatly advanced by the use of the new infrared photographs of the Ch'u Silk Manuscript. Upon comparison with parts of the classics preserved in certain Tun-huang manuscript material, it has been possible to shed new light on the calendar, astrology, and religious concepts of the Chan-kuo period.

1. REMARKS ON CALENDAR TERMS

(a) The ' Ten suns (days) '
Attention is drawn to the following passage in the Manuscript (A. 6-33 to A. 7-12):

1.   The character 猷 is composed of two parts. The top part consists of 尺 with an extra stroke, and this has an ancient form 𩲡 recorded in the *Shuo-wen*. The lower element is a variant form of 虫. There is then no doubt that the whole character 猷 is a variant form of 風.
    Individual character references to the tentative reconstruction of the Ch'u Silk Manuscript text (Barnard: Figure 4A, in present volume) are provided for readers interested in following up such details. [Ed].

The Emperor Chun then arranged the orderly movement of the sun and the moon. (The god) Kung Kung (共 工) to pace out[2] .... Ten suns (days) and Four seasons. (... 帝夋乃爲日月之行. ▰ 共工☐步, 十日四時.)

The term 'Ten Suns' (十日) appears in the *Ch'u-tz'u* (Chao-hun):

And ten suns that come out together, melting metal, dissolving stone. (Trans. D. Hawkes, *Ch'u Tz'u — Songs of the South*, p. 104)

It is also to be found in the *Chuang-tzu* and elsewhere.[3] According to the *Shan-hai-ching*:

Hsi-ho 羲和, the wife of Emperor Chun 帝俊 begot Ten Suns.*

This legend is similar to that in the Manuscript. The Ten Suns sometimes indicates the Ten Stems (i.e. the names of the days). Here the term is parallel to the Four Seasons and is obviously used as a calendar term.

(b) *The 'Four Seasons' and the 'Three Seasons'*

Each of the four characters comprising the names of the seasons in the Ch'u Silk Manuscript contain the element ⊘ : 日 *jih* 'sun' (B. 1-13 to 16; C. 9-3, C. 15-3, C. 21-3, C. 3-3). This particular feature is rarely found in transmitted literature. Only an occasional example is to be found in such sources as the *Han-chien* 汗簡 eg. 舟 as 冬 *tung* 'winter' and 甘 as 春 *ch'un* 'spring'. However in the Tun-huang manuscript of a commentary on the *Shang-shu* (p. 3315: 尙書釋文) there is an instance of the graph 昃 and of the

2. The character (A. 7-8) is quite clearly 步, which means 'paces'. *Cf*. the legend in the *Shan-hai-ching* when Yü made two of his officials Ta-chang 大章 and Su-hai 豎亥 count their paces in the four directions.

3. For a detailed survey regarding legends of the 'ten suns' see Kuan Tung-kuei 管東貴, 'Chung-kuo ku-tai shih-jih shen-hua chih yen-chiu' 中國古代十日神話之研究, *BAS*, Vol. 33.

* It is still customary in Chinese scholarly writing to omit bibliographical details and simply to record the title of the book from which a passage has been cited — sometimes the chapter may also be given. As most of the sources involved in the present paper are not available in Western language translation, the problem need concern only the sinological reader. Accordingly I have not undertaken the task of searching for the precise references here. [Ed.]

ku-wen form 奥. In the same manuscript the character *ch'un* 春 in *ku-wen* form is written as 旹. Another instance of this form (耂) is found in the Shou-ch'un-ting 壽春鼎 inscription (*Wen-wu* 1964.9, pp. 36, 40). In the Ch'u Silk Manuscript the graphs *ch'un* are written as 杍 with an additional stroke which is a variant form.

The term Three Seasons (三時) appears twice (B. 6-6, 7; B. 6-15, 16). In the *Tso-chuan* (Huan, 6: Legge, Vol. 5, p. 49) we find this term in a statement by Chi-liang 季梁 who prevented the Marquis of Sui 隨 from attacking the troops of Ch'u. Tu Yü 杜預 commented to the effect that the Three Seasons stood for Spring, Summer, and Autumn. It seems that 'Winter' was not included.

(*c*) *The Twelve Months*

The names of the lunar months appear in the Tun-huang manuscripts p. 4024 and p. 4042 which fragments were originally a continuous piece of text as I have shown in Figure 1. The resulting reconstruction is undoubtedly an enlarged version of the *Yüeh-ling* 月令, the 'monthly ordinances' of the *Li-chi* with the names of the twelve months as given in the *Erh-ya* 爾雅 prefixed to each quotation from the *Yüeh-ling*.

During the T'ang dynasty in the T'ien-pao reign-period (742-755), a new edition of the *Yüeh-ling* was made. The distribution of 72 periods, each of 5 days, was arranged following the method of $6\frac{1}{7}$ days in accordance with apocryphal *Yi-wei* 易緯.[4] Later on, Li Lin-fu 李林甫 and others edited the *Yüeh-ling* and added a commentary. They submitted a memorandum to the Emperor. A fragmentary copy consisting of about 23 lines, is now in the British Museum (Tun-huang M.S. 621).[5] Another fragment, Tun-huang M.P. 3306 is entitled *Yüeh-ling chieh-yi* (月令節義). These are newly discovered materials dating from the T'ang period relating to the *Yüeh-ling*.[6]

---

4. See Ch'üan Tsu-wang 全祖望, *Chi-ch'i t'ing-chi wai-pien* 鮚埼亭集外編 Ch. 35: Pa Li-chi shih-ching yüeh-ling 跋禮記右經月令.
5. See Wang Chung-min 王重民, Tun-huang ku-chi hsü-lu 敦煌古籍叙錄, p. 49.
6. Some quotations from the *Yüeh-ling* found in the *Sung hui-yao* 宋會要 are, according to Shen T'ao 沈濤, taken from the *Yüeh-ling* of the T'ang period.

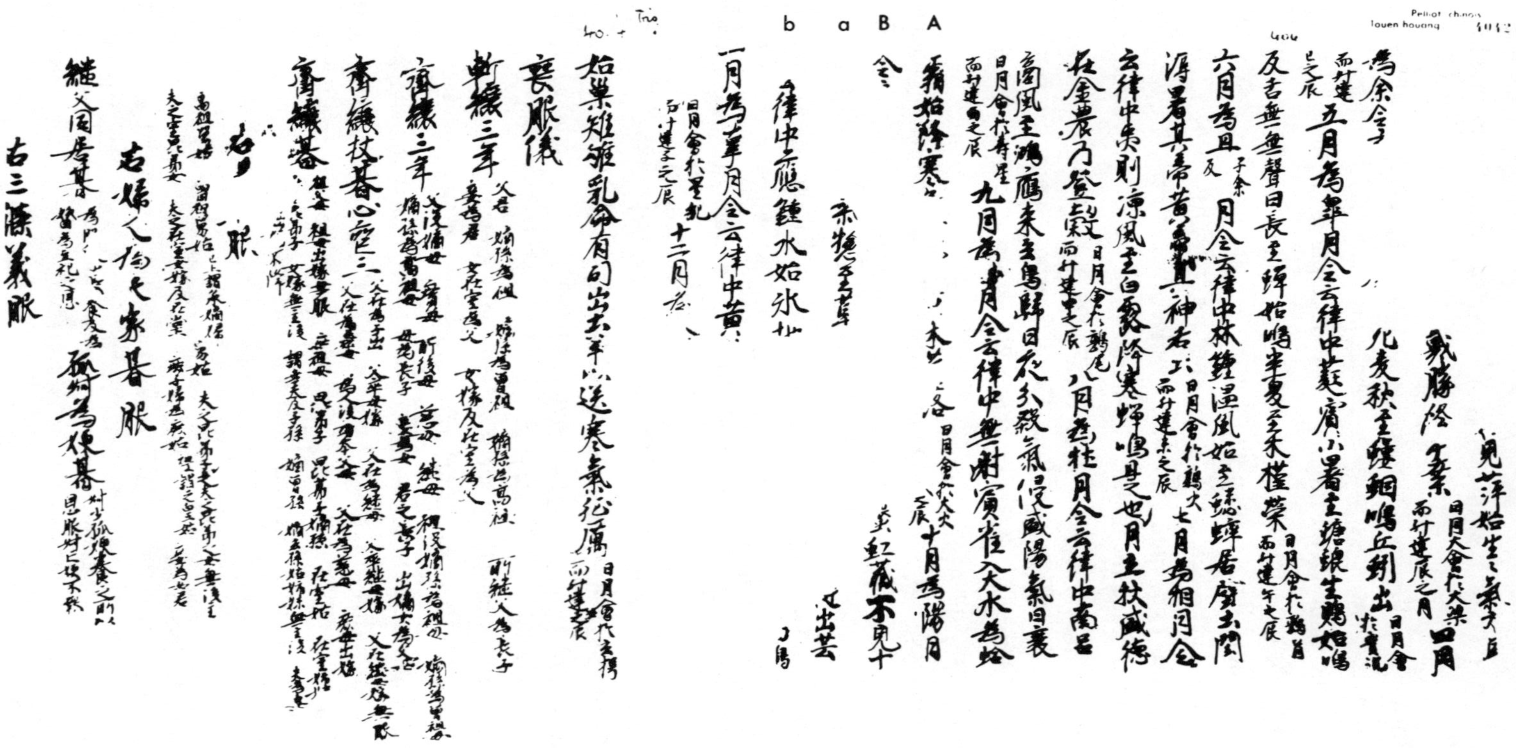

FIGURE 1. Tun-huang manuscripts P. 4024 and P. 4042 combined into their original and continuous form—lines A and B of P. 4024 are to be placed top and bottom of lines a and b of P. 4042.

	1st	2nd	3rd	4th	5th	6th	7th	8th	9th	10th	11th	12th
Erh-ya	陬	如	寎	余	皋	且	相	壯	玄	陽	辜	涂
Ch'u Silk Manuscript	取	女	秉	余	䓕 (㱃)	虘	金 (倉)	臧 (臧)	8	昜	姑	荼
Yüeh-ling (Tun-huang mss)				余	皋	且	相	壯		陽	辜	
Other Sources	娵 聚		窇	舒	高					疈		除

TABLE 1. *The several versions of the names of the Twelve Months.*

The names of the months in P. 4042 are identical with those in the *Erh-ya*, except the name of the eighth month which is written as 牡. This is in error for 壯 thus illustrating the possibility of occasional mistakes which may sometimes occur even in earlier sources.[7]

There are some special names of months occurring in inscriptions from the States of Ch'i and Ch'en, e.g. 冰月, 裖 (腜) which, presumably, were terms in current use in eastern parts of China.[8] On the other hand, the names for the twelve months used in the *Erh-ya* are the same as those used in the Ch'u Silk Manuscript. Much of the material in the *Erh-ya* is derived from the writings of Shih-tzu 尸子 said to be a native of Ch'u.[9] For these reasons, one may conjecture that the terms used in the *Erh-ya* were those current in the south of China. The names of twelve months in their various forms are illustrated in Table 1 above.

(d) The Intercalary Month

Reference to the intercalary month appears twice in the Ch'u Silk Manuscript. In one case the context is clear and reads as follows (B. 3–20 to 24): 月閏之勿行 *yüeh jun chi wu hsing* 'prohibited during the intercalary month'. In the *Ching-Ch'u sui-shih-chi* 荊楚歲時記 ('Annual Folk Customs of the State of Ch'u') by Tsung Lin 宗懍 there

7.　　Ku Yen-wu 顧炎武 mentions that in copies of Li Ch'ing-chao's 李清照 Chin-shih-lu hou-hsü 金石錄後序 printed in Shantung after the Wan-li reign-period, the characters 壯月 are often found corrupted to 牡丹 (see *Jih-chih-lu* 日知錄 [別字]). This corruption is the same as the one found in the Tun-huang manuscript version.
8.　　The character 裖 in bronze inscriptions, probably = 腜 meaning 'the twelfth month' (see *Fung-su-t'ung* 風俗通).
9.　　Note, for example, the Chapters Jen-yi 仁意 and Kuang-tse 廣澤 which have a great deal in common with the *Erh-ya*.

117

is a sentence similar to this record of the Ch'u Silk Manuscript which reads: 閏月不舉百事 'During the intercalary month, it is forbidden to do anything'.[10] It would seem that this was an old Ch'u custom.

By means of an intercalary month, the ancient Emperor Yao fixed the Four Seasons in order to make up a lunar year (*Shu-ching*: Legge, Vol. 3, p. 22). Tun-huang M.P. 3306 reads: 大數三年一閏, 細而言之, 八年三閏, 十九年九閏 'Roughly, there is one intercalary month in three years; more exactly, there are three intercalary months in eight years, or nine intercalary months in nineteen years', (It will be noted that 'nine' is obviously a mistake for 'seven'.)

(*e*) '*Coming of the Swallows*'

Another sentence in the Manuscript (C. 6–1 to 5) may be discussed in connection with the first month. It reads: 日取乙則至 'during the month of Ch'ü swallows will arrive'. The characters 大乙 *ta-yi* appear on an ivory vessel containing a diagram of the Seven Stars of Han period date.[11] The graph 乙 is to be read as 鳦 which appears in the *Shuo-wen* which also defines 乞 *yi* as 玄鳥 'black bird'.[12] The *Ching-Ch'u sui-shih-chi* says: 荆楚之俗, 燕始來, 睇 有入室者, 以雙箸擲之, 令有子, 'According to the Ching-Ch'u custom when the swallows begin to come, people who throw a pair of chopsticks at them upon seeing them enter a house, will have a son',[13]

2. THE MEANING OF YING (縄=盈) AND CH'U (紬=縮) AND DIVINATION BY IRREGULARITIES OF THE BROOM STAR

In the Ch'u Silk Manuscript there is the following paragraph of an astrological record which reads along these lines (B. 1–1 to 2–30):

Sometimes the sun and moon are not in their constant course. This is called *Ying* (gaining) and *Ch'u* (retreat-

---

10.　See Moriya Mitsuo 守屋美都雄 *Chūgoku kosaijiki no kenkyū* 中國古歲時記 の研究.

11.　See *Shuang-chien-yi ku-ch'i-wu t'u-lu* 雙劍誃古器物圖錄, B. 39a–b.

12.　The character 乙 should not be read as 巳 (祀) because the graph 祀 appears in the sentence 民祀不㳪 (B. 11–23 to 26) where the element is written as 巳 which is certainly different from 乙.

13.　This passage is quoted in Lo Yüan's 羅願 *Erh-ya-yi* 爾雅翼.

> ing). Spring, Summer, Autumn, and Winter have... and have their own regular way. When the order of the sun, the moon, and the heavenly bodies[14] is disturbed, gaining and retreating ... and the plants would become erratic ... ominous happenings. Heaven and earth will cause disasters(?). The *T'ien-p'ou* star 天棓[15] will tremble and fall down in ... direction. Then, the mountains and hillocks ... there will be streams and floods. Such (phenomena) are (seen) in the Po-po (孛孛).[16]

It is my opinion that 𦁐絀 should read as 盈縮. It is a special term found in ancient Chinese astronomy. The character 𦁐 appears in the *Shuo-wen* and the *Shuo-wen chi-yün* (集韻). It is a variant form of 縕.[17] The element 呈 is often interchangeable with 盈 as components of characters. Hence 𦁐絀 is equivalent to 盈絀 and 贏絀.[18] In the Ch'u Silk Manuscript the term 𦁐絀 is employed in the sense of a motion of heavenly bodies, so it should be read as 盈縮. According to Needham, a short retrogradation of a planet was called a 'retreat' (縮 *so*) and an unexpectedly rapid advance was called 'gaining' (贏 *ying*) or an 'urgency' (疾 *chi*).[19] There are two sources in which the details of the term 贏縮 are mentioned: (i) the T'ien-kuan-shu chapter of the *Shih-chi* which states: 'In order to measure the apparent forward motion 順 *shun* and the retrograde motion 逆

14. The phase 日月星辰 is frequently seen in the classics. The Canon of Yao says: 'to calculate and delineate the movements and appearances of the Sun, the Moon, the Stars and the Zodiacal spaces ...' (Legge, Vol. 3, p. 18).
15. A kind of 'edging-in star' such as the T'ien-ch'iang (天槍) and the T'ien-ch'an (天欃).
16. These two lines may be transcribed into modern characters as follows:

隹(惟)……日月則𦁐絀，不𢔶(得)亓(其)常。春夏秋备，又(有)
□又尚(常)。日月星辰，亂𠎫(達)其行。𦁐絀𠎫□，卉木亡尚。
……犬(夭=祆)，天陸(陸=地)乍(作)羕。天梠(棓)牆(將)乍湯(蕩)，
降于亓(其)方。山陵其𤔲，又(有)泉又迴(汩)，是胃(胃=謂)孛=。

17. *Cf.* for instance, (沈子) 逞 = 盈, (欒) 盈 = 逞.
18. For 贏絀, see *Hsün-tzu*: 緩急贏絀 (荀子非相).
19. See J. Needham, *Science and Civilization in China*, Vol. III, p. 399.

ni of Jupiter, it would be better to observe the movement of the sun and the moon. An unexpected rapid advance is called 'gaining', a short retrogradation is called 'retreat';[20] (ii) the T'ien-wen-chih chapter of the *Han-shu*: 'Whenever the five planets rise early, it is called *ying*, *ying* is the guest; whenever the planets rise late, it is called *so*, *so* is the host. The *ying* and *so* of the five planets can be reviewed through the appearance of Piao (杓 'the Dipper')'.[21]

The name T'ien-p'ou which is found in the star-map in the Tun-huang manuscript S3326 is drawn at the end of the diagram (see Needham, *op. cit.*, Vol. III, Pl. XXIV). According to the *Ho-tu* 河圖 as quoted by the T'ien-wen-chih chapter of the *Chin-shu* the spirits of Jupiter are the seven stars 'from T'ien-p'ou to Tsang-shui (自天 棓至蒼彗)'. The T'ien-kuan-shu says: 'The T'ien-p'ou always appears in the third month; its tail is about four feet long. When the Spirits of Jupiter appear on the north-east, there will be war in the Empire'. The term *shui-hsing* 彗星 occurs in the 'Nine Songs': 登九天兮撫彗星. 'He mounts the ninefold heaven and grasps the Broom Star' (trans. Hawkes, *op. cit.*, p. 41). In the Bibliographical section of the *Sui-shu* there are several works listed with the titles concerning divinations made in connection with the Broom Star.

The character 棓 can be deciphered as 棓 because of its identity with the graph 棓 in the inscribed tally of the Prince of E(鄂君節).

As there were treatises on the military affairs of the Yin-yang School (兵陰陽) compiled during the Chan-kuo period, this paragraph in the Ch'u Silk Manuscript might be regarded as belonging to the Ping-yin-yang School.[22]

20.   史記天官書：察日月之行，以揆歲星順逆。...歲星贏縮，...其趨舍而日 贏，退舍日縮‧贏，其國有兵不復；縮，其國有憂將亡。
21.   漢書天文志：凡五星早出為贏，贏為客；晚出為縮，縮為主人。五星贏縮，必有天應見杓。
22.   Note the explanatory caption under Peripheral figure No. 1 (C. 2-1 to 2-22): 'During the month of Ku, it will be propitious for war and for attacking cities, for gathering the people, for meeting the lords of the various States and for setting a norm for all affairs, and for the execution of unrighteous people. (曰姑：利戮伐； 可以攻城，可以聚衆，會諸侯，型百事，戮不義).— These sentences may be considered as the theory of the Yin-yang military school.

Furthermore, being a native of Ch'u, some of *Fan Li's* 范蠡 political ideas are derived from the astrological *ying-so* theme.[23] He points out that the success of human affairs must follow the way of Heaven and Earth. He mentions the term *ying-so* twice in his talk with Kou-chien Wang (勾踐王) of Yüeh. The name 玄月 — one of the twelve months in the Ch'u Silk Manuscript appears only in the *Erh-ya* and the *Kuo-yü* (Yüeh-yü 越語) where it appears once. Upon the basis of these facts, it would seem that the culture of Yüeh was under the influence of Ch'u.

3. THE RELATIONSHIP BETWEEN GODS AND MAN

It is said that Ch'ung 重 and Li 黎, the ancestors of Ch'u, ruled Heaven and Earth from generation to generation. Ch'ung acted as Governor of the South, administering the gods in Heaven and Li acted as Governor of the North administering man on earth. They divided the world into two halves, delimiting the spheres of activity pertaining to gods and men. This idea of the ' non-communication between heaven and earth' (絕地通天) would seem to be a concept traditional to the Ch'u kingdom.[24]

In the Ch'u Silk Manuscript the relationship between the ' Hundred Gods' and men is mentioned frequently. As in the case in the *Shan-hai-ching*, the Manuscript also records the two legendary Emperors, Ti Chun 帝俊 and Yen Ti 炎帝. The former regulated the movement of the sun and moon, while the latter ordered Chu Jung 祝融, the great ancestor of Ch'u, to have various things performed. Here the character *ti* means ' the superior ruler of Heaven', and the motion of the sun and the moon was caused by him. This meaning is quite close to that which appears in the records of the oracle bones of the Shang period.

23.   Fan-li was a native of San-hu 三戶 of Yüan City 宛; see the *Wu-Yüeh Ch'un-ch'iu* 吳越春秋.

24.   *Cf. Shu-ching*, Legge, Vol. III, pp. 593-4; *Kuo-yü*, Ch'u-yü — the conversation between Ch'ao Wang and Kuan Yi-fu; and the Ch'ung-li 重黎 in the *Fa-yen* 法言.

On the other hand, we find in the classics that after the Ch'un-ch'iu period, scholars began to have new ideas about the relationship between the gods and men. For instance Chi Liang 季梁 said: 'Men are the basis of the gods. The King should firstly bring human affairs to completion before devoting himself to the service of the gods'. (*Tso-chuan*, Legge, Vol. 5, p. 84) and Shih Yin 史囂 said: 'When a State is about to prosper, it listens to the people, and when it is about to decay, it listens to the gods' (*ibid.*, p. 120). These progressive ideas are in accord with the way of Chou. Confucius said, 'Devote yourself to what is right for the people. Respect the gods and spirits, but keep yourself at a distance from them'. This means that people and the rites should come first while the gods and their worship should be made a secondary consideration. However, the traditional ideas of the Ch'u people as recorded in the Ch'u Silk Manuscript show that they still followed the way of Shang and thus they appear more con-servative in comparison with other kingdoms. This is the important point in distinguishing the culture of Ch'u with that of Chou and Lu, particularly when dealing with ancient Chinese religion.

BIBLIOGRAPHY

Details of standard sources and reference works such as *Chin-shu*, *Chuang-tzu*, *Erh-ya*, *Fa-yen*, *Han-chien*, *Han-shu*, *Kuo-yü*, *Li-chi*, *Shuo-wen chieh-tzu*, etc. are not presented here as they concern only specialist readers.

Ch'üan Tsu-wang 全祖望
    Pa Li-chi shih-ching yüeh-ling 跋禮記石經月令 in his *Chi-ch'i t'ing-chi, wai-pien* 鮚埼亭集外編, Ch. 35.
Hawkes, D.
    1959   *Ch'u Tz'u — Songs of the South*, Oxford.
Kuan Tung-kuei 管東貴
    1962   'Chung-kuo ku-tai shih-jih shen-yü chih yen-chiu' 中國古代十日神話之研究, *BAS*, Vol. 33.
Legge, James
    1893   *The Chinese Classics*, Oxford, 2nd Edition, revised.
Moriya Mitsuo 守屋美都雄
    1963   *Chūgoku ko saijiki no kenkyū* 中國古歳時記の研究.
Needham, Joseph
    1959   *Science and Civilization in China*, Vol. III, Cambridge.
Tsung Lin 宗懍
    Ching-Ch'u sui-shih-chi 荆楚歳時記, 梁宗懍撰.
Wang Chung-min 王重民
    1958   Tun-huang ku-chi hsü-lu 敦煌古籍叙錄, Peking.
Yü Hsing-wu 于省吾
    1940   *Shuang-chien-yi ku-ch'i-wu t'u-lu* 雙劍誃古器物圖錄, Peking.

THE TWELVE GODS OF THE
CHAN-KUO PERIOD SILK MANUSCRIPT
EXCAVATED AT CH'ANG-SHA*

HAYASHI MINAO

Some time ago I published a long study of the text of the Ch'u Silk Manuscript based upon the Freer Gallery of Art panchromatic photographs and since have published corrections of many character details following receipt of prints from a trial run of infrared photographs (Hayashi, 1964; 1966). In the present survey, therefore, the emphasis is placed upon the Twelve Peripheral Figures rather than the text of the Manuscript. We shall first of all study these paintings with reference to transmitted literary sources.

1. CHARACTERISTICS OF THE TWELVE GODS OF THE MANU-SCRIPT SEEN IN LITERARY SOURCES

Let us commence by examining the conclusions of earlier scholars who have attempted to find literary parallels:

* Translated by Noel Barnard (and condensed from the Japanese hand-written manuscript in consultation with the author). The main text of the original manuscript (200 squares per page) totals 262 pages with an additional 90 pages of notes and bibliography. Space problems have necessitated a rather severe reduction in size but as the sections covering shamanism have recently appeared in print in somewhat the same form and coverage of subject matter (Hayashi: 1967) they have been greatly summarised. For the remainder of the paper I have had the unenviable task of still having to decide what to retain in full and what to summarise from the very interesting and informative assembly of materials Professor Hayashi has brought together. The original Bibliography is maintained in full because of its comprehensive coverage.
    Passages cited from the Shan-hai-ching (and other such traditional literature) should be regarded as tentative translations. The renderings given mainly follow Ho Yi-hsing's commentary which Hayashi also follows closely. In the descriptions of some of the fantastic animals, gods, demons, etc. in the Shan-hai-ching it is not always clear whether one or more of the creatures existed; thus my use of singular or plural forms may be open to question. [Ed.]

Peripheral Figure No. 1[1]

Jao Tsung-yi (1954 : 78 ; 1958 : 38) has regarded this deity as comprising the head of an ox and the body of a man, thus representative of the *Ti-wang shih-chi* 帝王世紀 (*circa* 270 A.D.) description of Shen Neng Shih 神農氏 whose alternative name — Yen Ti 炎帝 — occurs in the Manuscript (A. 6-1, 2). An Chih-min 安志敏 (1963 : 57) has cited the *Shan-hai-ching* passage : 'From the mountains of Shih-hu 尸胡 to the mountains of Wu-kao 無皋 . . . the gods all take the form of a human-like body with the horns of a ram.' (4.9a) so, too, Ch'en P'an 陳槃 (1953 : 195). But although the horns are like those of an ox (certainly not those of a ram) the head is square and accordingly rather unlike that of an ox. The identifications in both cases lack support in respect of essential details in the paintings themselves. Thus there are no grounds for paralleling the Manuscript representation with the above traditional description of Shen Nung Shih.

Peripheral Figure No. 2

This creature Ch'en interprets as a deity biting upon a snake held in its mouth and has quoted the *Shan-hai-ching* passage : 'In the Ta-huang 大荒 ('distant places, far beyond the seas') there is a mountain called *Pei-chi-t'ien-kuei* 北極天櫃 . . . and there are also gods which champ snakes in their mouths and grasp them. They take the form of a human body with a tiger's head ; four hoofs terminate their long shanks. The name by which they are known is : Chiang-liang 彊良.' (17.4b). An is of the same opinion. However, the object in question issuing from the creature's mouth hardly appears to be a snake ; furthermore, it is not held in the hands and the head is not that of a tiger, if anything it is like that of a man or a monkey. Jao (1954 : 79) considers the creature to comprise a being with one arm and a long tongue which it holds and quotes the *Shan-hai-ching* passage : 'There was a man called Wu Hui 吳回, strange (in profile from the) left as

---

1.   The reference numbers used throughout this paper when citing the Peripheral Figures or the Manuscript text follow Barnard's reconstruction reproduced in his Figures 4B and 4C.

he had no right arm.' (16.8b). However, when we examine the infra-red photographs now available it is clear that the painting has both arms rendered. Shang Ch'eng-tso (1964 : 18) quotes a seemingly relevant passage from the *Shan-hai-ching* but he is quite mistaken in his inter-pretation of the drawings.

Peripheral Figure No. 7

Both Ch'en (1953 : 194) and Jao (1954 : 74; 1958 : 38) have cited the *Shan-hai-ching* passage describing three-headed deities : 'Shao-shih 小室 and T'ai-shih 太室 are both peaks of the K'u Mountains ... the gods (dwelling) therein take the shape each of a human face and three heads ...' (5.28b). Also in the *Huai-nan-tzu* 准南子 (4 :14) the description of three-headed people in a southern land is referred to.* An (1963 : 57) and Shang (1964 : 17) also follow this point.

Peripheral Figure No. 8

Ch'en (1953: 194) rather curiously misinterprets the drawing and cites a *Shan-hai-ching* record (7.11a) of a country with people with one arm, one eye, and one nostril apiece. In the *Huai-nan-tzu* (4.13) there is also record of a country of one-armed people. The infrared photographs now show clearly enough the nature of the misunderstandings here.

Peripheral Figure No. 9

Jao (1954 : 79) interprets the figure as an animal with a very long horn, comparing it with the wood sculptured monsters bearing deer's antlers which have been excavated from Ch'ang-sha tombs and refers to T'ang period *ming-ch'i* with pairs of horns and also to the *Sui-shu*

---

* It should be further observed that this *Shan-hai-ching* passage does not fully accord with the representation of the three-headed Peripheral Figure — nothing is said as to the shape of the body, simply the fact that the deities have three heads, each with a human face 其神狀皆人面而三首. Prior to this passage and immediately following it is reference to the fact that the bulk of the gods residing in the K'u-shan area have the body of a pig and the face of a man. Whether in this context the three-headed deities with human faces also are to be read as having the body of a pig is not entirely clear. However the *Huai-nan-tzu* reference is quite unambiguous : 三頭民 'three-headed people' and the reference is to 'people' not to supernatural beings (*KBTK* ed., 4.14). [Ed.]

隋書 account of the 12 kinds of horned animals used to repel evil spirits from the palace. An (1963 : 57) regards it as a creature with two long horns and with one arm and quotes the passage from the *Shan-hai-ching* just referred to (7.11a). Actually the figure, as may be seen in the new photographs, comprises the body of a bird with human heads. Thus the earlier interpretations offered do not accord with details as now evident to us.

Peripheral Figure No. 10

An regards this figure as one with a single foot and with a long tongue and then quotes various literary sources speaking of a one-legged creature : the *k'uei* 夔. However, the Manuscript figure actually has two legs and so far as the characteristics of the demon known as *k'uei* in pre-Ch'in times are concerned I have presented evidence elsewhere (Hayashi, 1960: 34-8) that there is no resemblance to Peripheral Figure No. 10. Peripheral Figures Nos. 2, 9, and 10 each have a long tongue protruding which feature Jao (1954 : 79 ; 1958 : 38-9) and An (1963 : 69) compare with the wooden sculptures from the sites of Ch'ang-sha and Hsin-yang of Chan-kuo period date which also possess protruding tongues and which they refer to as 'tomb guardians' (鎮墓獸 *chen-mu-shou*) thus taking them to be gods with the power to drive away evil spirits.

With the exception of a number of acceptable associations which have been noted above in respect of the three-headed man in Peripheral Figure No. 7 and the tongue - protruding motifs in Nos. 2, 9, and 10, the majority of the views given by the earlier scholars cited are difficult to substantiate. This is, of course, partly due to the lack of clarity of the materials upon which they worked. Yet even upon the basis of the most recent photographs of the Manuscript which are clearer by far, this method of searching for precise parallels amongst the recorded characteristics of pre-Ch'in period deities as preserved in the *Shan-hai-ching* and other such sources — with the particular features of the Ch'u Silk Manuscript deities now distinctly evident — might well become an unproductive undertaking. For instance, in seeking to associate Peripheral Figure No. 7 with the three-headed deities mentioned in the *Shan-hai-ching* a problem arises in respect of the character *kao* (C. 13-1 ; C. 14-2) written alongside this figure which we otherwise know to be the name of the god of the fifth month as recorded in the *Erh-ya* 爾 雅. Furthermore, it may be observed in the *Shan-hai-ching* that different deities may be described in almost similar terms. This, too, raises a question of some relevance. The method of research attempted to date which has been to seek among the classics for attributes that seem to match the pictures of the Peripheral Figures and in an *a priori* manner ascribe these attributes to the Ch'u Silk Manuscript figures, becomes practically meaningless.

To find out the character of the Peripheral Figures in the Ch'u Silk Manuscript, we must first look into the Manuscript itself as a source from which inferences may be drawn. This we shall now attempt to do.

Alongside each of the Peripheral Figures is written three characters, the first one of which functions as the name of the Peripheral Figure and coincides with one of the names of the twelve month deities as preserved in the *Erh-ya*, while the second and third characters in these 'caption headings' indicate the nature of their jurisdiction over the month. In speculating thus in an earlier paper I cited such examples as the following : in C. 9, the first character is the name of the deity, the second character means 'supervise', and the third character means 'spring'. Similarly C. 15 has the first character as the name of the deity and the second character is 'supervise' and then we have the character 'summer'. So, too, in the case of C. 21 in respect of 'autumn' and C. 3, in respect of 'winter' (Hayashi, 1964 : 48). Then in the long texts alongside each figure is assessed in detail whether certain things were permissible or not, whether certain proceedings would be lucky or unlucky. As to the second and third characters in the captions in relation to these long texts, however, I was somewhat vague in my assessment of their significance but as a result of the clearer photographs and the revisions I have recently made upon the basis of the trial run infrared photos (Hayashi, 1966), it seems now that my thoughts were not entirely wrong. For instance, in the case of C. 1, the second and third characters if read as they stand and without additional radicals, will not, of course, give any meaning but when we take into account the content of the long text associated with this caption which speaks of the advantages attending military incursions in this month, the feasibility of attacks against city walls, of supervision of the multitudes, of entering into covenants with other Princes, of formulating regulations, and of killing the unrighteous, we may see it possible to interpret these characters by adding the 'hand' radical to the second one (thus 扮 *pan* which may mean 'control', 'ally with') and reading the third character as *chang*3 'senior' in the sense of 'Leader of the Princes'. If we do this, then the sense of the caption will correspond well with the content of the long text. Similarly, the second and third characters in C. 5, C. 7, C. 11, and C. 17 may each be demonstrated to comprise a brief indication of the functions or duties of each particular deity as elaborated in the long texts alongside each Peripheral Figure.*

If the preceding observations are correct we may conclude that each Peripheral Figure is accompanied by a comparatively long text explaining the particular rôle of the deity and its influence over fortunes — good or bad — in the associated month, and then alongside each in the form of a title or caption is written first the single character name of the deity — the majority of these names coincide with those of the twelve months as given in the *Erh-ya* — the next two words,

---

* The associated data is as follows: C. 5 取于下 with C. 6 曰取巳 [祀] 則至 ...; C. 7 女拔武 with C. 8 曰女可以出師敦邑, 不可以受女, 取臣妾 ...; C. 11 余取 [娶] 女 with C. 12...取 [娶] 女為邦芺; C. 17 倉莒 [莫] 得 with C. 18 曰倉不可以川☒, 大不訢于邦, 又須, 灾于上下.

As translation of both the cited passages and the discussion detailing supporting evidence for the transcriptions and interpretations proposed would require extensive explanation,I have presented briefly Hayashi's discussion covering only the C. 1 and C. 2 passages above. There are also a number of instances where authorities lack agreement (*cf.* Jao Tsung-yi's remark on the graph 曰 [C. 6: 3] p. 114 above) which situations require elaboration by the translator. As these are problems of interest to only a small number of specialists there is little need to go into details here. Reference will, however, be made to these matters in some detail in my translation and notes on the Manuscript text in *The Ch'u Silk Manuscript*. [Ed.]

as we have noted, comprising simply a terse summary of the main attributes of the deity. Accordingly, it seems valid to regard the Peripheral Figures as gods controlling the fates individually of each of the twelve months of the year. Although in the classics there is no record of actual deities with such names and which are associated with the twelve months of the year, nevertheless, there are to be observed other traditions suggesting that there were, indeed, such deities as I have pointed out in respect of *Lun-heng* 論衡 and *Hou Han-shu* 後漢書 data elsewhere (Hayashi, 1964 : 84, Note 31).

Accepting then that the *Erh-ya* names of months are also, as illustrated in the Ch'u Silk Manuscript, the names of gods who had jurisdiction over the fates for each month, we have yet to explore their exact nature. One possibility that comes to mind is that there may have been a legend to the effect that there were twelve moons which came one after the other into the sky and which each had its supervisory deity; these become gods of the months and as such, it might be assumed, appear as the Twelve Deities in the Ch'u Silk Manuscript. This might seem reasonable upon the basis of the well-known legend of there being 'ten suns'. However, amongst the classics there is no indication of such a concept as 'twelve moons' except for the following passage in the *Shan-hai-ching* which tends to suggest the possibility of the existence of such a concept : 'There, the ladies are about to (?) bathe the moon. Chang-hsi 常羲, wife of the Emperor Chün 帝俊 gave birth to the twelve moons. Thence they commenced (the practice of) moon-bathing.' (16.6a)*

In the oracle-bone texts of Shang there are records of sacrificial ceremonies concerned with the sun (Hu Hou-hsüan, 1944 : 2, 11–13)

---

* In attempting to interpret this passage it would seem necessary to take into account the relevant data in the entry and commentaries referring to the 'birth of ten suns' (15.6a). Of particular interest is the comment that the giving birth to 'ten suns' is: 'so to speak, to give birth to ten sons (子) each named after a day (日) ...' Upon this basis *yüeh* 'moon' above should probably be rendered as 'months' rather than 'moons'. However, some illustrated editions of the *Shan-hai-ching* show, in reference to this passage, a picture of a woman about to place a moon in a bathing basin thus following one of several interpretations that the ambiguities of the Chinese text allows. [Ed.]

but nothing in respect of the moon.[2] It would seem that in comparison with the sun there was little concern in China towards the moon in ancient times.

There is little in the actual content of the Manuscript which might demonstrate a relationship of the deities drawn around the periphery of the Manuscript with the months of the year. And although the names of the twelve months as recorded in the *Erh-ya* are written alongside the Peripheral Figures, nevertheless, in Section B of the Manuscript where we find references to the months in terms of the 'first month', the 'second month', the 'third month', the 'fourth month', and the 'fifth month' (B. 3-25 to 3-29; 4-6 to 4-9) there is no sign of the month-deity names as such being employed in the two major texts.

Accordingly, it would appear that the names which we find in the *Erh-ya* applied to the twelve months, were not actually applied to the months of the year at the time when the Ch'u Silk Manuscript was compiled. Possibly this was because they were highly literary and elegant terms which at the time were not in everyday use and, even if such were the case, the fact remains that the Manuscript was a sort of high-brow book of mysteries wherein such terms would be employed as a matter of course (Hayashi, 1964 : 87). If these terms were in everyday use it would be difficult to explain why the months in Section B of the Manuscript recorded in regard to fortunate and unfortunate happenings should be referred to only as the 'first', the 'second', the 'third', etc. months in contradistinction to Section C which uses the month-names.

Taking such observations into consideration it would seem that the twelve month-names of the *Erh-ya*, which we see in the Manuscript as the names of the Twelve Deities were not originally connected with the months of the year — these Twelve Deities seem to have had a different origin and their various supervisory functions over

2.   Ch'en Meng-chia 陳夢家 (1936 : 102-3) sought to prove the existence of sacrificial rites to the moon on the basis of the graph 夕 *hsi* 'evening' and cited several post-Han sources in support of his contention. But these being strongly influenced by the Yin-Yang concepts of later times are hardly sufficient forms of evidence. Furthermore the *hsi* sacrifices in oracular texts are directed to ancestral gods and gods of natural phenomena — they are clearly not concerned with the moon.

the fates of men and events later were allocated each to a particular month of the year along the lines of the explanatory texts beside each of the Peripheral Figures and their names became those also of the months of the year at a later stage. But, at the time of the compilation of the Ch'u Silk Manuscript this association of the deity's names with the particular months of the year had not yet been fully effected.

As we have observed earlier, the concept of divine beings having jurisdiction over the fates for each month of the year existed in Han times following different traditions from that preserved in the Ch'u Silk Manuscript. However, the use of a 'month' as the unit of time, during which fortunes and misfortunes were to be assessed, has much older origins. In the Shang period, divinations were made for 'days' and also for 'ten-day weeks'. This is common knowledge but occasionally we find the 'months' employed as a unit of time covering a period of divination.[3] Thus, it is clear enough that the concept of deities with powers over fates for periods of a month was already established as early as Shang times.

2. THE ORIGINS OF THE TWELVE GODS IN LITERARY SOURCES

As we do not find in the traditional literature the names of the Twelve Gods recorded with any divine characteristics associated with them, it is difficult to demonstrate directly evidence concerning their origins. In the Shan-hai-ching, however, we may draw attention to the listings of several shamans (巫 wu) with names following the title, wu, which seem to hint towards parallels with the names of the Twelve Gods of the Manuscript: 'To the east of K'ai-ming 開 明 are Wu-P'eng 巫彭, Wu-Ti 巫抵, Wu-Yang 巫陽, Wu-Li 巫履, Wu-Fan 巫凡, and Wu-Hsiang 巫相. They are on either side of the corpse of an E-yü 窫窳 and each holds in his hand an elixir of immortality to ward off the onset of death. The E-yü is a creature

3.   Cf. the following oracles in Tung Tso-pin 董作賓 (1948–53: 450; 1948L3129): 口三月其雨·于四月其雨 'Will it rain in the third month?' 'In the fourth month will it rain?' 戊午卜. 今九月史. 于十月史. 'On the day wu-wu (55) an enquiry was made: In the present ninth month will we send someone on service (abroad)?', 'In the tenth month will we send someone on service (abroad)?'

which comprises the body of a snake with a human face. It was slain by Erh-fu-ch'en 貳負臣.' (11.6a). In another section is the following passage: 'In Ta-huang — far beyond the seas — there is a mountain called Feng-chü-yü-men 豐沮玉門. Where the sun and the moon set there is Mt. Ling 靈山. Here the ten shamans: Wu-Hsien 巫咸, Wu-Chi 巫卽, Wu-Fen 巫肦, Wu-P'eng 巫彭, Wu-Ku 巫姑, Wu-Chen 巫眞, Wu-Li 巫禮, Wu-Ti 巫抵, Wu-Hsieh 巫謝, and Wu-Lo 巫羅 make their ascents and descents from Heaven to earth. Every kind of medicinal herb is to be found in the vicinity.' (16.3a).[4]

Notwithstanding the fact that these two groups of shamans resided in mountains of different names, there is much in common: both groups resided far away in the Western Regions, both are connected with the elixir of immortality, more than half the names of the Six Shamans have parallels amongst the names of the Ten Shamans. It is thus not difficult to recognise here two different traditions originating from the same source. Amongst these names, furthermore, there are five which coincide very closely with the names given to the Peripheral Figures in the Ch'u Silk Manuscript (see Table 1) so much so that it would appear more than a matter of sheer coincidence — rather it would seem to indicate a further tradition branching from the same source. In the *Shan-hai-ching* the most notable of these five is Shaman Hsien. He appears in another literary source, the 'Annals of Yin' in the *Shih-chi* where he is recorded as a minister of one of the Kings of Shang (中宗太戊) and his name has been parallelled with entries amongst oracle bones recording sacrifices to a person with divine characteristics called Hsien Wu 咸戊 — since Lo Chen-yü (1927: A, 13) wrote, these both have been taken to be identical with Wu-Hsien of the *Shan-hai-ching*. Ch'en Meng-chia has suggested that the character 戊 *wu* is an official rank (1956: 365) but, as I have demonstrated elsewhere (Hayashi, 1967: 205), this is

4.   Ho Ying-hsing 赫懿行 in his commentary on this passage associates the names 巫肦 and 巫禮 with those of 巫凡 and 巫履 considering them to be of the same two persons — this seems to be quite acceptable. He further pairs 巫謝 and 巫相 which, however, has no phonetic basis of identity.

not possible. Nevertheless, there remains the strong probability that Hsien Wu (咸戊) of the oracular records is the same person as Wu-Hsien (巫咸) recorded in literary sources of later ages — there are several reasons: in oracle-bone texts a divinity called *hsien* is considered to be no other than Hsien Wu (Ch'en Meng-chia, 1956: 365); the *Shuo-wen* has under the graph 巫 *wu* the entry: 'In antiquity, Wu-Hsien was first to practice shamanism.'; the graph 巫 *wu* appears in oracle bone inscriptions as a rank of office; in the Preface to the Shang-shu (尚書序) the commentary on the section 咸有一德 *Hsien yu yi-te* states: 'Wu-Hsien ... his name was Hsien, he was a shaman

Names of the Twelve Month Deities	The *Erh-ya* Equivalents	The 'Ten Shamans' *Shan-hai-ching*	The 'Six Shamans' *Shan-hai-ching*
—	—	巫咸	—
—	—	巫卽	—
—	—	巫肦 *pan*	巫凡 *fan*
秉 *ping*	丙 *ping*	巫彭 *p'eng*	巫彭 *p'eng*
姑 *ku*	辜 *ku*	巫姑 *ku*	—
—	—	巫眞	—
—	—	巫禮 *li*	巫履 *li*
—	—	巫抵 *ti*	巫抵 *ti*
叔 *cha*	且 *ch'ieh*	巫謝 *hsieh*	—
—	—	巫羅	—
昜 *yang*	陽 *yang*	—	巫陽 *yang*
倉 *ts'ang*	相 *hsiang*	—	巫相 *hsiang*

TABLE. 1. Parallel names amongst the Twelve Month Deities of the Ch'u Silk Manuscript, the Erh-ya month-names, and the names of Shamans in the Shan-hai-ching.

of the Yin [i.e. Shang] period ...' Taking all these into consideration it would seem that Hsien of the oracular records (i.e. Hsien Wu) obtained the rank of 巫 *wu* 'Shaman' and thus came to be called Wu-Hsien. There does not, unfortunately, exist information as to the nature of his divine attributes.

In the *Tsu-Ch'u wen* 詛楚文 (of 313 B.C.) Wu-Hsien is recorded: 大神巫咸 'The Great Spirit Wu-Hsien' and in his name both Ch'u and Ch'in swore to maintain friendly relations (see Jung Keng, 1934: 4); thus we see him as a powerful deity worshipped widely from north to south China. In this connection, we might also observe amongst the literary sources compiled after the Chan-kuo period numbers of geographical names incorporating the name Wu-Hsien which are located in various areas of China (Hayashi, 1967 : 205). In the Li-sao 離騷 of the *Ch'u-tz'u* there is the passage : 'Wu-Hsien was to descend just as evening approached. With an offering of fine spiced rice I went to welcome him. All the gods shading (the setting sun) descended in readiness for his coming and at the same time from Chiu-yi 九疑 Mountain the spirits came crowding to meet him.' (*KBTK* Vol. 22, 1. 36). The Chiu-yi Mountain in southern Hunan where Wu-Hsien was to descend was also said, according to the commentary of Wang Yi 王逸, to be the burial place of the mythical Emperor Shun 舜.

In Han times Ch'u was well known for the strong influence of shamanistic cults in the region : 'South of the Yangtze River ... they believe in shamans and spirits and time after time engage in licentious sacrificial ceremonies.' (*Han-shu*, Ti-li-chih. 8). The Preface to the 'Nine Songs' (Li-sao) of the *Ch'u-tz'u* records a similar observation and then continues : 'In their ceremonies male and female shamans play music, sing, and dance to give pleasure to the gods.' So, too, the story in the Li-sao cited above referring to the descent of Wu-Hsien to Chiu-yi Mountain in order to express his views to Ch'ü-yüan 屈原, the author of the *Ch'u-tz'u* elegies, was no doubt constructed against a background of customs that existed throughout Ch'u where, when the occasion demanded, there could be felt no relief from one's anxieties unless the descent of the gods could be invoked to give counsel on matters of good or bad fortune through the mouths of shamans.

In the Chan-kuo period and the Han period particular mountains were associated with particular gods and the sacrificial ceremonies to each deity were marked by special gifts and sacrificial offerings ; numerous examples are recorded in the *Shan-hai-ching*. South of the Yangtze River where there was so much emphasis upon shamanistic deities, it would appear that the mountains where the gods were believed to descend or to reside — where the sacrifices were conducted in honour of them and where there lived the male and female shamans whose business it was to invoke their descent — belonged to large companies of such shamans. In the *Hou-Han-shu*, in the Biography of Sung Chün 宋均,

is the following account: 'In Chün-ch'iu-hsien 逡遵縣 there are the two mountains T'ang 唐 and Hou 后 to both of which the people offer sacrifices. The shamans select youths and maidens from amongst the people and marry them to the deities of opposite sex. Each year they are replaced by newly selected brides and grooms. Those once having been betrothed to the gods dare not marry again amongst the people. Many times ordinances (against this practice) have been issued but no one dares to violate the custom.' Although this account is to be regarded as an extreme example of the power that shamans held over a community, it is difficult to believe that a situation of this kind was one limited solely to the two mountains in question. We may assume that in practically every locality where there existed mountains upon which the gods descended each was in the possession of a band of shamans who, to greater or lesser degrees, maintained strong influences over the nearby communities.

Wu-Hsien was one such 'divine shaman'. In the commentary of Wang Yi on the earlier quoted Li-sao passage is the statement: 'Wu-Hsien in ancient times was a divine shaman (shen-wu).' The term shen-wu requires consideration. It appears in the Yüeh-chüeh-shu 越絶書 (8.8b) as follows: 'In the eastern [i.e. lower] stretches of the Yangtze, the place called Wu-tsang 巫葬 is the abode of the descendants of the divine shaman Wu Tu (神巫無杜) of Yüeh. When he died Kou-chien [King of Yüeh, 497-65 B.C.] had him buried in the centre of the river — the shamans and the gods wanted to take advantage of this to overturn the boats of the Wu 吳 people...' It seems evident here that the attribute of divinity to Wu Tu came into being through his descendants, while amongst a group of shamans the same term may well have been one that would have been applied to a legendary ancestral god. Thus the statement 'Wu-Hsien in ancient times was a divine shaman,' was naturally one which was designated by his descendants and it may be assumed that a group of shamans existed whose task it was to make offerings to him and to invoke his descent.

Thus we may observe fairly clearly down to the close of the Eastern Chou period the nature of the deity called Wu-Hsien; he was an actual person who lived in the Shang period, he came to be revered as the progenitor of shamanism, over an extensive area of the country he was accepted as a powerful god, mountains upon which he was believed to descend are scattered throughout many parts of the land. Then towards the end of the Chan-kuo period groups of shaman who regarded themselves as his ancestors conducted sacrifices to him and invoked his descent to advise them on questions of fate.

Amongst the shamans of the *Shan-hai-ching* one other regarding whose attributes we can conduct enquiries in classical sources is Wu-Yang — he figures in the Chao-hun 招魂 'The Summoning of the Soul' of the *Ch'u-tz'u* wherein he speaks of himself as one dealing with dreams. At first glance it might seem that there is little connection between dreams and invocations to the soul but man in antiquity thought differently. As noted in the Cheng Hsüan 鄭玄 commentary to the Chou-li 周禮 in explaining a passage concerning the method of attending to three types of dreams: 'The dream is the soul's coming into consciousness, it may be used in divination.' (24.4a). Differing thus when man is awake, the soul could detach itself from the body and independently move about. Dreams thereby engendered were in the province of the *Chou-li* officer, *Ta-pu* 大卜.

According to the preceding and other such related data it may be demonstrated that Wu-Yang in the rôle of an official in charge of the interpretation of dreams would inevitably have been concerned with the practice of issuing summonses to souls. If we take into account the rôle he is given in the Chao-hun we may surmise that throughout the Ch'u territories he was regarded as a divine shaman of considerable fame.

A further member of the *Shan-hai-ching* shamans, Wu-P'eng, is noted by the 3rd-4th century A.D. commentator Kuo P'u 郭璞 as having been listed in the *Shih-pen* 世本, a lost book, where he was stated to be the founder of the art of medicinal healing (*cf.* Yen Yi-ping, 1951).

These then are the only three of the 'Six Shamans' and the 'Ten Shamans' of the *Shan-hai-ching* regarding whose nature it is possible to achieve some understanding; however, a point that deserves attention is that while each became a divine shaman and originally had the rôle of an ancestor, each had his own special sphere of importance : Wu-Hsien in the pledging of oaths and covenants, Wu-Yang in the interpretation of dreams and the invocation of souls, and Wu-P'eng in the healing arts. The three shamanistic posts of the *Chou-li* also manifest the same feature (Hayashi, 1967 : 208).

Viewing the situation along these lines, it may be permissible to assume that the different names amongst the 'Six Shamans' and the 'Ten Shamans' accordingly imply that each engaged in different duties ; and originally, furthermore, in the mountains where they were in the habit of descending, the various groups of shamans who called upon the deities to descend probably each drew upon several divine shamans — the choice of deities favoured differing from one group to another. Thus may we account for the correspondences and differences of divine shamans' names in the two sections of the *Shan-hai-ching*. When these two sections were compiled, presumably at different times and places, the authors followed certain traditions and principles and selected respectively the totals of 'six' and of 'ten' divine shamans from amongst the existing shamanistic deities scattered throughout the States (Hayashi, 1967 : 208).

Accordingly, the antecedents of the Twelve Peripheral Figures painted around the edges of the Ch'u Silk Manuscript may perhaps be reconstructed as follows : they were deities selected from the same primary sources as were the 'Six Shamans' and the 'Ten Shamans' of the *Shan-hai-ching* and from other relevant primary sources but with different principles underlying the selection and were aligned with the twelve months of the year. This is the reason that they manifest names in common with the *Shan-hai-ching* Shamans. Their functions as arbitrators of the fates of men for each month and differing in essentials from one month deity to another — is a feature which is highly characteristic of the divine shamans. These Twelve Gods of the Ch'u Silk Manuscript presiding thus over the fortunes of each of the twelve months of the year would, no doubt, have been selected from shamanistic deities originating from many and various places. In accordance with the 'Five Elements' (五 行 *wu-hsing*) theorising as to the norms of conduct of mankind stipulated for each of the twelve months, so the divine shamans would have been selected whose attributes more or less coincided with these norms and then they were aligned with the appropriate months of the year. Differences between the two traditions reflect differences attending the principles of selection.

When it came to the painting of the Peripheral Figures in the Manuscript the 'Five Elements' school which first established the systematized concept of the Twelve Gods of the Month did not create the shapes of the deities nor their names from out of the air. Throughout the country, as recorded in the *Shan-hai-ching*, the people actually worshipped gods manifesting all kinds of shapes; unless the representations accorded with these, it would probably have been impossible to have gained general acceptance. The systematizing of deities into groups, such as the group of twelve in the Ch'u Silk Manuscript, is not restricted to this particular document only. Throughout China, and in many places, the practice was current in Chan-kuo times.

From amongst the many locally worshipped gods five were eventually selected on the basis of the 'Five Elements' theory and were organised into the concept of the 'Five Emperors' — this was the period when the systematization of myths and legends was being established (Hayashi, 1967 : 209-10).

3. SHAMANISM IN THE SHANG PERIOD

The origin of shamanism may be traced back into the Shang period and actual records of shamans are well attested in the oracle bones where we find, too, the commencement of the practice of systemizing the shamans into numerical groups. Furthermore, when we look at the representations of the Twelve Gods in the Ch'u Silk Manuscript we may notice amongst the paintings certain elements that have been preserved since Shang times. Regarding the former I have discussed the matter at some length and with copious illustration in my paper ' Chūgoku kodai no shinpu' (1967 : 210-224) to which several references have already been made in the above paragraphs and will omit consideration here. As to the latter, however, the subject will be surveyed in the following section.

4. THE ORIGINS OF THE TWELVE GODS IN THE CH'U SILK MANUSCRIPT FROM THE POINT OF VIEW OF THE PAINTINGS

Now we shall compare the Peripheral Figures in the Ch'u Silk Manuscript with other relevant archaeological materials. It will be appreciated, however, that unlike the remains from Egypt or Mesopotamia, those in and around China with which we might make comparisons, are of very limited extent.

Peripheral Figure No. 3

The comparison will commence with Peripheral Figure No. 3 which coincides in name with the first of the month-names recorded in the *Erh-ya*.* The fabric of the Manuscript is badly torn and sections missing thus making reconstruction of the original form difficult; however, the lower right-hand part of the body of this creature which is shaped like a heart, is comparable to the torsos of the birds comprising Peripheral Figures Nos. 4 and 9. It would seem evident that it originally depicted the body of a bird. Above this the head would have been placed ; upon comparison with Peripheral Figure No. 9, traces of what might be considered to be the neck and the forehead (with horns) are discernible. Alongside there remains a long S-shaped protruberance which may be possibly a tongue or the tail of a snake. To the left are the remnants of what is probably a kind of snake, the head of which,

---

* Numbering of the Peripheral Figures has been effected in accordance with the earlier research of Jao Tsung-yi which is now being gradually superceded by the generally accepted *Erh-ya* month-name sequence, the correspondence of which with the Peripheral Figure names was first observed by Li Hsueh-ch'in 李 學 勤 (*WW* 1960.7). As the numbers are intended to function purely as a means of reference it has been considered unnecessary to revise them in terms of the Erh-ya sequence. With the forthcoming publication of *The Ch'u Silk Manuscript* the reference numbers as employed in the several relevant papers in the present volume will become standard. Up to now four different methods of numbering have been advocated. [Ed.]

with the antenna-like feature, may be compared with Peripheral Figures Nos. 6 and 11. As will be noted later these are taken to be snakes with their forked-tongues protruding. Below the head of the snake and to the left of the extension of its body are two claw-shaped features and to the right are lines which seem to be part of an arm. Claw remnants appear to the right of the character 取 in the 'caption title'.

Notwithstanding the mutilation of this part of the Manuscript, it is evident that the picture comprises a bird and a snake as its main components — this coupling immediately brings to mind the Chan-kuo period motif comprising a snake gripped in the claws of a bird which may even be pecking at it.[5] Although the picture, or rather this possible interpretation thereof, seems acceptable, the analysis attempted here is by no means to be regarded as conclusive.

Peripheral Figure No. 4

This figure comprises a double-body, single-neck, four-headed creature with rectangular-shaped eyes, a crescent above each rectangular-shaped head, a single leg with three-claws for each body, and a three-feathered tail at the bottom of each body. The neck appears like a carpenter's square and is reminiscent of the form of neck in Peripheral Figure No. 7. As a whole the two bodies and the leg on each may be regarded as those of birds. It should be noted, however, that a single leg in this case, is probably to be interpreted as a pair of legs. It was common practice in Chan-kuo period representations of four-legged animals to draw only two legs which were intended to indicate the actual presence of four legs (*cf.* Peripheral Figure No. 12). There does not appear either in literature or in transmitted art from the Chan-kuo period, record or representation of any creature comparable to the present one.

5. A further Ch'u example to which reference may be conveniently made here is the beautifully carved lacquered screen from Tomb No. 1, Wang-shan, which is illustrated in William Watson's paper above (p.   , Figure 8). Amongst the Middle States may be observed such examples as in the bronze Hu-vase (59: 23) in the uppermost and lowermost bands of décor excavated from Tomb No. 59, Liu-li-ko (Kuo Pao-chün, 1959: Pl. 93).

Peripheral Figure No. 5

The creature represented here is not entirely clear. The head is rectangular-shaped and with rectangular-shaped eyes while a long line drawn across the lower part of the face is doubtless the mouth. Part of the body, an arm, and part of a leg may be discerned. There is unfortunately insufficient detail for us to be able to make comparisons with other materials. However, as in the case of Peripheral Figures Nos. 1 and 4, the rectangular-head characteristic may be of significance. Amongst the figures painted in lacquer on the frame of a *se*-harp unearthed at the Ch'ang-t'ai-kuan 長 臺 關 site of Hsin-yang 信 陽, Tomb No. 1, may be noted a creature with a bird-like body and a rectangular or, rather, a 'four-cornered' head (Figure 1).*

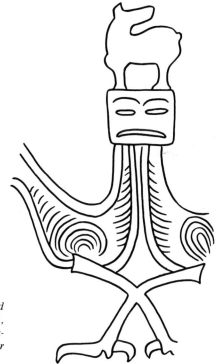

FIGURE 1. *Mythical creature depicted in lacquer in a* se-*harp from Tomb No. 1, Ch'ang-t'ai-kuan, Hsin-yang—a rectangular-shaped head on a bird's body (after Ch'en and Chia, 1958).*

* A comprehensive assembly of the *se*-harp figures may be studied in Chang Kwang-chih's paper above (Figure 6). [Ed.]

141

In the *Shan-hai-ching* attention may be drawn to the following passage : 'And to the east, a distance of 150 *li*, is the mountain called Chi-shan 岐 山 ... the god, She-t'o 涉 蠱, lives there. He has a human body and a square face and three legs.' (5.31b). While in *Mo-tzu*, it may also be recollected, there is a reference to Duke Mu of Ch'in who, while in the Temple, saw enter a strange being with the body of a bird and with a square head. The apparition frightened him and he ran outside;[6] thus it is evident that a 'square', 'rectangular', or 'four-cornered' head may have been something of considerable awe to people of that time – just what its significance was is not, however, clear.

Peripheral Figure No. 6

This figure comprises the intertwined bodies of two snakes — the lower portion of which was misplaced and has since been corrected — with a single head comprising two heart-shaped units combined as one. As may be observed in representations of snakes commonly found from Shang times to the Chan-kuo period (Hayashi, 1960 : Figs. 13–17) the head appears as though belonging to a poisonous variety with its seemingly inflated neck. In the distended upper part of the head appears a pair of bulging white objects which are probably the eyes. One might, indeed, wonder if the lower heart-shaped unit of the head of this Peripheral Figure is an exaggeration of the somewhat comparable curled horn-like members of the single-head double-bodied snake in Figure 2 A. At the top of the head may be observed the finely drawn antenna-like forked tongue of the creature. In various art forms of the Shang period, particularly amongst the dragon-like decorative elements in bronze vessels, may be observed examples of a similar forked or split tongue (2 B). In oracle-bone script, too, the character for 'tongue' has the same split form (2 C). Even in representations of human-like forms (2 D) we find examples amongst the oracle-bone script which incorporate forked or split tongues as

6.   The original text speaks of Duke Mu of Cheng (鄭). Sun Yi-yang 孫 詒 讓 in his *Mo-tzu chien-ku* 墨 子 閒 詁 has demonstrated that this is an error for Duke Mu of Ch'in (秦)— this interpretation is followed here.

FIGURE 2. Single-head double-bodied snakes and the forked tongue. A: detail of décor in a vase excavated at Liu-li-ko, Tomb No. 60, showing curled horn-like features on the head of a ble-bodied snake (after Kuo Pao-chün, 1958: Pl. 84); B: décor detail of dragon-head with ruding forked tongue (after Umehara, 1933: Pl. 129); C: two oracle-bone graphs depicting a ed tongue (CKWP items 3199, 3200); D: graphs incorporating anthropomorphic figure with ed tongue (CKWP items 1079); E: single-head double-bodied snake in the décor of the Tso-Ta Fang-Ting (after Jung Keng, 1936: Pl. 43); F: remnants of the décor on a wooden vessel Tomb No. 1001, Hou-chia-chuang 侯家莊, Anyang (after Liang and Kao, 1962: Fig. 29).

I have pointed out in an earlier paper (1953: 212).[7] It would thus seem that the Ch'u Silk Manuscript representations of the split tongue accord with a tradition going back to Shang times.

7. Attention may be drawn to the country of 'branched-tongues' 岐舌國 referred to in the Shan-hai-ching (6.4a) which Kuo P'u in his commentary explains as: 'the inhabitants all had "branched tongues"—the term 支舌 is sometimes found, too.'
    This legend may refer to people with tongues exhibiting the phenomenon in Peripheral Figure No. 5.

The single-head double-bodied snake was known as Chih (蟠) or Fei-yi (肥遺) in Chan-kuo times and was believed to be the form assumed by a god who resided in dried-up marshes and river-beds. Representations are known as early as Shang and Western Chou times: the example in Figure 2 E is one that often turns up, while 2 F which is incomplete in the upper section is, nevertheless, clearly a single-head double-bodied creature. The latter is of Shang provenance and the intertwined nature of the two bodies is a feature in common with the Ch'u Silk Manuscript version. In the *Shan-hai-ching* the reference to the Fei-yi is as follows: 'And again to the north, a distance of 80 *li*, is the mountain called Hun-hsi 渾夕 which lacks grass and trees but has large quantities of copper and jade. Here the Hsiao River 囂水 commences, and flowing to the northwest, wends its way to the sea. And here there is a snake with two bodies and a single head. It is given the name, Fei-yi, and when it appears there will then occur a severe drought in that country.' (3.8a).

In the Ch'u Silk Manuscript the name given to this creature is 余 *yü* (C. 11-1) thus differing from the *Shan-hai-ching* deity which is associated with drought. In the *Shan-hai-ching* the name, *Fei-yi*, is also applied to a bird: 'And again to the west, a distance of 70 *li*, is the mountain called Ying 英 ... there are birds like quail in shape with a yellow body and red beak. They are called Fei-yi and if eaten will stop ulcers. They can be used to kill intestinal worms.' (2.4a). Note also the term Fei-yi in the following passage written as 肥蟠 and suggested in the commentary to be identical with the single-head double-bodied snake of Hun-hsi: 'And again to the west, a distance of 60 *li,* there is the mountain called T'ai-hua 太華 ... neither birds nor animals live there. There is, however, a snake called Fei-yi with 6 feet and 4 wings. When it appears there is a severe drought throughout the world (天下).' (2.2a).[8] This creature is, of course, quite different from the Hun-hsi deity but may

8. In Kuo P'u's commentary on this passage is a note to the effect that during the reign of T'ang (湯) of the Shang period [*circa* 1750 B.C. in the orthodox chronology] this creature was seen on the foothills of Mt. Yang.

be compared in part to the Ch'u Silk Manuscript version with its 4 wing-like protruberances though feet are lacking. A possible example of a single-head double-bodied snake with wings (?) of Chan-kuo period date appears in Figure 3.

FIGURE 3. Single-head double-bodied snake with wings (?) as depicted in a jade girdle pendant (after Umehara, 1958: Pl. 48 upper left).

It is interesting to observe thus, in the *Shan-hai-ching*, creatures of entirely different form bearing the same name, as well as creatures of the same species but differing somewhat in certain physical aspects. Then upon comparison with an identical form of creature, as in the Ch'u Silk Manuscript, an entirely different appellation is employed. Data are far too few to allow a correct reconstruction of the genealogical situation underlying the processes — probably ranging over many centuries — that resulted in this confusion.

Peripheral Figure No. 7

The three-headed man to which reference was made earlier in this paper has already been noted in terms of its correspondence with the relevant descriptions in the *Shan-hai-ching* and the *Huai-nan-tzu* as noted by earlier writers. Amongst contemporaneous archaeological and literary sources, there are not at present available examples of a three-headed creature in a form corresponding with Peripheral Figure No. 7. But there are close associations in matters of detail to which we shall draw attention. It may be noted that the top of each head of the three-headed figure tends to be flat. This remarkable

145

feature is also to be noted in respect of Peripheral Figures Nos. 2, 8, and 9 which likewise are flat-headed. In the *Shan-hai-ching* is the following entry : ' Chu-jung 祝融 descended and settled on the Chiang River. He begot Kung-kung 共工 ; Kung-kung begot Shu-ch'i 術器 ; Shu-ch'i's head was flat on top.' (18.10a). As will be observed later this feature which at the time was considered to be extraordinarily rare amongst mankind is one that has origins in the Shang period.

On the top of each head are painted fine parallel lines rising vertically then bending outwards on either side — probably the hair of the creature 'standing on end'. A similar stance of the hair may be observed in other Chan-kuo period representations of supernatural beings such as the finely incised Lien-casket figure (Figure 4). Unkempt,

FIGURE 4. Demon with hair standing on end—incised in a bronze Lien-casket excavated at Liu-li-ko, Tomb No. 1 (after Kuo Pao-chün, 1959: Fig. 29).

untied hair seems, in ancient China, to have been a characteristic as-cribed to ghosts and gods in Shang and Chou times as I have demon-strated elsewhere (Hayashi, 1960). The feature and its association with the awesome Peripheral Figure No. 7 is unmistakably depicted in the Çh'u Silk Manuscript.

The crescent-shaped hands terminating the outstretched arms of the three-headed man, which at first glance might be taken to be the claws of animals, are probably intended to be human hands. They may be compared with contemporary pictures on the harp from Ch'ang-t'ai-kuan mentioned before, wherein the hands of various anthropomorphic figures are drawn in the same way (see Figure 5 A–B). Other of the Peripheral Figures in the Ch'u Silk Manuscript such as Nos. 1 and 2, also have this same feature. It would seem that the drawing of the hand in the Ch'u cultural area was generally made in this crescent manner. The peculiar spur-like shape effected at the elbows of Peripheral Figure No. 7 is also characteristic of the figures in the above-mentioned harp (Figure 5 C, E). The leaf-shaped foot, to be observed in Peripheral Figure No. 7 and in other Peripheral Figures in the Manuscript, is also characteristic elsewhere amongst contemporary representations of anthropomorphic figures. A striking example may be noted in Figure 5 D which is taken from a Ko-dagger-axe found recently in Hupei Province near Ching-men-hsien 荊門縣.[9] As the figures of men on the Ch'ang-t'ai-kuan harp are executed with normal feet, it would appear accordingly that the leaf-shaped foot was one especially associated with supernatural creatures in the Chan-kuo period. As already observed, other than literary records of three-headed men, there is virtually nothing in the way of illustrations of Chan-kuo period origin embodying three-headed beings. However, in the Shang period, we may note an oracle-bone character which may be of some significance (Figure 5 H). It comprises a 'man' (5 I) and where the head would appear, there are placed three head-like units (5 J);thus the complete graph may well have been intended to represent a three-headed man.[10] Perhaps even a flat-headed aspect might be inferred if we may consider the element ⊔

9.   The entire body of this creature is covered with scales. On the top of its head two long palm-leaf-like fronds bend downwards from either side and between them stands a wedge-shaped object. Attached to each of its ears is a curved snake; in the right hand it holds a two-headed dragon and in the left a four-legged dragon; a snake wound round the waist functions as a belt. Between its opened-out legs is a further four-legged dragon. The creature's leaf-shaped feet stand upon the 'sun' and a 'three-day-old moon'. Several of these features are individually present amongst various of the archaeological portrayals of gods and demons and are described in such literary sources as the *Shan-hai-ching* but the combination of so many of them in the one being is unknown elsewhere.

10.   Shirakawa Shizuka has suggested that these units are either 'heads' or 'mouths' and further discusses the possibility that they may portray containers (carried on the heads) in which the written records of prayers to the gods are placed (1956: 69–70).

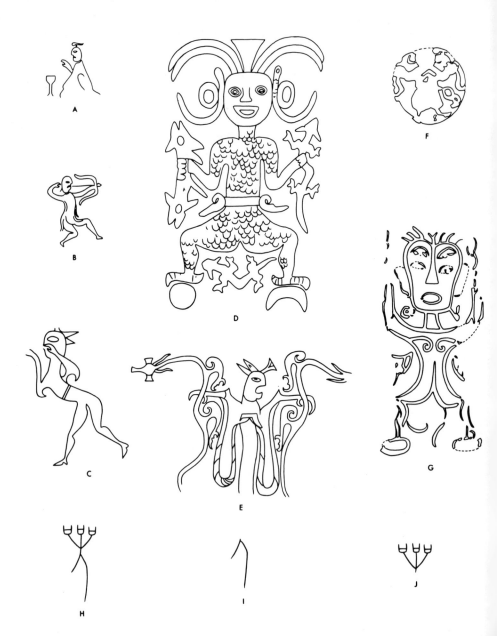

FIGURE 5. *Crescent-shaped hands, spur-shaped elbows, leaf-shaped feet, three-headed men, etc.*
A–C, E: from the Ch'ang-t'ai-kuan se-*harp (after Ch'en and Chia, 1958); D: décor on a Ko*
dagger-axe — for complete figure see William Watson above (Figure 7, 2) — excavated at Ching
men-hsien, Hupei (after Wang Yü-t'ung, 1963: Pl. 1); F: pictorial seal with figure holding a snake
in each hand (after Ch'en Chieh-ch'i, 1922: 30.48) G: from a bronze sword (after Liu T'ai-chih,
1935: 10.101); H–J: oracle-bone graphs depicting three-headed men (after CKWP item 4277).

148

(which is usually 'mouth') being a calligraphic development from the form ⎵. As such the graph ⍑ may have represented a human body surmounted by three flat-topped heads and there being, of course, no such actual creature it would, doubtless, represent a supernatural being. This particular character does not, it is significant to observe, appear in the divinatory texts proper among the oracle bones but is found entered as a State name of one of the tribute-paying States subservient to City Shang which is recorded in respect of tribute payments (Hu Hou-hsüan, 1966 : A3.21-2, 59-60, 62, 65). Accordingly, it would appear that the character may portray features of the people, or of a god revered in that particular country. It seems reasonable thus to suggest that the concept of the three-headed man may have origins dating back into the Shang period.

Peripheral Figure No. 8

This has a flat head and like the central head of the three-headed man, the outline of the face is formed by two lines. The mouth is rectangular in shape with teeth bared in a frightening appearance. Both arms are spread outwards and the forearms are crescent-shaped. The arms seem to be contracted with the forearms reversed so as to face upwards but exactly how to interpret this aspect of the drawing is difficult. However, attention may be drawn to a couple of *Shan-hai-ching* passages in which reference is made to people of a particular country who had forearms in a reversed position : ' The country, Jou-li 柔 利, is east of the land of one-eyed people. The inhabitants have each only one arm and one leg which are reversed at elbow and knee and are crooked. The leg is on top.' (8.1a). Note also : ' In the Ta-huang — far beyond the seas — there is a mountain called Jih-yüeh 日 月 山 . . . there are a people with their forearms reversed who are known as T'ien-yü 天 虞.' (16.6a). The two lines hanging from the ends of the crescent-shaped forearms of Peripheral Figure No. 8 may possibly represent snakes and thus accord with the passages cited earlier in this paper from the *Shan-hai-ching* and these by no means comprise all such records. In this connection, attention may be drawn again to the Ch'ang-t'ai-kuan harp figures amongst which one is especially deserving of note holding as it does two dragon-like creatures — one in each hand (Figure 5 E). In a Chan-kuo period seal, too, is a figure holding two snakes (5 F). There are however, no other drawings, particularly with snakes held in the hands, with which comparisons of Peripheral Figure No. 8 may be made. The feet of this deity, it may be observed, differ considerably from the feet of the other deities in the Ch'u Silk Manuscript and their exact significance is difficult to assess. Between the legs appear two tail-like objects, the purport of which likewise escapes us. However, in Figure 5 G, taken from a Chan-kuo period sword, may be observed between the legs of this four-eyed creature two similar appendages which may possibly be identical in significance to those just described in Peripheral Figure No. 8.11

Peripheral Figure No. 9

This deity has the flat head to which we have already referred and like the preceding figure its teeth are bared; it has a very weird appearance. From the head rise two somewhat curled ram-like horns but there being no such comparable examples either in literary or in archaeological sources perhaps we should interpret them as crest-like feathers. Below the head is a long bird-like neck and a tongue-like object commencing, however, from the chin and thus in all probability a beard. The body is heart-shaped and has three tail-feathers at the bottom and a single leg drawn to the left. Although the single leg may be considered to indicate two legs, it will be noted that Peripheral Figure No. 10 has actually two legs drawn; thus we cannot, in the present case, be absolutely certain whether or not it was the artist's intention to portray a single leg. Roughly speaking, however, we may regard this deity as comprising a bird's

11. In the Yi-nan tomb is an engraved stone slab in the southern wall of the middle vault depicting a four-eyed man and there is a caption below bearing his name: 蒼頡 Ts'ang Chieh (Tseng Chao-yü, etc. 1956: Pl. 52). Ts'ang Chieh is described in the *Lun-heng* 論衡 as having 'four eyes. He served Huang Ti "the Yellow Emperor" as a scribe (see details in Tseng Chao-yü, etc. p. 39). Although this engraved stone confirms the Han-time tradition as transmitted in the *Lun-heng* there are, of course, no grounds to propose an identity between 5 G and Ts'ang Chieh.

150

body with a human-like face. In the traditional literature there is a considerable number of references to deities of this particular form. The relevant accounts which appear in such works as the *Shan-hai-ching*, *Mo-tzu* 墨 子, *Lü-shih ch'un-ch'iu* 呂 氏 春 秋, etc. have been conveniently assembled together by Yang Kuan 楊 寬 (1941). Although they are by no means uncommon, there is no record of any of these deities with the name 倉 *ts'ang* (C. 17-1 ; C. 18-2) as in the Ch'u Silk Manuscript, or anything approaching it. So far as the single foot aspect is concerned there are only the following two passages in ancient literary sources: 'Again to the west, a distance of 70 *li*, there is the mountain called Yü-tz'u 㺄 次 ... there are birds in the shape of an owl with human-like face and a single leg. They are called T'o-fei 橐 𩿤.' (*Shan-hai-ching* 2.5b) ; and in the same source : 'Pi-fang 畢 方 birds ... they have (the bodies of a) bird, human-like face, and a single leg.' (6.2a). In another entry in the *Shan-hai-ching*, however, the Pi-fang birds lack in their description the presence of a human-like face (2.26a).

In a late Chan-kuo period mirror there may be observed amongst the decorative elements a single-leg bird (Figure 6 A), while in Figure 6 B may be noted a rendering of a single-leg bird of Eastern Han date ; these might be associated with the single-leg Pi-fang birds lacking human-like faces. For an example of such creatures with human-like faces there is a late Ch'un-ch'iu period example (6 C). From the chin of this creature hangs a beard of triangular shape, the neck is covered with scales and from the base of the neck a single leg is shown stretched out horizontally, but upon comparison with the other animal inter-twined with it (which has two legs shown) it is evident that a single leg is intended to represent a pair of legs. Below the leg is the feathered body and below this the tail feathers. In various respects, this creature may be compared with Peripheral Figure No. 9 in the Ch'u Silk Manu-script notwithstanding the fact that it lacks the long plume-like feathers on the head. The beard-like appendage on the chin, the horizontally extended leg, and the curled shape at the 'knee' are corresponding fea-tures. Other examples of bird-like creatures with bearded human-like faces may be observed in engraved stone tomb facings of Eastern Han date. In Figure 6 (D-E) such examples are presented. In each of these

A

C

B

E

D

F

cases the creatures possess two legs but lack plumes surmounting their heads. The example in (6 F) dates back to the Shang period: it is a jade piece in The Sackler Collections. The lower part comprises an example of the commonly found 'phoenix' or 'owl' shape but the upper section comprises a human head on the back of which there are S-shaped protruberances of the same kind as found on Shang period 'phoenixes' (Hayashi, 1966: 15-18). These may perhaps be regarded as the forerunner of the long plumes which we see in Peripheral Figure No. 9. An important point, however, is the fact that evidence of this kind indicates quite early origins of the concept of human-head, bird-bodied creatures. Accordingly, this jade-piece is especially valuable.

As may be observed from the preceding discussion, examples ranging from Shang times to the Chan-kuo period are by no means few in numbers. Although we are unable to find examples so far as name, character, and physical appearance are concerned that match in every respect the features of the Manuscript deity, nevertheless, it is not to be doubted that the latter is a deity of similar type to those cited.

Peripheral Figure No. 10

The head of this creature may be described as being like that of a dragon. Upon comparison with the head of the dragon in Figure 7 (A) a marked degree of similarity may be observed. There are slight differences in the degree the lower jaws jut out, the thickness of the 'ears', and the manner in which the Manuscript version is not clearly defined in terms of a boundary-line between ears and head.

The 'snub' effect of the nose may be noted as a commonly occuring form in dragon-heads in early Eastern Chou bronze décor with the eye usually placed below the feature (7 B). In Peripheral Figure No. 10 it is uncertain, however, as to whether there was originally an eye in the

FIGURE 6. Single-leg birds and birds with human-heads and with beards. A: décor on a bronze mirror (after Palmgren, 1948: Pl. 35, 3); B: stone engraving from the Yi-nan 沂南 tomb (Tseng Chao-yü, etc., 1959: Pl. 76); C: decoration on a Hu-vase supposedly excavated at Li-yü-ts'un 李峪村 (after Shang hai po-wu-kan, 1964: II. 69); D: detail from engraved stone facing of a tomb, Hsü-chou 徐州. Kiangsu (KK 1964.10: Fig. 5, 2); E: stone engraving from the Yi-nan tomb (Tseng Chao-yü, etc., 1959: Pl. 62); F: jade ornament in The Sackler Collections (J-231).

FIGURE 7. *Characteristics of dragon-heads. A: example from the lacquer paintings on the Ch'ang-t'ai-kuan* se-*harp (after Ch'en and Chia, 1958); B: décor detail from the Ch'en Hou Hu-vase* 陳厌壺 *(after Tch'ou, 1924: Pl. 15).*

head of this creature owing to destruction of the silk material in the area where an eye would be expected to appear. From the mouth there protrudes a long, thin tongue which may also be compared with the same feature in the dragon-head in 7 B — one commonly found in early Eastern Chou times.

The body of this deity has very much the appearance of a sweet potato. Hairs are painted along its back. Because of the mutilated silk fabric it is uncertain whether the creature has a tail-like appendage or not. To the left of the body are two thin legs like those of a small bird. Because of the nature of the legs and the similar burly nature of the body of the bird in Figure 6 B we may possibly regard the body of this deity also as that of a bird. Dragon-head bird-bodied beings are mentioned in the *Shan-hai-ching*: ' All told, the Ch'üeh 䧿 [鵲] Mountains commencing from the Mountains of Chao-yao 招 搖 to the Ch'i-wei 箕 尾 Mountains, amount to a total of ten, and extend for 2,950 *li*. The

gods all have the shape of a bird's body with the head of a dragon.'
(1.5a), also : 'All told, the Tung-t'ing 洞庭 Mountains commencing
from the Mountains of Pien-yü 邅遇 to the Jung-yü 榮余 Mountains ...
The gods all have the shape of a bird's body and the head of a dragon.'
(5.53a).

Unfortunately, however, we cannot be completely certain that
the Manuscript deity comprises the combination of a bird's body with
a dragon-head. Furthermore, there do not appear to be many relevant
items to be found amongst archaeological remains with which comparison might be made.

Peripheral Figure No. 11

This creature has two heads on a fork-shaped neck. Each head
is more or less 'double' heart-shaped and from the tip of the head
a forked tongue protrudes. As noted earlier, this form of head may
be identified as that of a snake. The double neck connects with the
body but on account of considerable damage to the silk fabric its
exact nature is difficult to reconstruct. Four feet, two on each side
of the body which do not meet the opposite members as pairs but
are placed at irregular positions may be noted. And at the bottom
is a tail-like object with round markings like the dapple pattern on
a deer.

Unlike the reconstruction prepared by Noel Barnard, I consider
the creature to have a thin meandering, snake-like body (Figure 8 A)
thus being consistent with the snake-heads surmounting it.

The curve from the body to the tail in this reconstruction might
also be considered in relation to that of the dragon-like animal held
in the left hand of the deity drawn in Figure 5 D. Note also the
legs of the two similar animals held by the mythical creature in 5 E
— each leg has a curved hook-like protruberance which is a kind of
feather. If my reconstruction is correct, the deity in the Manuscript
may be termed a double-head four-legged snake. The double-headed
snake known as Hui (虺, 蟣, or 虺), a deity with supernatural powers,
I have discussed in an earlier paper (1960 : 41-2).

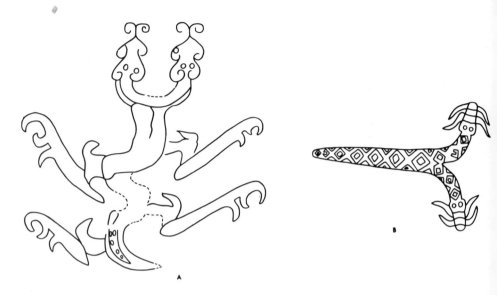

FIGURE 8. Single-body double-headed snakes. A: author's reconstruction of Peripheral Figure No. 11 [cf. Barnard, Figure 4 above, for variant version]; B: décor on Ko-dagger-axe from Ch'eng-ku 城固, Shensi (after WW 1966.1: 2).

So far as double-headed snakes are concerned there are two types that come to mind: first, one comprising a long-bodied creature with a head at either end of the body and secondly, the type with two heads at the one end of the body. There are literary references to which attention might be drawn describing the latter type of double-headed snake in the *Erh-ya*, where the term 枳首蛇 *chih-shou-she* (equivalent to 岐首蛇) occurs and also in the *Shan-hai-ching*: 'There are a people known as the Miao-min 苗民. They have gods comprising the body of a snake which is as long as a chariot shaft and with human-like heads — there is a head on the left and another on the right.' (18.6a). Although these references concern double-headed snakes, they are unlike the creature with which we are now dealing in that they do not have legs at all. Nevertheless, in the *Shan-hai-ching* we may note a passage with record of four-legged snake-like creatures. But, in these cases the creatures do not have two heads — they are single-headed creatures: 'And again to the west, a distance of 370 *li*, there is the mountain called Lo-yu 樂游山 where the T'ao River 桃水 comes out ... in its waters are many Hua 鰧 fish. They are shaped like snakes

156

and have four legs and they eat fish.' (2.23a). Representations of double-headed snakes are few. In the decoration on a *Ko*-dagger-axe reproduced in Figure 8 B, the heads are thin and with long drooping 'moustaches' on either side — at first glance the heads do not appear to be snake-like. However, upon comparison with the head of the single-head double-bodied snake in 9 D which has similar features it seems acceptable to regard the heads in 8 B as those of a snake. The diamond pattern of 'scales' on its body is one commonly found on snakes in Shang and Western Chou décor and otherwise the provenance details show this weapon to be of Shang or early Western Chou date.

The double-headed snake (but without four legs) is to be noted amongst the wood sculptures from the Wang-shan 望 山 site, Chiang-ling 江 陵, Hupei (Figure 9 A). This example has a long tongue protruding from each head. The heads are back-to-back and their S-shaped necks merge together to form a single neck which is set in a square stand. Although the available photographs are poorly reproduced it is, nevertheless, evident that the sculpture is close in major details to the well-known wooden figure now in The Sackler Collections (9 B). This too might be called a double-headed snake. On each head is affixed a pair of deer antlers. In the second example the creature has a pair of hands raised in an upright position placed alongside the mouth of each of its heads. Salmony (1954 : 8–11) some years ago described the heads of this particular sculpture as being a form of *t'ao-t'ieh* but this is not possible. As he saw it, the head seemingly lacked the lower jaw but it is not actually the case as one may observe from the side view. The lower jaw in Chan-kuo period dragons and other such creatures is often unobtrusive as in 9 C and placed immediately behind the eyes ; the comma-shaped 'ears' as seen from the side are not to be regarded as ears but may be compared with the curled spiral-shaped members on the forehead of the single-head double-bodied snake in 9 D. Thus there is little ground to see these creatures as a kind of *t'ao-t'ieh* ; furthermore, the heads do not appear to be reminiscent of an animal such as a tiger or other feline but rather they would appear to have a reptilian character. However, attached to the heads there are deer's antlers and the protruding tongues of these wood sculptured creatures are

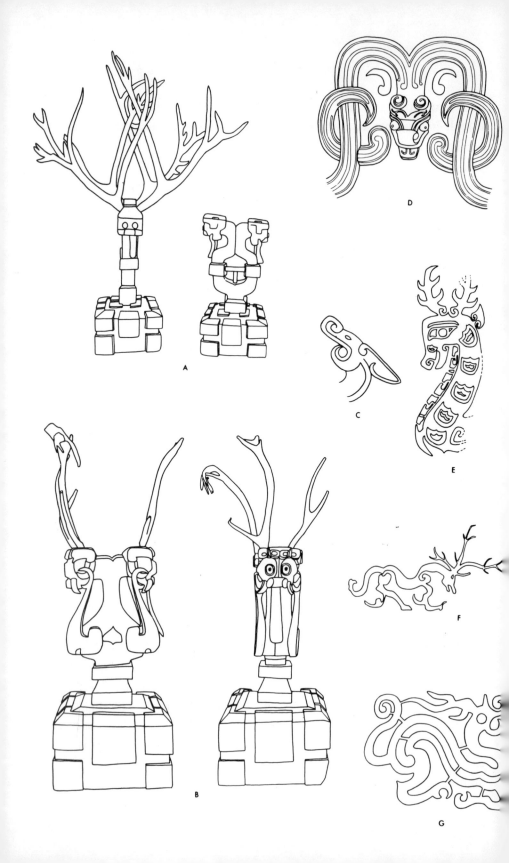

A

B

C

D

E

F

G

not those of snakes as in the case of Peripheral Figure No. 11 but rather the tongues of animals. In the single-head double-bodied snake décor of a bronze vessel of late Western Chou style (9 D) it may be observed that the protruding tongue of this snake-like creature is essentially identical with the tongues in the wooden sculptures. The association of this kind of tongue with single-head double-bodied snakes thus has origins as early as Late Western Chou.

A major variation in detail between the wood sculpture creatures cited here and Peripheral Figure No. 11 is the presence of antlers in the case of the former. Regarding the wood sculptures Jao Tsung-yi (1958a) draws attention to a commentary note in the *Shih-chi* which defines an animal called Fei-chü 蜚 虡 (also written 蜚 遽) as : ' a supernatural animal comprising the head of a deer and the body of a dragon.' But the Fei-chü has only a single head while the wood sculptures certainly lack any semblance to a deer's head apart from the antlers. A carved bone from the Shang site Hou-chia-chuang 侯 家 莊, Anyang, may be better cited in comparison with the Fei-chü description (9 E). Two other examples (9 F–G) respectively of Chan-kuo and Ch'un-ch'iu date are in some respects, but not entirely, remi-niscent of the Fei-chü description. It is, however, sufficiently clear that the wood sculptures have little in common with the Fei-chü description.

Salmony (1954 : 7-16) in his discussion on Figure 9 B and a Yi-ewer 匜 in the Seattle Art Museum which he thought contained representations of dancers wearing antlers and engaged in dances to promote good harvests, is somewhat off the mark in certain details. But in proposing that the antlers may indicate the power of protection because of their association with tomb guardian figures from Ch'ang-sha excavations, he was surely correct.

FIGURE 9. Single-body double-headed creatures with antlers. A: wood sculpture from Tomb No. 1 Wang-shan (after WW 1966.5: Pl. 20); B: painted wood sculpture now in The Sackler Collections (S-2069); C: detail from a jade girdle pendant excavated from Ch'ang-t'ai-kuan, Tomb No. 1 (after WW 1957.9: Pl. 9); D: décor detail from the Sung Hu-vase 頌 壷 (after Jung Keng, 1934a: Pl. 87); E: incised décor on bone artifact from Tomb No. 1001, Hou-chia-chuang, An-yang (after Liang and Kao, 1962: Pl. 210, 9); F: decoration on a bronze Chien basin excavated from Tomb No. 75, Liu-li-ko, Hui-hsien, Honan (after Kuo Pao-chün, 1959: Pl. 100); G: décor element in a bronze Hu-vase (after Umehara, 1936: Pl. 17, 2).

Deer antlers surmount the Ch'ang-t'ai-kuan 長臺關 wooden guardian figures. These have pointed ears, large round red eyes, teeth and large fangs exposed in a wide mouth, and a long protruding tongue hanging down to the waist (Figure 10 A). Both hands clutch a snake at jaw level; the creature is apparently in the process of devouring it. The forepaws and hind paws are armed with long claws but strangely the creature is seated in a human-like posture (*seiza* ; *cf.* Ch'en Ch'i-lu, below p. 420). Attention may be drawn to the previously quoted *Shan-hai-ching* passage (17.4b) describing the Chiang-liang deity (p. 124) which, with the exception of its lack of antlers, otherwise matches the Ch'ang-t'ai-kuan figure very closely. In his commentary on this passage Ho Yi-hsing notes the correspondence of the name Chiang-liang with one of the *Hou Han-shu* (Li-yi-chih 禮儀志) listings of the 'Twelve Gods', namely Chiang-liang (強梁 [also 強良, 彊梁, 彊良]) who in concert with another of these demons lived upon the dismembered corpses of criminals. Seen in this rôle, the Chiang-liang accords well with the Ch'ang-t'ai-kuan sculpture which it is assumed was placed in the tomb in the expectation of its carrying out a similar function. As An Chih-min (1963 : 57) observes it would seem that tomb guardians of this kind may have developed later into the 'Twelve Gods' whose function was to pursue and to expel wicked demons from the Inner Palace. He also notes the similar bronze figure from Hsin-cheng 新鄭 which originally functioned as a vessel-stand (Figure 10 B) with snake-like supports issuing from its mouth (and grasped in the hands) and extending from its horns. The creature stands upon a pair of coiled snakes. We know that this particular strange animal is not derived from the State of Ch'u.

Literary references relevant to the double-headed snake aspect of Figure 9 A, the Chiang-liang association with 10 A, etc. do not mention deer antlers. Deer antlers being a peculiar feature of ogres were probably not at first incorporated in the general body structure

FIGURE 10. Tomb guardians and deer antlers. A: example from Ch'ang-t'ai-kuan, Tomb No. 1 (after reconstruction in Kodansha, 1963: 6); B: the figure of a Chiang-liang (?) from Hsin-cheng, Honan (after Sun Hai-p'o, 1937: 133); C: deer antlers on stand, Ch'ang-t'ai-kuan Tomb No. 2 (after KK 1958.11: Pl. 6).

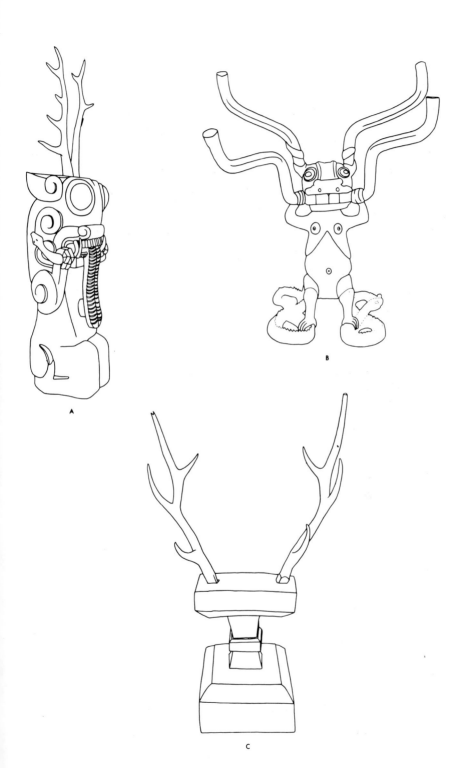

A

B

C

of the representations of gods that came to wear them but were later added in order to accentuate their supernatural powers. Support for this hypothesis might be claimed in respect of 10 C, a plain stand bearing deer antlers only. Also the small antler imbedded in a lead stand found in the Chan-kuo period Chao-ku-ts'un 趙固村 Tomb No. 1 (*Hui-hsien Report*: Pl. 94, 23-5) regarded by the reporters as an attachment to a form of tomb guardian (p. 120) but if this were so the stand would be redundant; thus it seems best to consider the object as a tomb guardian in its own right in the same way as 10 C. From Tombs Nos. 12 and 14 in Fen-shui-ling, Ch'ang-chih 分水嶺長治, Shansi, painted deer antlers were excavated; the reporters observed that the lower ends had been sharpened as though to be inserted into the heads of tomb guardians but no evidence appears as to whether they were used in stands or in sculptured figures.

The appearance of antlers thus on their own seems to prove that they were believed to have had some kind of supernatural power. Further, in the tomb from which the guardian creature (Figure 10 A) was excavated there was found a 'waist-pit' (腰坑 *yao-kang*) containing the skeleton of a small deer. The custom involving the burial of a dog in a small pit located below the deceased's waist was common in Shang times and the significance of the practice — to protect or to warn the tomb occupant of danger — is generally known and accepted. Although the custom in Eastern Chou times is much less commonly found than in Shang, it nevertheless persists. In a tomb excavated at Lo-yang, deer were found buried together with the deceased, no doubt a practice which had similar meaning to people of that period.

What then was the significance of the deer in ancient China? There is a considerable amount of material, both archaeological and literary concerning this question. Space, however, is insufficient to allow a comprehensive consideration here. Thus I draw attention only to the archaeological data such as we have already reviewed. Just as dogs were sacrificed in the Shang period and were placed with the deceased person in his tomb, so too, deer were buried in tombs in Eastern

Chou times. Apparently the belief was that the animal would warn the occupant of the tomb when any dangerous spirits were about to invade the premises. It is clear, too, that the practice of burying deer's antlers or images of deities crowned with antlers in tombs was not limited to Ch'u but, in fact, appears in sites in Honan and Shansi in the older cultural areas. Salmony's impression that it was solely a Ch'u custom which was derived from India now requires revision.

Peripheral Figure No. 12

At first glance, this creature appears to be a drawing of a bird-headed animal. Rising from the head is a pair of feather-like objects similar to those in Peripheral Figure No. 9. The parrot-like beak and the long thin neck are features which indicate this section of the creature to be drawn after a bird. The body is deer-like but the long thick tail is not that of a deer. Not even the similar species *Elaphurus davidianus* with its long tail reaches anywhere near this length. The legs are those of an animal but the feet are not clearly discernable. Although two legs only are drawn, it would be as well to regard these as representing four limbs. Along the body may be observed a long, thick stripe reminiscent of that on a tapir (貘 *mo*: *tapirus indicus*). Amongst Chan-kuo period illustrations in bronze and in ceramics there are several which approximate the features in Peripheral Figure No. 12. That in Figure 11 A is very close except that it has wings while the feather crest on its head is more like that of a phoenix rather than the double crest in the Ch'u Silk Manuscript illustrations. Figure 11 B, taken from a vessel excavated at Liu-li-ko Hui-hsien, is similar to that in 11 A. Here, however, instead of wings may be observed on the long neck of this creature several feather-like objects. Figure 11 C which is a section of a long, complicated, repeated pattern shows some of the features that may be compared with Peripheral Figure No. 12. The body is long and thin and at the curves of the body are wings — the feature is one similarly found in dragons — but the way in which the beak curves and the shape of the feather crest are very close to the same items in the Ch'u Silk Manuscript deity.

FIGURE 11. *Bird-headed animals. A: detail from décor on a bronze* Hu-*vase (after Umehara, 1936: Pl. 1); B: detail from décor on a Chien-basin from Tomb No. 75, Liu-li-ko (after Kuo Pao-chün, 1959: Pl. 100); C: detail from décor on a bronze* Hu-*vase (after Umehara, 1960: II. Pl. 386); D: incised décor in pottery* Hu-*vase from Huai-jou-hsien* 懷柔縣, *Peking (after KK 1962.5: Pl. 7, 1).*

Figure 11 D which is taken from the incised decoration in a pottery vessel of Chan-kuo period date unearthed near Peking, has features in common although it lacks a double feather crest on the creature's head. Amongst tomb paintings of gods and demons of Eastern Han times, creatures of similar appearance are often found (*cf.* Tseng Chao-chüeh, 1956: Pls. 43, 61, 66, etc.). In literary sources this type of bird-head animal-bodied creature is often described under the term Fei-lien (飛 廉). In the *Han-shu* is a description which in many essentials corresponds remarkably well with the features in

Peripheral Figure No. 12 : 'Chin Cho 晉 灼 stated : " The body is like that of a deer, the head like a sparrow, it has horns and the tail of a snake, it is patterned like a leopard ".' The commentary goes on to say that the Fei-lien was a divine animal which could call up winds and clouds. 'Sparrow' in this connection is probably to be understood as 'phoenix' (Hayashi, 1966 : 25) while 'horns' is to be read as in the *Shuo-wen* gloss : 'Huan (萑) is an owl ... with horns of feathers.' Although the *Shuo-wen* describes the leopard's coat as having round patterns — which feature does not accord with the Manuscript painting — the *Erh-ya* states : '貘, 白豹' thus defining 'tapir' as a 'white leopard'. When we take these points into account it would appear that Chin Cho's description of the mythical Fei-lien accords fairly well with details of Peripheral Figure No. 12. However, we must keep in mind that some other descriptions of the Fei-lien suggest an entirely different creature — for instance, there is one which speaks of the Fei-lien as comprising a bird's body and the head of a deer. Variations in detail of this kind, as I earlier observed, appear not infrequently amongst the sources we have consulted. Attention may be drawn to the associations in literary sources of the Fei-lien in the Middle States area but whether in these accounts it is the same creature as described by Chin Cho is not certain. In the *Shih-chi* the tradition of the Fei-lien may also be traced back into Shang times but we have no archaeological illustrations depicting the form of the Fei-lien as it may have been imagined by Shang period artists.

Peripheral Figure No. 1

This creature has the horns of an ox and the head is rectangular-shaped and reminiscent of the term we discussed earlier in respect of rectangular-headed people. The eyes are unusual in that they are aligned in vertical position. This feature is probably that referred to in the *Shan-hai-ching* as 直目 *chih-mu* 'upright eyes' or 從 [縱] 目 *tsung-mu* 'vertical eyes' : 'The Mei (袜＝魅) is a creature with a human body, black head, and vertical eyes.' In his commentary Ho Yi-hsing suggests the Mei was possibly the same as 'the beasts with pigs' heads, vertical eyes, and disarranged hair ...' (12.3a) which

165

are described in the *Ch'u-tz'u* (*KBTK* 10.26). Also there is the following description : 'Beyond the Northwestern Ocean and north of the Red River there lies Chang-wei 章尾山 Mountain. Here there reside gods with human faces, snake bodies, and are red in colour. Their eyes are upright . . .' (17.9a). In the centre of the forehead of Peripheral Figure No. 1 is a small triangular patch, the significance of which cannot be assessed. The outstretched arms are similar to those in Peripheral Figure No. 7. The legs of the short body were originally misplaced and in recent reconstructions have been corrected. Between the two legs and also under the arm-pits appears in each case a small hook-like object. A similar feature may be noted under the arms and behind the legs in the drawing of the bird-head human-bodied demon in Figure 12 A. In

FIGURE 12. *Revised reconstruction of Peripheral Figure No. 1 with 'spurs.' A: detail from décor on bronze* Hu-*base (after Jung Keng, 1941: Fig. 238); B: Peripheral Figure No. 1 as revised by the author.*

this latter case, because the creature has the head of a bird, we may perhaps regard these hook-like objects as being spurs. With this thought in mind, I propose the reconstruction of Peripheral Figure No. 1 as given in my Figure 12 B which varies slightly from that proposed by

Barnard. I take the legs to be bow-legged in shape. This possibility is also to be noted in respect of a *Shan-hai-ching* passage which speaks of bow-legged people : 'Han-liu 韓流 had a long neck and ... ears [謹 耳 — meaning uncertain], a human face with a pig's snout, his body was covered with scales and his legs were like felloes of a wheel. His feet were trotters.' (18.2a).*

Accordingly, Peripheral Figure No. 1 has a most unusual shape comprising as it does a square-shaped head with ox-horns and vertical-eyes, a very short body with bow-legs, and spurs under the arm-pits and between the legs. There is no literary description of mythical creatures with all these characteristics. As I observed earlier, the interpretations made by other scholars to the effect that Peripheral Figure No. 1 comprises an ox's head and a human body has no support in fact. It is interesting, nevertheless, to find in the Shang period vestiges of such a concept. The oracle-bone graphs in Figure 13 may be interpreted as a standing human figure with an ox's head

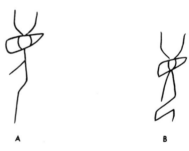

FIGURE 13. Oracle – bone graphs comprising an ox's head on a human body (after CKWP item 44341.)

A   B

(13 A) and a kneeling human figure also with an ox's head (13 B). Possibly these may be taken to indicate something of the origins of the much later concept of the mythical Shen-neng, particularly in

---

* Kuo P'u's gloss states that in the term 渠股 *ch'ü-ku* the graph *ch'ü* means 車輞 *ch'e-wang* 'tyre of chariot wheel' which is to say 跰 脚 *chien-chiao* 'calloosed legs'. This gloss does not, however, seem to take into account the more appropriate meaning of both *ch'ü* and *wang*, namely 'felloes'. Hayashi has discussed the possibility of 跰 being read in the sense of 跰 躚 *chien-hsien* 'stagger', 'totter', or similarly as 蹁 躚 *p'ien-hsien*. The *Shuo-wen* glosses *p'ien* as 'unusually shaped feet'. It would seem to me preferable, however, if we are to regard the graphs *chien-chiao* in Kuo P'u's gloss as being some what off the mark (as Hayashi quite rightly does in a long note on this point) simply to follow the original text which seems clearly to mean 'bow-legged' rather than to seek to reconstruct the last two graphs — whatever the approach, however, the interpretations will be similar. [Ed.]

view of the fact that these characters are used invariably as place names in Shang oracle bone–script. It is, however, quite improbable that there is any direct connection with the Manuscript figure.

Peripheral Figure No. 2

This deity is also flat-headed and around the outline of the head is painted a narrow band — in these respects it is similar to Peripheral Figure No. 8. However, from the mouth protrudes a thin tongue split to the left and to the right and there are differences in the shape of the ears. But the ears, or what appear to be ears, are rather like those of an ox or some other creature in contrast to the human-like ears of Peripheral Figure No. 8. Above the head there rises two objects like fronds of pampas grass. The arms which are like those in Peripheral Figure No. 7 stretch outwards to the left and to the right but one arm is raised somewhat higher than the other. The body is very short and so, too, the legs. The feet are like those in Peripheral Figure No. 7 — leaf-like in shape. As we cannot define exactly whether the head is that of a human being or of an animal, and likewise the body, there remains little that we can use as a basis for searching for comparable descriptions in literary sources. Figure 14 A which is taken from the Ch'ang-t'ai-kuan harp to which we have several times referred, has several features in common with the Manuscript figure — the shape of the head and the ears (?) is similar and so, too, the short stumpy body. Unfortunately the area above the creature's head has suffered damage and we cannot be sure whether there was originally a pair of plumes or some such sort of crest.

FIGURE 14. Anthropomorphic figures with ox-like ears and others with crest-plumes. A, B: examples with ox-like ears in the Ch'ang-t'ai-kuan se-harp (after Ch'en and Chia, 1958): C– G: various bronze inscription versions of anthropomorphic figures with crest-plumes (C, after Yü Hsing-wu 1957: 349 [Ku-beaker ins.]; D: after Lo Chen-yü 1936: XV. 33 [Chüeh-wine-cup ins.]; E: after Uü Hsing-wu 1957: 27 [Ting-cauldron ins.]; F: after Lo Chen-yü 1936: XVIII. 19 [P'ou-vase ins.]; G: after Yü Hsing-wu 1957: 504 [Fang-Yi-casket]); H: chariot appliqué excavated at Yi-tu-hsien 益都縣., Shantung (after Shan-tung wen-wu hsuan-chi: Pl. 84) I: Fang-Ting-cauldron with human face found near Ch'ang-sha (after Kodansha, 1963: 49]; J: jade figure (after Kodansha, 1963: 54]; K: jade figure (after WW 1959.7: 65]; L: jade figure excavated Tomb No. 1, Lo-yang western suburbs (after KK 1959.12: Pl. 4, 1).

A B C D E

F G H

I

K J L

The head of a dragon seen again in front of the demon's breast in Figure 14 B, also on the same harp, evinces practically identical details. Although, no doubt little more than a coincidence it is interesting to observe that the position and stance of the arms is quite close to that of the Manuscript deity. From the top of the head rises a wedge-shaped object similar to that in 5 D. Possibly it may be regarded as a kind of feather.

In Shang times, we find amongst the clan-sign type of inscriptions in bronze vessels, several examples of figures similar to Peripheral Figure No. 2 in the Ch'u Silk Manuscript. One that is very close in respect of the two feathers rising from the head may be studied in Figure 14 C. But as this is derived only from a rubbing, we cannot be absolutely sure as to the genuineness of the inscription. Although a little different in the mode of drawing, the representations in 14 D–G may be accounted more appropriate for comparison, not only because of the two plume-like objects arising from the heads but also because of the squat nature of the body and the open-thigh position in each case. The feature is also present in 14 H, a chariot fitting and again in 14 I, a square *Ting*-cauldron with the plume-like objects appearing just above the ears on either side of the head. In a study of various renderings of the phoenix (Hayashi, 1966a) I speculated upon the same plume-like elements as in the above cited illustrations as comprising crest-plumes. We have thus the problem of human-like creatures with crest-plumes issuing from their heads identical with those of phoenixes. It would seem clear enough that these do not portray ordinary men — the placement of the face in 14 I in the position normally occupied by the *t'ao-t'ieh* would certainly suggest a supernatural status in this case.

Notwithstanding the recognisable variations in respect of the crest-plumes in Peripheral Figure No. 2, it is evident that there were in Shang times demons in human shape wearing pairs of plumes. As in the case of the Manuscript deity the Shang examples also depict a fat body and a similar tendency towards flat-topped heads — such similarities can hardly be regarded as merely coincidental.

Other than these Shang period examples, we may also note an early Western Chou figurine (14 J) a jade carving of late Western Chou to early Ch'un-ch'iu date (14 K) and a Chan-kuo period decorative element from a bronze vessel (14 L). The second of these examples has the crest-plumes branching into a highly complex pattern; both hands and feet are apparently rendered as feathers. Although they do not necessarily depict the same god they do indicate the tradition of supernatural beings with phoenix crest-plumes continuing from Shang times through to the Chan-kuo period.

A further outstanding feature attending Peripheral Figure No. 2 is, of course, the long, thin, protruding tongue which it will be noted is absent amongst the cited crest-plume examples. The protruding tongue motif may be found embodied in the decoration of a middle Shang period style *Tsun*-vase (Figure 15 A). This was excavated at Anhwui a few years ago and is probably the earliest manifestation of the protruding tongue motif. The representation of the tongue here, may be compared also with my earlier Figures (2 C–D). There do not seem to be further Shang period artifacts or décor with human appearance embodying the protruding tongue motif but amongst oracle-bone characters we may observe the examples 夸 and 夋 both of which comprise the body of a man with an animal head from which a split tongue protrudes. The characters are employed either as geographical names or as the names of tribes. The oracle records containing them date in the Wu Ting 武丁 period (*circa*. 1200 B.C. in the orthodox system) and as the two graphs are close in structure, they may even be the same graph.

From the Shang period down to Chan-kuo times, materials are very scarce relating to the protruding tongue motif. Then in the Chan-kuo period wooden sculptures with both deer antlers and protruding tongues appear. Possibly belonging to the same tradition is a pottery 'tomb-guard' of Eastern Han date found in a tomb in Canton (Figure 15 B). The long, wide, protruding tongue is partly lost ' thus its original length is uncertain; both arms are long and are terminated by animal hooves which rest on the ground. Its two feet are very short and are

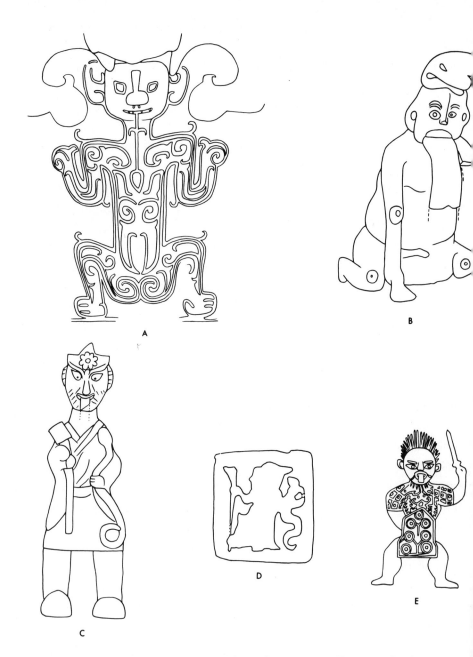

FIGURE 15. *The protruding tongue motif from Shang times to Han. A: detail from a Ts...*
beaker unearthed at Chu-chai-ch'ü 朱砦區, *Fu-nan* 埠南, *Anhwei (after photo taken by auth...*
cf. WW *1951.1); B: pottery figure excavated in the eastern suburbs of Canton (after* WW *195...*
Pl. 4); C: pottery figure excavated near Hua-lung-ch'iao 化龍橋, *Chungking (after* KK *195...*
Pl. 7, 10); D: pictorial seal (after Ch'en Chieh-ch'i, 1922: XXX. 38); E: figure on lugs of yel...
glazed P'ou-vase excavated near Yi-wu-hsien 義烏縣, *Chekiang (*KK *1965.3: Pl. 1, 3).*

172

folded under the body towards the rear.' (*WW* 1955.6 : 68).* Accordingly the continuation of the protruding tongue motif into Eastern Han times may be demonstrated.

Figure 15 C is also of Eastern Han date and was unearthed in Chungking. The same association of a snake and a military weapon held in the hands, is to be noted in 15 D taken from a Han period seal. Lastly, we may note in 15 E a warrior forming part of the décor on the lugs of a yellow glazed P'ou-vase of Western Han date unearthed in a Chekiang site. He is wearing armour, his hair is on end, and in one hand brandishes a sword and in the other a shield. His tongue is protruding and his features are terrifying in appearance.

The Han period materials cited manifest tongues of a higher order of animals than in the case of Peripheral Figure No. 2 and there are some differences in the body, too. They are presented here, however, not only to illustrate the continuation of the motif in these later times but also the ferocity of expression so clearly associated with the tongue protruding motif. Such would seem to be also the significance of the motif in Chan-kuo times.

Now to summarise this investigation of the origins of the Twelve Deities in the Ch'u Silk Manuscript. Table 2 will serve to indicate briefly the correlations of material, both archaeological and literary, which I have assembled in this paper. As Peripheral Figures Nos. 3 and 5 are insufficiently clear for the purposes of the investigation, we may assess the significance of our findings on the basis of 10 of

---

* The presence of 'joint-marks' on the knees and elbows of this unusual figure brings to mind the extensive survey on this subject ('Joint-marks') published by Carl Schuster some years ago. It also raises a point of further interest in that it comprises only the third such example derived from China (*cf.* Ch'en Ch'i-lu, this volume, Figure 7 L and M and regarding the Tien-style figures in L see Schuster, *op. cit.* pp. 30-1) which has come to light or has been considered in terms of 'joint-marks'. So far as I recollect there is very little that one may point to in the Chinese scene which clearly bears witness to the presence of 'joint-marks' and of the 3 items just mentioned two are of southern Chinese origin and both datable no earlier than Han. As to the Sumitomo drum it is best left aside (but not out of sight) until more can be ascertained as to its antecedents. The point is, therefore, that China is probably not the source of origin of this motif. But the two Chinese (and very much South Chinese) examples which we can really depend upon indicate an entry of the motif into the Chinese scene. As we can date these two artifacts, this information will be found of interest in a wider Southeast Asia/Pacific context. [Ed.]

the 12 Peripheral Figures only. It will be noted thus, in our Table, that approximately one third of the deities can be correlated with other Chan-kuo period illustrative materials together with Chan-kuo period and later literary data while approximately the same proportion of correlations have been found amongst materials which may be taken to have origins in the Shang period. Taking into account, therefore, the overall paucity of evidence prior to Ch'in and Han times, it may be allowed that these results are not without reasonable

	Peripheral Figures Numbers:											
	1	2	3	4	5	6	7	8	9	10	11	12
Data in Literary Sources						○	○	×	○	×	×	○
Illustrations in Chan-kuo Period Artifacts	○					○		×	○		×	○
Illustrations in pre-Chan-kuo Period Artifacts	○					○	○		○			

○ : possibly applicable data
× : data applicable but of uncertain validity

TABLE 2. Associations of archaeological and literary data with the Twelve Month Deities of the Ch'u Silk Manuscript.

significance. Although the origins of many of the materials that have been drawn upon in this paper are not properly provenanced, nevertheless, we would be wise to regard such materials in general as originating from various parts of China and not restricted to the confines of the State of Ch'u only. Furthermore, as much of our evidence comes from decorative motifs in various artifacts, there is no reason to believe that the area of belief in a particular deity was restricted to the area in which a particular artifact was recovered. We may regard too, the slight variations in details in the representation of the deities, as an indication of the diversity of approaches and concepts in a particular area of manufacture. The artisans in each such area would, of course, incorporate in the décor they applied to vessels and artifacts the forms of gods and demons best known to the area.

Accordingly we may conclude that the Twelve Deities in the Ch'u Silk Manuscript were not solely characteristic of the Ch'u State but there were deities with identical attributes which were extensively revered throughout the Middle States of ancient China. Representations of them were depicted widely. From my investigation of the literary sources, the same conclusion has seemed justifiable. Furthermore, I have suggested that the Twelve Peripheral Figures have probably originated from shamans who became deified and were selected and systematized into a group of twelve divine beings in accordance with the concepts of those responsible for editing the materials in this way. Throughout the territory of ancient China we may be sure that there were many deities with attributes in common with those of the Manuscript month-deities. Unfortunately, however, the correspondence of names relevant to this problem, is not as well attested as one would wish. This paucity of names is also a problem attending the correlations between literary data and that of the Manuscript in respect of the shamanistic deities. But this, no doubt, reflects the difficulties one may expect to attend the nature of literary sources of the kind with which we are concerned. As I have observed, the same form of deity is often given a different name in a different locality, while the same name may be applied to different forms of deities in different localities. Yet, in this rather complicated situation, we do find amongst the relevant but rather rare literary sources an appreciable number of records of their names and also quite a few illustrations of the deities amongst the fortuitously excavated materials. When it comes to a precise association of the names with the archaeological pictorial data can we not perhaps claim that there are actually several such cases?

When we look into this situation it would seem, as a result of our investigation amongst archaeological sources of illustration, that we should regard particular instances where the Peripheral Figure names and those of the shamanistic deities cannot be parallelled in our searches amongst available materials to be simply due to the limitations of archaeological finds to date.

5. THE ORIGINS OF THE CH'U REGION CHARACTERISTICS AS REFLECTED IN THE TWELVE MONTH DEITIES OF THE CH'U SILK MANUSCRIPT.

The Ch'u cultural area which gave birth to the Manuscript was regarded by the people of the Middle States as a primitive and barbarous country — a view maintained by them which emphasises the different character of the Ch'u region but one which in these terms cannot, of course, be accepted.

At an early stage the Ch'ü-chia-ling Culture with its Yang-shao-Lung-shan antecedents spread widely over the lower reaches of the Hanshui in Hupei where the Ch'u came into being (Figure 16). Upon

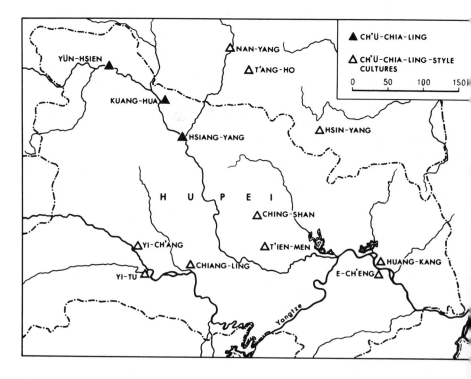

FIGURE 16. The distribution of Ch'ü-chia-ling sites and several others evincing similar style the Ch'u area. After: KK 1965.1: 41–2 for Yi-tu, KK 1959.1: 11 for Hsin-yang; the remain(after Hsin Chung-kuo ti k'ao-ku shou-huo.

THE CH'U SILK MANUSCRIPT: THE TWELVE GODS

this foundation Middle Shang cultural influences advanced into the area. In the northern sector of Hunan there have been remarkable discoveries of Late Shang settlements. In contrast to the frequently found records amongst Late Shang oracle-bone inscriptions concerning military expeditions into the Huai-ho basin further to the east, there are no instances recorded of invasions into the former area. The peoples of the lower reaches of the Huai-ho accommodating themselves to Middle Shang cultural influences became powerful and apparently were prepared to resist the might of Shang. In the Hupei-Hunan area, however, Shang settlements were successfully established and developed into a commercial base from whence various products from the south were gathered for despatch to the Royal Court. After the fall of Shang some contact with the northern States continued up to Middle Western Chou times but thereafter contacts seem to have ceased (Figure 17).

The preservation and the development of Shang culture which had thus entered the Ch'u territory may be observed in the nature of the titles of office numbers of which are unknown in Middle States' contexts of Western Chou times but are found in Shang oracle-bone records. Certain elements of bronze décor and the large *cheng*-bells (鉦) from Ch'u sites also bear witness to Shang origins. The myths and legends of ancient times that appear in the T'ien-wen section of the *Ch'u-tz'u* may also be considered to have been brought into the Ch'u area some time following the Ch'ü-chia-ling cultural incursion and prior to Middle Western Chou times — they were not imported from the northern States commencing in Middle Ch'un-ch'iu times as is usually supposed.

According to critical comments issuing from Chou writers the Shang respected the gods and gave priority to the sacrificial ceremonies, an attitude that is well attested in the oracle-bone inscriptions. From Chan-kuo to Han times criticisms in almost similar terms directed against the customs of Ch'u have come down to us thus witnessing another aspect of the probable source of such characteristics in the Ch'u culture. Amongst the Middle States during the Chou period it was man who was given priority rather than the gods — the change

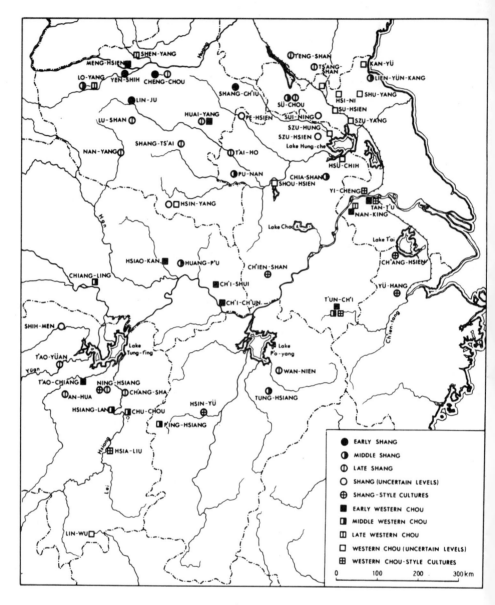

FIGURE 17. *The distribution of Shang and Western Chou culture sites in Central China.*

of direction of the Chou culture was thus towards an emphasis upon the systemization of society.

The people of the Middle States — a stage ahead in culture — in calling the Ch'u a barbarian country saw, in effect, a State of Ch'u whose cultural phase was actually a retention of the original character

178

of the Shang. Regardless of their differing attitudes towards the gods, the deities to whom sacrifices were made throughout the Middle States and in Ch'u had features in common originating as far back as Yangshao times. It is because of this that the deities painted on the Ch'u Silk Manuscript exhibit parallels with the gods of the States to the north. If we are to recognise regional characteristics specifically of Ch'u origin in the Twelve Gods of the Manuscript, we should not be concerned with the apparent differences as they appear at first glance but rather with the customs of Ch'u so strongly influenced by shamanism wherein the Ch'u people selected and systematized shamanistic deities into a group of Twelve Gods.

BIBLIOGRAPHY

Japanese Sources
Hayashi Minao 林巳奈夫
1953 'In-Shū seidōki ni arawareru ryū ni tsuite' 殷周青銅器に現れる龍について, *Tōhōgakuhō* 東方學報 (Kyōto), 23 (pp. 181-218).
1958 'Anyō Inkyo no honyūdōbutsugun ni tsuite' 安陽殷虛の哺乳動物群について, *Kōkotsugaku* 甲骨學, 6 (pp. 16-54).
1960 'In-Shūjidai no ibutsu ni arawasareta kishin, 殷周時代の遺物に表はされた鬼神, *Kōkogaku zasshi* 考古學雜誌, 46.2 (pp. 105-32).
1961 'Sengokujidai no gazōmon (1)' 戰國時代の畫像紋 (一), *Kōkogaku zasshi*, 47.3 (pp. 27-49).
1963 'Kandai danshi no kaburimono' 漢代男子のかぶりもの, *Shirin* 史林, 46.5 (pp. 80-126).
1964 'Chōsa Shutsudo Sengoku hakushokō' 長沙出土戰國帛書考, *Tōhōgakuhō* (Kyōto) 36 (pp. 53-97).
1965 'Chūgokukodai no bunka' in *Sekai no bunka*: *Chūgoku*, 中國古代の文化, 世界の文化・中國, Tōkyō, (pp. 76-109).
1966 'Chōsa shutsudo Sengoku hakushokō hosei' 長沙出土戰國帛書考補正, *Tōhōgakuhō* (Kyōto), 37 (pp. 509-14).
1966a 'Hōō no zuzō no keifu' 鳳凰の圖像の系譜, *Kōkogaku zasshi*, 52.1 (pp. 11-28).
1967 'Chūgokukodai no Shinpu, 中國古代の神巫, *Tōhōgakuhō* (Kyōto), 38 (pp. 199-224).
Hoshikawa Kiyotaka 星川清孝
1961 'Soji no kenkyū' 楚辭の研究, Tenri.
Kaizuka Shigeki 貝塚茂樹
1947 'Kiboku to Zei' 龜卜と筮, Tōhōgakuhō (Kyōto), 15.4 (pp. 25-86).
1959-60 *Kyōto Daigaku Jimbun kagakukenkyūjo zō kōkotsumonji* 京都大學人文科學研究所藏甲骨文字, Kyōto.
Kōdansha 講談社版
1963 *Sekai Bijutsutaikei・Chūgoku Bijutsu* (1) 世界美術大系・中國美術 (一), Tōkyō.

Mizuno Seiichi 水野清一
1948 'Gazōin ni tsuite' 畫像印について, Tōhōgakuhō (Kyōto) 16 (pp. 135-40).
Shirakawa Shizuka 白川靜
1956 'Saisho kankei jisetsu' 載書關係字說, Kōkotsu kimbungaku ronsō 甲骨金文學論叢, 4 (pp. 40-95).
1962 'Anshū rokki tsūshaku' 安州六器通釈, Kōkotsu Kimbun ronsō, 10 (pp. 1-60).
1966 Kimbun tsūshaku 金文通釈, Hakutsuru bijutsukanshi 白鶴美術館誌, Vol. 14.
Takeuchi Yoshio 武内義雄
1943 'Eki to Chūyō no kenkyū' 易と中庸の研究, Tōkyō.
Umehara Sueji 梅原末治
1933 Ōbeishūcho Shinakodōseika 歐米蒐儲支那古銅精華 [彝器部], Kyōto.
1936 Sengokushiki dōki no kenkyū 戰國式銅器の研究, Kyōto.
1955 Kogyoku zuroku 古玉圖錄, Kyōto.
1960-62 Nipponshūcho Shinakodōseika 日本蒐儲支那古銅精華 [彝器], Kyōto.

Chinese Sources

Anon.
1955 'An-hui Ssu-hsien Hao-hsien fa-hsien ku-ch'i shih-ch'i ch'i Han-mu' 安徽泗縣亳縣發現骨器石器及漢墓, WW 1955.6: 121-2.

An Chih-min and Ch'en Kung-jou
1963 'Ch'ang-sha Chan-kuo tseng-shu ch'i ch'i yu-kuan wen-t'i, WW 1963.9: 48-60

An-hui-sheng wen-hua-chü wen-wu kung-tso-tui 安徽省文化局文物工作隊
1959 'An-hui T'un-hsi Hsi-Chou mu-tsang fa-chüeh pao-kao' 安徽屯溪西周墓葬發掘報告, KKHP 1959.4: 59-88.

Chai T'ai-ting 齋泰定
1955 'Ho-nan Lo-yang, fa-hsien hsün-lu ti mu-tsang yi-tso' 河南洛陽發現殉鹿的墓葬一座, WW 1955.9: 195.

Chang Shou-lin 張壽林
1930 'Shang-sung k'ao' 商頌考, Chün-hu ch'i-k'an 濬湖期刊, 2: 11-19.

Chang Yung-nien 張永年
1962 'Kuan yü "Hu-shu wen-hua" ti jo-kan wen-t'i' 關于 "湖熟文化" 的若干問題 KK 1962.1: 32-6.

Ch'en Chieh-ch'i 陳介祺
1922 Shih-chung-shan-fang yin-chü 十鐘山房印舉, Shanghai.

Ch'en Meng-chia 陳夢家
1936 'Ku-wen-tzu chung chih Shang-Chou chi-ssu' 古文字中之商周祭祀, Yen-chin, hsüeh-pao 燕京學報, 19: 91-155.
1936a 'Shang-tai ti shen-hua yü wu-shu' 商代的神話與巫術, YCHP 20: 485-576.
1956 Yin-hsü pu-tz'u tsung-shu 殷虛卜辭綜述, Peking.
1956a 'Hsi-Chou t'ung-ch'i tuan-tai (5)' 西周銅器斷代 (五), KKHP 1956.3: 105-27.

Ch'en P'an 陳槃
1953 'Hsien-Ch'in Liang-Han po-shu k'ao [fu-lu: Ch'ang-sha Ch'u-mu chüan-chih ts'ai tseng chiao-pien hsiao-chi]' 先秦兩漢帛書考 [附錄: 長沙楚墓絹質采繪照片小記, 歷史語言研究所集刊] BAS 24: 193-5.

Chi Fu-t'o 姬佛陀
1916-18 Chien-shou-t'ang so ts'ang Yin-hsü wen-tzu 戩壽堂所藏殷虛文字.

Chiang-su-sheng wen-wu kuan-li wei-yüan-hui 江蘇省文物管理委員會
1955 'Chiang-su Tan-t'u Yen-t'un-shan ch'u-t'u ti ku-tai ch'ing-t'ung-ch'i' 江蘇丹徒 墩山出土的古代青銅器, WW 1955.5: 58-61.
1956 'Chiang-su Tan-t'u Yen-t'un-shan Hsi-Chou-mu ch'i fu-tsang-k'ang ch'u-t'u

hsiao-ch'i-wu pu-ch'ung ts'ai-liao' 江蘇丹徒煙山西周墓及附葬坑出土的小器物補充材料, *WW* 1956.1 : 45-6.

1958 'Hsü-chou Kao-huang-miao yi-chih ch'ing-li pao-kao' 徐州高皇廟遺址清理報告, *KKHP* 1958.4 : 7-18.

1964 'Chiang-su Hsü-chou T'ung-shan wu-tso Han-mu ch'ing-li chien-pao' 江蘇徐州銅山五座漢墓清理簡報, *KK* 1964.10 : 504-19.

Chiang-su-sheng wen-wu kung-tso-tui 江蘇省文物工作隊

1961 'Chiang-su Hsin-hai Lien-shih-ta-ts'un hsin-shih-ch'i shih-tai yi-chih k'an-ch'a-chi' 江蘇新海連市大村新石器時代遺址勘查記, *KK* 1961.6 : 321-3.

Chiang Hsüan-yi 蔣玄佁

1949 *Ch'ang-sha*, Shanghai.

Chin Hsiang-heng 金祥恒

1959 *Hsü chia-ku-wen pien* 續甲骨文編, Taipei.

Chu P'ei-chang 祝培章

1961 'Shen-hsi Ch'eng-ku fa-hsien ti ch'ing-t'ung-ch'i' 陝西城固發現的青銅器, *WW* 1966.1 : 1-2.

Chung-kuo k'o-hsüeh-yüan k'ao-ku yen-chiu-so 中國科學院考古研究所

1962 *Hsin Chung-kuo ti k'ao-ku shou-huo*, Peking.

1962a 'Hu-pei Ch'i-ch'un Mao-chia-tsui Hsi-Chou mu-kou chien-chu' 湖北圻春毛家嘴西周木構建築, *KK* 1962.1 : 1-9.

1965 *Chia-ku-wen pien* 甲骨文編, Peking.

1965a 'Ho-nan Yen-shih Erh-li-t'ou yi-chih fa-chüeh chien-pao' 河南偃師二里頭遺址發掘簡報, *KK* 1965.5 : 215-24.

Fan Ju-sen 范汝森

1959 'Shang Chou shih-tai chi-chien yü-tiao' 商周時代幾件玉雕, *WW* 1959.7 : 65.

Ho-nan-sheng wen-hua-chü wen-wu kung-tso tui 河南省文化局文物工作隊

1956 'Cheng-chou Pi-sha-kang fa-chüeh chien-pao' 鄭州碧沙崗發掘簡報, *WW* 1956.3 : 27-39.

1957 'Wo-kuo k'ao-ku-shih-shang ti k'ung-ch'ien fa-hsien, Hsin-yang Ch'ang-t'ai-kuan fa-chüeh yi-tso Chan-kuo ta-mu' 我國考古史上的空前發現, 信陽長台關發掘一座戰國大墓, *WW* 1957.9 : 31-2.

1957a 'Ho-nan Shang-ts'ai ch'u-t'u ti yi-p'i t'ung-ch'i' 河南上蔡出土的一批銅器, *WW* 1957.11 : 66-9.

1959 'Ho-nan Hsin-yang San-li-tien yi-chih fa-chüeh pao-kao' 河南信陽三里店遺址發掘報告, *KKHP* 1959.1 : 1-11.

1961 'Ho-nan Meng-hsien chien-hsi yi-chih fa-chüeh' 河南孟縣澗溪遺址發掘, *KK* 1961.1 : 33-9.

Ho-nan-sheng wen-wu kung-tso-tui 河南省文化工作隊

1958 'Hsin-yang Ch'ang-t'ai-kuan ti-erh-hao mu ti fa-chüeh' 信陽長臺關第二號墓的發掘, *KK* 1958.11 : 78.80.

Hsü Chung-shu 徐中舒

1935 'Ku-tai shou-lieh t'u-hsiang k'ao' 古代狩獵圖像考, 慶祝蔡元培六十五歲論文集, Vol. 2 : 000-618. Peking.

1936 'Yin-Chou chih chih shih-chi chih chien-t'ao' 殷周之際史蹟之檢討, 歷史語言研究所集刊, *BAS* 7.2 : 137-64.

Hsieh Yao 薛堯

1963 'Chiang-hsi chin-nien ch'u-t'u ti chi-chien ch'ing-t'ung-ch'i' 江西近年出土的幾件青銅器, *KK* 1963.8 : 416-18.

Hu Hou-hsüan 胡厚宣

1934 'Ch'u-min-tsu yüan-yü tung-fang k'ao' 楚民族源於東方考, 史學論叢, 1.

1944   *Chia-ku-hsüeh Shang-shih lun-ts'ung* 甲骨學商史論叢, 初集, 成都. Ch'eng-tu.
1951   *Chan-hou nan-pei so-chien chia-ku lu* 戰後南北所見甲骨錄, Peking.
Hu Jen-ch'ao 胡人朝
1958   'Ch'ung-ch'ing-shih Hua-lung-ch'iao Tung-Han chuan-mu ti ch'ing-li' 重慶市化龍橋東漢磚墓的清理, *KK* 1958.3 : 42-3.
Hu-nan-sheng po-wu-kuan 湖南省博物館
1966   'Hu-nan-sheng po-wu-kuan hsin fa-hsien ti chi-chien t'ung-ch'i' 湖南省博物館新發現的幾件銅器, *WW* 1966.4 : 1-6.
Hu-pei-sheng wen-wu-chü wen-wu kung-tso-tui
1966   'Hu-pei Chiang-ling san-tso Ch'u-mu ch'u-t'u ta-p'i chung-yao wen-wu', *WW* 1966.5 : 33-55
Hu Wen 胡文
1966   'An-hui T'un-hsi yu ch'u-t'u ta-p'i Hsi-Chou chen-kuei wen-wu' 安徽屯溪又出土大批西周珍遺文物, *WW* 1966.6 : 52.
Hua-tung wen-wu kung-tso-tui 華東文物工作隊
1954   'Ssu-nien-lai Hua-tung-ch'ü ti wen-wu kung-tso ch'i ch'i chung-yao ti fa-hsien' 四年來華東區的文物工作及其重要的發現, *WW* 1954.8 : 3-34.
Jao Tsung-yi 饒宗頤
1954   'Ch'ang-sha Ch'u-mu shih-chan shen-wu t'u-chuan k'ao-shih, *JOS* I. 1 : 69-84
1958   *Ch'ang-sha ch'u-t'u Chan-kuo tseng-shu*, Hong Kong
1958a   'Ch'ang-sha Ch'u-mu po-hua shan-kuei-t'u pa' 長沙楚墓帛畫山鬼圖跋, 金櫃論古綜合刊, I : 60.
1959   *Yin-tai chen-pu jen-wu t'ung-k'ao* 殷代貞卜人物通考, Hong Kong.
Jung Keng 容庚
1934   *Ku-shih-k'o ling-shih* 古石刻零拾, Peking.
1934a   *Wu-ying-tien yi-ch'i t'u-lu* 武英殿彝器圖錄, Peking.
1936   *Shan-chai yi-ch'i t'u-lu* 善齋彝器圖錄, Peking.
1941   *Shang-Chou yi-ch'i t'ung-k'ao* 商周彝器通考, Peking.
Kao Chung-ta 高仲達
1965   'Hu-pei Yi-tu Kan-chia-ho hsin-shih-ch'i shih-tai yi-chih' 湖北宜都甘家河新石器時代遺址, *KK* 1965.1 : 41-2.
Kao Chih-hsi 高至喜
1960   'Shang-tai jen-mien fang-Ting' 商代人面方鼎, *WW* 1960.10 : 57-8.
1963   'Ning-hsiang Huang-ts'ai fa-hsien Shang-tai t'ung-ch'i ho yi-chih' 寧鄉黃材發現商代銅器和遺址, *KK* 1963.12 : 646-8.
K'ao-ku yen-chiu-so Lo-yang fa-chüeh-tui 考古研究所洛陽發掘隊
1959   'Lo-yang Hsi-chiao yi-hao Chan-kuo-mu fa-chüeh-chi' 洛陽西周一號戰國墓發掘記, *KK* 1959.12 : 653-7.
K'o Ch'ang-chi 柯昌濟
1933   *Chin-wen fen-yü pien* 金文分域編, 餘園叢刻.
K'o Chi-kung 葛治功
1965   'An-hui Po-kang-yin-ho ch'u-t'u ti ssu-chien Shang-tai t'ung-ch'i 安徽泊崗引河出土的四件商代銅器, *WW* 1965.7 : 23-5.
K'o Chieh-ping 葛介屏
1959   'An-hui Pu-nan fa-hsien Yin-Shang shih-tai ti ch'ing-t'ung-ch'i 安徽埠南發現殷商時代的青銅器, *WW* 1959.1 (inside front and rear covers).
Ku Chieh-kang 顧頡剛
1941   'Chan-kuo Ch'in-Han-chien jen ti tso-wei yü pien-wei' 戰國秦漢間人的造偽與辨偽, 古史辨, 7.A : 1-64.
1941a   'Shan-jang-chüan-shuo ch'i yü Mo-chia k'ao' 禪讓傳說起於墨家考, 古史辨, 7.B : 30-107.

Kuan Yü-ts'ui 關玉翠
1966　'Pi-yang-hsien ch'u-t'u ti liang-chien Hsi-Chou t'ung-hu' 沁陽縣出土的兩件西
　　　周銅壺, WW 1966.1 : 56-7.
Kuang-chou-shih wen-wu kuan-li wei-yüan-hui 廣州市文物管理委員會
1955　'Kuang-chou-shih tung-chiao Tung-Han chuan-mu ch'ing-li chi-lüeh 廣州東郊東
　　　漢磚墓清理紀畧, WW 1955.6 : 61-76.
Kuo Jo-yü 郭若愚, etc.
1955　Yin-hsü wen-tzu chui-ho 殷虛文字綴合, 科學出版社,
Kuo Pao-chün 郭寶鈞
1951　'1950 nien ch'un Yin-hsü fa-chüeh pao-kao' 1950 年春殷虛發掘報告, KKHP 5 :
　　　1-61.
1959　Shan-piao-chen yü Liu-li-ko 山彪鎮與琉璃閣, 考古學專刊乙種第十一號, 科學
　　　出版社, Peking.
Kuo Ping-lien 郭冰廉
1958　'Hu-pei Huang-p'o-yang-chia wan ti ku-yi-chih t'iao-ch'a' 湖北黃坡楊家灣的古
　　　遺址調查, KK 1958.1 : 56-8.
1958a　'Hu-pei Huang-p'o Kuang-shan-shui-k'u-kung-ti fa-hsien yü ch'ing-t'ung ch'i' 湖
　　　北黃坡廣山水庫工地的發現與青銅器, KK 1958.9 : 72-3.
Kuo Mo-jo 郭沫若
1937　Yin-ch'i ts'ui-pien 殷契粹編, Tōkyō.
1958　'Kuan-yü E-chün-ch'i chieh ti yen-chiu' 關于鄂君啓節的研究, WW 1958.4 : 3-6.
Kuo Te-wei 郭德維
1964　'Hu-pei Huang-p'o P'an-lung-ch'eng Shang-tai yi-chih ho mu-tsang' 湖北黃坡盤
　　　龍城商代遺址和墓葬, KK 1964.8 : 420-1.
Kuo Yüan-wei 郭遠謂
1965　'Chiang-hsi chin-liang-nien ch'u-t'u ti ch'ing-t'ung-ch'i' 江西近兩年出土的青銅
　　　器, KK 1965.7 : 273-5.
K'ung Fan-yin 孔繁銀
1959　'Shan-tung T'eng-hsien Ching-t'ing mei-kuang teng ti fa-hsien Shang-tai t'ung-ch'i
　　　ch'i ku-yi-chih mu-tsang' 山東滕縣井亭煤礦等地發現商代銅器及古遺址墓
　　　葬, WW 1959.12 : 67-8.
Li Hsiao-ting 李孝定
1965　Chia-ku-wen-tzu chi-shih 甲骨文字集釋, 中央研究院歷史語言研究所專刊之十
　　　五, Taipei.
Li Chien 李健
1963　'Hu-pei Chiang-ling Wan-ch'eng ch'u-t'u Hsi-Chou t'ung-ch'i 湖北江陵萬城出土
　　　西周銅器, KK 1963.4 : 224-5.
Li Wei-yin 李蔚然
1960　'Nan-ching fa-hsien Chou-tai t'ung-ch'i' 南京發現周代銅器, KK 1960.6 : 41.
Li Ya-neng 李亞農
1950　Yin-ch'i chih-yi hsü-pien 殷契撫佚續編, Peking.
Liang Ssu-yung and Kao Ch'ü-hsün 梁思永・高去尋
1962　Hou-chia-chuang 2.1001 hao mu 侯家莊 2.1001 號墓, Taipei.
Lin-yi wen-wu shou-chi-tsu 臨沂文物收集組
1965　'Shan-tung Ts'ang-shan-hsien ch'u-t'u ch'ing-t'ung-ch'i' 山東蒼山縣出土青銅器,
　　　WW 1965.7 : 27-30.
Liu E 劉鶚
1899　T'ieh-yün ts'ang-kuei 鐵雲藏龜
Liu Chang-sun 劉長孫 etc.
1965　'Hu-pei Hsi-shui fa-hsien liang-chien t'ung-ch'i' 湖北浠水發現兩件銅器, KK
　　　1965.7 : 369-70.
Liu T'i-chih 劉體智
1935　Hsiao-chiao ching-ko chin-wen t'o-pen 小校經閣金文拓本.

Liu Tung-ya 劉東亞
  1964   'Ho-nan Huai-yang ch'u-t'u ti ch'ing-t'ung-ch'i ho t'ao-ch'i' 河南淮陽出土的青
         銅器和陶器, *KK* 1964.3 : 163-4.
Lo Chen-yü 羅振玉
  1927   *Tseng-ting Yin-hsü shu-ch'i k'ao-shih* 增訂殷墟書契考釋.
  1936   *San-tai chi-chin wen-ts'un* 三代吉金文存.
Ma Ch'eng-yüan 馬承源
  1965   'Tsai-lun "Ta-wu wu ch'i" ti t'u-hsiang' 再論 "大武舞戚" 的圖象, *KK* 1965.8 :
         413-5.
Ma Ch'üan 馬全
  1955   'Ho-nan Chien-yang ch'ing-li-le yu Hsi-Chou chih Sung teng tai ti hsü-tuo mu-
         tsang' 河南澗陽清理了由西周至宋等代的許多墓葬, *WW* 1955.5 : 116-7.
Nan-ching po-wu-yüan 南京博物院
  1960   '1959 nien tung Hsü-chou ti-ch'ü k'ao-ku t'iao-ch'a' 1959 年冬徐州地區考古調
         查, *KK* 1960.3 : 25-9.
  1960a   'Chiang-su Hsin-yi San-li-tun ku-wen-hua yi-chih ti-erh-tz'u fa-chüeh chien-chieh'
         江蘇新沂三里墩古文化遺址第二次發掘簡介, *KK* 1960.7 : 20-2.
  1960b   'Chiang-su-sheng shih-nien-lai k'ao-ku kung-tso chung ti chung-yao fa-hsien' 江
         蘇省十年來考古工作中的重要發現, *WW* 1960.7 : 1-11.
  1964   'Chiang-su P'ei-hai-ti-ch'ü k'ao-ku t'iao-ch'a 江蘇邳海地區考古調查, *KK* 1964.1 :
         19-25.
Ni Tzu-li 倪自勛
  1961   'Lin-jü Hsia-tien fa-hsien Shang-tai wen-hua yi-chih' 臨汝夏店發現商代文化遺
         址, *WW* 1961.1 : 75.
P'ei Ch'i 裴琪
  1958   'Lu-shan-hsien fa-hsien yi-p'i chung-yao t'ung-ch'i'. 魯山縣發現一批重要銅器,
         WW 1956.5 : 73-4.
Pei-ching-shih wen-wu kung-tso tui 北京市文物工作隊
  1962   'Pei-ching Huai-jou-ch'eng pei-tung-chou Liang-Han mu-tseng' 北京懷柔城北東
         周西漢墓葬, *KK* 1962.5 : 219-39.
Shan-tung-sheng wen-wu kuan-li ch'u 山東省文物管理處
  1959   *Shan-tung wen-wu hsüan-chi* 山東文物選集, 普查部分, Peking.
Shang Ch'eng-tso 商承祚
  1933   *Yin-ch'i yi-ts'un* 殷契佚存, Nanking.
  1964   'Chan-kuo Ch'u po-shu shu-lüeh', *WW* 1964.9 : 8-20 [see Chang, p. 00 : 82].
Shang-hai po-wu-kuan 上海博物館
  1964   *Shang-hai po-wu-kuan ts'ang ch'ing-t'ung-ch'i* 上海博物館藏青銅器, Shanghai.
Sun Hai-p'o 孫海波
  1937   *Hsin-cheng yi-ch'i* 新鄭彝器, Peking.
T'an Ch'i-hsiang 譚其驤
  1962   'E-chün-Ch'i chin-chieh ming-wen shih-ti' 鄂君啓節銘文釋地, 中華文史論叢,
         II : 169-190. Peking.
T'ang Lan 唐蘭
  1935   *Ku wen-tzu-hsüeh tao-lun* 古文字學導論, Peking.
  1965   'Yin Ta-ho-Fang-Ting (Jen-mien-Ting)' 殷大禾方鼎 (人面鼎), 人民中國, 1965.10 :
         120.
  1966   'Hsi-Chou hui-yi-wen Tsun' 西周虺蝪紋卣, 人民中國, 1966.3 : 120.
T'ien-chin-shih wen-hua-ch'ü wen-wu tsu 天津市文化局文物組
  1964   'T'ien-chin-shih shou-chi ti Shang-Chou ch'ing-t'ung-ch'i 天津市收集的商周青
         銅器, *WW* 1964.9 : 33-6.

Tseng Chao-yü 曾昭燏 etc.
  1956   *Yi-nan ku-hua-hsiang-shih-mu fa-chüeh pao-kao* 沂南古畫像石墓發掘報告, Peking.
  1959   'Shih-lun Hu-shu wen-hua' 試論湖熟文化, *KKHP* 1959.4 : 47-58.
Tung Tso-pin 董作賓
  1945   *Yin li-p'u* 殷曆譜, Nan-hsi.
  1948   *Yin-hsü wen-tzu chia-pien* 殷虛文字甲編, Nanching.
  1948-53   *Yin-hsü wen-tzu yi-pien* 殷虛文字乙編, Taipei.
Wang Chi-ying and Mou Yung-k'ang 汪濟英 • 牟永杭
  1965   'Che-chiang Yi-wu fa-hsien Hsi-Han mu' 浙江義烏發現西漢墓, *KK* 1965.3 : 152-4.
Wang Chih-min 王志敏 etc.
  1956   'Chieh-shao Chiang-su Yi-cheng kuo-ch'u fa-hsien ti chi-chien Hsi-Chou ch'ing-t'ung-ch'i' 介紹江蘇儀徵過去發現的幾件西周青銅器, *WW* 1956.12 : 31-2.
Wang Hsiang 王湘
  1947   'An-hui Shou-hsien shih-ch'ien yi-chih t'iao-ch'a pao-kao' 安徽壽縣史前遺址調查報告, *KKHP* 2 : 179-250.
Wang Shih lum 王士倫
  1965   'Chi Che-chiang fa-hsien ti t'ung-nao, yu-t'ao-chung ho Yüeh-yü-shih-mao' 記浙江發現的銅鐃, 釉陶鐘和越玉石矛, *KK* 1965.5 : 256-7.
Wang Yü-t'ung 王毓彤
  1963   'Ching-men ch'u-t'u ti yi-chien t'ung-ko' 荊門出土的一件銅戈, *WW* 1963.1 : 64-5.
  1963a   'Chiang-ling fa-hsien Hsi-Chou t'ung-ch'i' 江陵發現西周銅器, *WW* 1963.2 : 53-5.
Yang K'uan 楊寬
  1941   'Chung-kuo shang-ku-shih tao-lun' 中國上古史導論, 古史辨, 7A : 65-404.
Yang Shu-ta 楊樹達
  1954   *Pu-tz'u ch'iu-yi* 卜辭求義, Peking.
Yen Yi-p'ing 嚴一萍
  1951   'Yin-ch'i cheng-yi' 殷契徵醫, 甲骨金文叢考三四, 再錄.
Yin Huan-chang 尹煥章
  1954   'Ts'ung fa-hsien ti wen-wu chung t'an Hua-tung-ch'ü ku-wen-hua kai-k'uang' 從發現的文物中談華東區古文化概況, *WW* 1954.4 : 26-30.
  1963   'Huai-yin-ti-ch'ü k'ao-ku t'iao-ch'a 准陰地區考古調查, *KK* 1963.1 : 1-8.
  1964   'Hung-tse-hu chou-wei ti k'ao-ku t'iao-ch'a' 洪澤湖周圍的考古調查, *KK* 1964.5 : 220-6.
Yin Ti-fei 殷滌非
  1954   'An-hui-ti-ch'ü ssu-nien lai fa-hsien ti k'ao-ku ts'ai-liao' 安徽地區四年來發現的攷古材料, *WW* 1954.4 : 31-4.
  1958   'Shou-hsien ch'u-t'u ti "E-chün-Ch'i chin-chieh"' 壽縣出土的 "鄂君啓金節", *WW* 1958.4 : 8-11.
Yu Ch'ing-han 游清漢
  1958   'Ho-nan Nan-yang Shih-li-miao fa-hsien Shang-tai yi-chih' 河南南陽十里廟發現商代遺址, *KK* 1958.7 : 370.
Yü Hsing-wu 于省吾
  1957   *Shang-Chou chin-wen lu-yi* 商周金文錄遺, Peking.
Yü Wei-ch'ao 俞偉超
  1963   '"Ta-wu X-ping" t'ung-ch'i yü Pa-jen ti "Ta-wu" wu', *KK* 1963.3 : 153-5

Western Sources
Barnard, Noel
    1969   *The Ch'u Silk Manuscript* [in preparation — copies of reconstructions in Plates XI–
            XXI consulted].
Chalfant, Frank H.
    1935   *The Couling-Chalfant Collection of Inscribed Oracle Bones*, Shanghai.
    1939   *The Hopkins Collection of Inscribed Oracle Bones*, Shanghai.
Mikawa, H. and A. Kollantz
    1966   'Zur Ur- und Vorgeschichte des Schamanismus', *Zeitschrift für Ethnologie* **B.**
            92, H. 2: 161-93.
Palmgren, N.
    1954   *Selected Chinese Antiquities from the Collection of Gustaf Adolf*, Stockholm.
Salmony, A.
    1954   'Antler and Tongue, An Essay on Ancient Chinese Symbolism', *Artibus Asiae*,
            Supplement XIII, Ascona.
Tch'ou, Tö-yi
    1924   *Bronzes Antiques de la Chine appartenant à C.T. Loo*, Paris et Bruxelles.

WESTERN ELEMENTS IN THE ART OF CH'U

WILLIAM SAMOLIN

This discussion deals with certain elements in the art of the Ch'u which indicate definite Western influences. In general these elements were amalgamated with earlier Chinese stylistic features, some of which date back to the Shang period. The art of the Ch'u thus provides a means to detect one of the streams of foreign influence which penetrate the Chinese culture sphere as well as some clues as to the source of the stream. Foreign elements, some originating at great distances, have entered the Chinese milieu from at least the middle of the second millennium B.C. There are also indications of a reverse flow in which Chinese elements or even Western elements modified by Chinese taste and practice move back in the direction from whence they came.[1]

The phenomenon of current and counter-current does not involve a uniform process but seems rather to resemble a series of pulses. The first prominent pulse appears to have taken place in the first half of the second millennium B.C. This corresponds to the emergence of the Chinese Bronze Age in the Shang period. At that time we witness not only the appearance of bronze artifacts indicating a very sophisticated metallurgy but also the chariot and other elements of material culture previously known in Western Asia. The fact that this corresponds to the period of the great expansion of Indo-Iranian peoples in which the chariot played an important rôle may not be a coincidence. Some bronze weapons with tubular

---

1. For Chinese elements in finds at Pazyrk V, cf. S.I. Rudenko. *Kul'tura Naseleniya Gornovo Altaya v Skifskoe Vremya,* '1953. Note treatment of feet on swans, Pl. CVIII; sphinx, especially the grotesque tail, Pl. CVIV and the silk saddle cloth showing a bird on a flowering plant, Pl. CXVIII. The last noted is in a style close to that of the Ch'ang-sha lacquers, *cf.* Cheng Te-k'un, *Chou China,* 1963, Pl. 42.

sockets found in Shang context are practically identical to weapons from Iran and Western Asia. It is worth noting that similar weapons make their first appearance in Egypt during the Hyksos period (R. Maxwell-Hyslop, *IRAQ*, 11 (1949), Pl. XXXVII). The Hyksos, who were Amurrite princes, not Indo-Iranians, seem to have made contact with Indo-Iranian charioteers toward the end of their rule at which time the chariot appears in Egypt (J. van Seters, *The Hyksos,* 1966, pp. 182-7). An axe from the Sackler Collections on display in the Faculty Room at Columbia University is quite similar to one from Syria at the Metropolitan Museum of Art. The Sackler piece was obtained as part of an Ordos collection. Some Shang and Chou weapons with obvious Chinese features still bear the clear stamp of Western influence.

The two succeeding pulses which have greater bearing on the problem at hand take place in the period between the ninth and fifth centuries B.C. The present state of our knowledge does not permit a close determination of the hiatus between them. Though there are some obvious inter-relationships each represents a distinctly different tradition. The first is related to the Hallstatt Culture of Central Europe, that is phases C and D of the sequence at the well-known burial site not far from Salzburg, Austria. Hallstatt culture is a late Bronze /early Iron Age type. The second tradition is related to the Scythian cultural sphere and represents the complex associated with the Eurasian 'animal-style'.

In the seventh century B.C. a new decorative style characterizes Chinese bronzes. It represents an elegant baroque phase in which new elements are combined with some long extinct. At present it is not clear whether this style represents a deliberate archaistic movement inspired by a new vigorous affluence or else is the result of the rapid development of a provincial region in which archaic elements survived after passing out of use in the older central region. This baroque style, designated Huai by Bernhard Karlgren who first studied it in depth, was named after the river valley in which it either originated or else proved to be the most productive region.

By the time the new style is well developed the Huai-ho Valley is included in the territory of the State of Ch'u. This great feudal State had its nuclear region in the Han-shui and the middle Yangtze. The Ch'u territory thus provided a route of advance for influences from the northwestern borderlands into what is now central China since the Han-shui originates in southern Shensi, flows across the base of the province in an easterly direction into northern Hupeh and then turns southeast to join the middle Yangtze. It may well be that the origins of the Huai style are to be sought back in the direction of the headwaters of the Han-shui.

The new decorative elements which are superimposed on the archaic Chinese features are the following: granulation or dotted bands forming outlines, granulation or dotted surfaces, S-shaped double-spirals, and circles on the bodies of animals. Karlgren referred to the granulation filling in Huai style as 'an idea of the Ordos animal style borrowed by the Huai style'. He considers this to be an element of particular importance in his investigation (*BMFEA*, 13, p. 28). He adds that the use of a granulation line as a filling of a band is a Huai style feature which appears in the seventh-sixth centuries B.C. As an example he offers the outline of a dragon on a *kuei*. In this case Karlgren fails to mention the S-shaped double-spirals which fill the body of this highly stylized dragon (Figure 1). It should be noted that bands and areas of granulation, spirals, and circles on the bodies of animals though present in Ordos art are not characteristic of the Eurasian 'animal-style'. Circles on the bodies of animals do not appear to be a Sarmatian feature as A. Salmony suggested (*Sino-Siberian Art in the Collection of C.T. Loo*, 1933, p. 35) but rather a Hallstatt and Luristan feature (Figures 2-7).[2] Granulation bands and areas are also a feature of Phrygian art and the Scythian 'animal-style' of Hungary rather than the more easterly regions of the 'animal-style' complex.[3] On the other hand, pear-

2.   Figure 2 is an Ordos piece now in the Sackler Collections, *cf.* W. Samolin and I.M. Drew, *Monumenta Serica*, XXIV (1965), Pl. 4C; Table III, ref. no. 6118.
3.   E. Akurgal, *Phrygische Kunst*, 1955, Taf. 22, 32; B. Thomas (ed.), *Archäologische Funde in Ungarn*, 1956, Pl. opp. p. 142 for gold stag of Tapoiszentmarton.

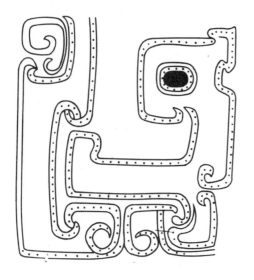

FIGURE 1. Granulated band and rubbing of same area illustrating presence of S-shaped double-spirals. After B. Karlgren, BMFEA 13, Fig.5b.

shaped figures on the bodies of animals is a common characteristic of the eastern province of the Eurasian 'animal-style'.[4]

The appearance of these decorative features in Central and Western Europe, on the one hand, and in China, on the other, in the same chronological setting is not likely to be a coincidence, particularly since it can be associated with the presence of bands of horse-riding warriors who diffuse elements of material culture which can be associated with the Pontic region at an earlier date.

The hypothesis of a migration from the Pontic region attracted linguists who became involved in the Tokharian problem after the discovery of Tokharian and Saka texts in East Turkistan at the turn of the century. Before long, fragmentary evidence from Chinese,

4.   Illustrations with examples abound in the numerous publications dealing with the Eurasian 'animal-style'. The most frequent occurrence is on bordered plaques usually rectangular in shape.

FIGURES 2-7. Examples of granulated bands, granulated areas, spirals, and circles in Hallstatt and Luristan animal figurines:- 2: Sackler Collections; 3: after M. Mellinck (ed.), Dark Ages and Nomads c. 1000 B.C., Istanbul 1964, Pl.XVIII, Fig.2; 4: ibid. Pl.XVII, Fig.2; 5: ibid Pl.XVIII, Fig.1; 6: after Y. and A. Godard, Bronzes du Luristan, Collection E. Graeffe, La Haye, n.d., Pl. 11, Cat.247; 7: after K. Kromer, Hallstatt, Prähistorische Kunst Vienna, 1963, Taf.41.

190

2

3

4

5

6

7

Greek, and Assyrian sources was collected to support this hypothesis. The parallel archaeological evidence was collected by Robert Heine-Geldern whose name has become intimately associated with this theory. Rather early in his investigations Heine-Geldern attributed the arrival of these Western elements in the Chinese cultural sphere to the mysterious people known to the Greeks as Kimmerians, to the Assyrians as Gimmari, and to the compilers of Genesis as Gomar.[5] The present writer believes he detected references to Kimmerians on the borderlands of China. They also seem to be associated with another ethnic designation used by the Ionian geographers and their successors, the Issedones. The same fragmentary evidence supports the view that the Tokharians were also part of the Kimmerian complex. It is quite possible that the term Kimmerian is a political rather than an ethnic designation.[6]

At all events, the development which brought Pontic elements to East Asia also brought them to Central and even Western Europe. In both regions these elements arrived earlier and made deeper penetration than those associated with Scythian expansion. Karl Jettmar and others have suggested that some of the Pontic elements in Hallstatt Culture are of East Asian origin. This is quite possible since there is no reason to believe that East-West contacts and transfer of influence moved in one direction. Similarities between Hallstatt and Chinese artifacts have been noted by Olov Janse in the early thirties.[7]

5. Even a brief indication of the extensive literature on the Tokharian and related problems is beyond the scope of this discussion. A convenient summary may be found in Heine-Geldern, *Saeculum*, 2, (1951), pp. 225-55.
6. W. Samolin, *Palaeologia*, IV, Osaka 1955; also *CAJ*, IV, 1 (1958); H. Kothe, *Klio*, 41 (1963).
7. Jettmar calls attention to the use of the cruciform tube as an element of horse furniture in Shang context, *cf.* Jettmar, *Art of the Steppes*, 1967, p. 219. Cruciform buttons and tubes are a common feature of the European Hallstatt Culture. With respect to buttons it should be noted that while there are no Chinese elements in the décor of the European examples, there are elements of European décor in Chinese examples. A cruciform button allegedly from the Huai-ho Valley contains the guilloche and the S-shaped spiral, *cf.* Janse, *BMFEA*, 4, Pl. III, 4a, b. Since the guilloche is common in the Aegean and Western Asia since Middle Bronze, it indicates that here the flow of influence was not all east to west. The guilloche is also found on a socketed celt from Yünnan, *cf.* Janse, *BMFEA*, 2, Pl. I, 3.

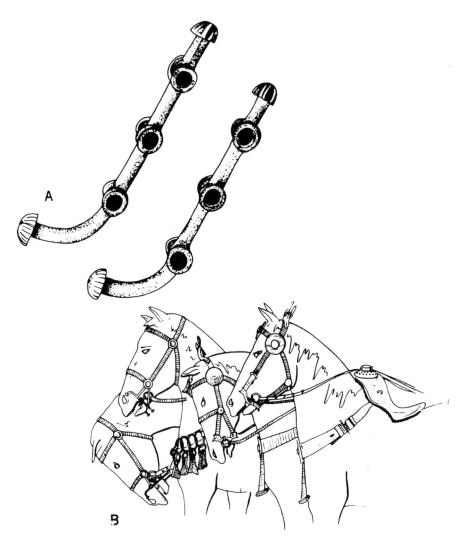

FIGURE 8. A: *triple-perforated psalia from Yugoslavia. After D. Garasanin,* Katalog Metala, *Belgrade 1954, Pl.LI, No.6. B: similar psalia from Belgium. After M.E. Mariën,* Trouvailles du Champ d'Urnes et des Tombelles Hallstattiennes de Court-Saint-Etienne, *Bruxelles, 1958, Fig.46.*

A serious consideration of the Kimmerian and Tokharian problem would be beyond the scope of this discussion. It is nevertheless *à propos* to indicate some chronological route markers. In the West the Hallstatt complex is characterized by artifacts associated with horse riding such as the psalia illustrated in Figure 8, cruciform buttons and tubes, and belt-segments formed of plaques consisting of a repetition of elements covering an area as in Figure 9.

193

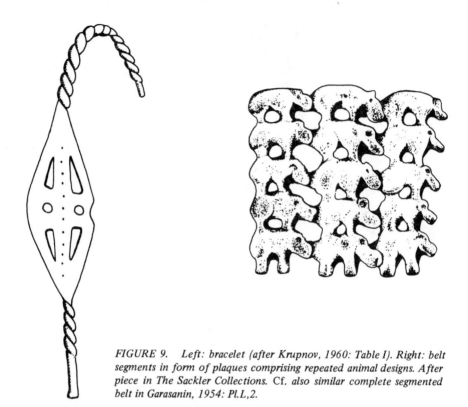

FIGURE 9. Left: bracelet (after Krupnov, 1960: Table I). Right: belt segments in form of plaques comprising repeated animal designs. After piece in The Sackler Collections. Cf. also similar complete segmented belt in Garasanin, 1954: Pl.L,2.

Two other characteristic features are long slashing swords as in Figure 10, and the flat-shouldered axe.

A provisional chronological-typological frame of reference must be established before one can attempt to indicate the source of these elements. Let us first consider the psalia of the type illustrated in Figure 8. It is straight with one end curved in an arc of a circle. It has three perforations and mushroom-shaped end-caps. Straight or slightly curved psaliae with three perforations and end caps appear in the western part of the North Caucasus in the eleventh-eighth centuries B.C. The psalia of the type illustrated in Figure 8 designated as a Thrako-Kimmerian type by Garasanin has been found not only in Yugoslavia but also in the Danubian region, the Rhineland, and in Belgium.[8] A similar type but with two per- forations is found among the artifacts of the eastern group of the

8.　M. E. Mariën, *Trouvailles du Champ d'Urnes et des Tombelles Hallstattiennes de Court- Saint-Etienne*, 1958, Figs. 18, 46, 50; G. Kossack, *Jahrbuch des Römisch-Germanischen Zentral Museums*, 1, 1953.

central region of the North Caucasus.[9] This would suggest a move from the Pontic region to Europe and then a reverse current since the modified form of the Thrako-Kimmerian psalia is found in the same chronological horizon as a bracelet of a type common in the Balkans and the lower Danube.[10]

Second, consider the long slashing sword. The slashing sword with the blade broadened near the tip is a characteristic weapon of the Central European Urnfield Culture. The spread of this culture had much to do with the disturbances which marked the late second millennium B.C. in the Mediterranean World. The long slashing sword, a weapon particularly suited to cavalry does not appear until the very end of the Urnfield phase, i.e., the Hallstatt period. A Greek sarcophagus from Klazomenae dated sixth century B.C. or earlier illustrates horsemen wielding long slashing swords of Hallstatt type. It should be noted that the headgear of the rear rider in Figure 10, if

FIGURE 10.   The long slashing sword, a typical cavalry weapon.
After I.M. D'yakonov, Istoriya Midii, Moscow 1956, Fig. 41.

not also that of the one in front, suggests a 'Kegelhelm', a type known in the Aegean in the eighth-seventh centuries B.C. (A. Snodgrass, Early Greek Armour and Weapons, 1964, Pl. 4, 5).

Finally, the shouldered axe is the Hallstatt feature which most strongly associates the complex with the Pontic region and Anatolia, a point stressed by Kothe (Klio, 41 (1963), p. 21). As a matter of

9.   See Table I in E.I. Krupnov, Drevnyaya Istoriya Severnovo Kavkaza, 1960 (front of p. 137), west zone horse furniture, early stage.
10.   See Table I (loc. cit.) eastern zone decorative objects, late stage, third row from top, also note forms in Table II, IVa-c in A. Benac and B. Cŏvič, Glasinac, Dio II Zelijezno Doba, 1957.

fact, the shouldered axe is known in Anatolia and Syria-Palestine since the Late Bronze Age (Y. Yadin, *The Art of War in Bible Lands,* 1963, Vol. I, p. 184). Thus the pre-Scythian cavalry people who diffused the distinctive Hallstatt features to Central Europe and Western Europe as well as China must have emerged from the Pontic region. The available information indicates these cavalry people were the Kimmerians who, as the Ionian geographers inform us, preceded the Scythians as masters of the Pontic Steppe.[11]

FIGURE 11. Mounted archers. After D'yakonov, op.cit. Fig. 40.

11.   The tables referred to in notes 9 and 10 above are after I.M. D'yakonov, *Istoriya Midii,* 1956, Figs. 41 and 40 respectively. Though D'yakonov puts a question mark after the designation 'Kimmerian', the designations are justified. A line drawing of figures on the François vase in E.H. Minns, *Scythians and Greeks,* 1913, Fig. 8, p. 54 shows a kneeling archer attired in the same manner as the horse-archers in Figure 11, labelled *KIMERIOS.*

BIBLIOGRAPHY

Akurgal, E.
    1955   *Phrygische Kunst*, Ankara.
Benac, A. and Čović, B.
    1957   *Glasinac, Dio II Zeliiezno Doba.*
Cheng Te-k'un
    1963   *Chou China, Archaeology in China*, Vol. III. Toronto.
D'yakonov, I.M.
    1956   *Istoriya Midii*, Moscow.
Garasinin, D.
    1954   *Katalog Metala*, Belgrade.
Godard, Y. and A.
    n.d.   *Bronzes du Luristan, Collection E. Graeffe*, La Haye.
Heine-Geldern, R.
    1951   'Das Tocharerproblem und die Pontische Wanderung', *Saeculum*, Vol. II.
Janse, O.
    1930   'Notes sur quelques épées anciennes trouvées en Chine', *BMFEA*, Vol. 2.
    1932   'Tubes et boutons cruciformes trouvés en Eurasie', *BMFEA*, Vol. 4.
Jettmar, K.
    1967   *Art of the Steppes*, New York.
Karlgren, B.
    1941   'Huai and Han', *BMFEA*, Vol. 13.
Kossack, G.
    1953   *Jahrbuch des Römisch-Germanischen Zentral Museums*, Mainz, Vol. 1.
Kothe, H.
    1963   'Die Herkunft der kimmerischen Reiter', *Klio*, Bd. 41.
Kromer, K.
    1963   *Hallstatt, Prähistorische Kunst*, Vienna.
Krupnov, E.I.
    1960   *Drevnyaya Istoriya Severnovo Kavkaza*, Moscow.
Mariën, M.E.
    1958   *Trouvailles du Champ d'Urnes et des Tombelles Hallstattiennes de Court-Saint-Etienne*, Brussels.
Maxwell-Hyslop, R.
    1949   'Western Asiatic Shaft-hole Axes', *Iraq*, Vol. II, Pt. 1.
Mellinck, M. (ed.)
    1964   *Dark Ages and Nomads c. 1000 B.C.*, Istanbul.
Minns, E.H.
    1913   *Scythians and Greeks*, Cambridge.
Rudenko, S.I.
    1953   *Kul'tura Naseleniya Gornovo Altaya v Skifskoe Vreyma*, Moscow.
Salmony, A.
    1933   *Sino-Siberian Art in the Collection of C.T. Loo*, Paris.
Samolin, W.
    1955   'The Historical Ethnology of the Torim Basin before the Turks', *Palaeologia*, Vol. IV, No. 1. Osaka.
    1958   'Ethnographic Aspects of the Archaeology of the Torim Basin', *Central Asiatic Journal*, Vol. IV, Pt. 1. The Hague-Wiesbaden.

Samolin, W. and Drew, I.M.
    1965   'Eurasian Animal Style Plaques I', *Monumenta Serica*, Vol. XXIV.
van Seters, J.
    1966   *The Hyksos*, New Haven, Conn.
Snodgrass, A.
    1964   *Early Greek Armour and Weapons*, Edinburgh.
Thomas, B. (ed.)
    1956   *Archäologische Funde in Ungarn*, Budapest.
Yadin, Y.
    1963   *The Art of War in Bible Lands*, New York.

THE LACH-TRUONG CULTURE—
WESTERN AFFINITIES AND CONNECTIONS
WITH THE CULTURE OF ANCIENT CH'U

OLOV R. T. JANSE

Recent discoveries made in the Dong-son and Oc-eo sites have revealed important Western affinities in the Vietnamese cultural heritage. In the light of this new knowledge the Lach-truong cultural elements need to be closely re-examined. The results of carefully conducted excavations in Vietnam, analysed and evaluated by comparative media, have disclosed important Western elements and ideas of which some were channelled to Lach-truong via China, especially through the Ch'u cultural area, fused with the Tocharer-Italo-Celts' cultures and even with Shamanism.[1] The relics represented in the Vietnamese itinerary collection: *Art and Archaeology of Vietnam, Asian Crossroads of Cultures* (Catalogue publication No. 4430) exhibited in Washington, D.C. in 1961 under the auspices of the Smithsonian Institution give evidence of the Indo-Hellenistic and Near-Eastern influences.

The little-known port of Lach-truong in the province of Thanh-hoa is the location where thirty years ago we brought to light predominantly vaulted brick tombs, some dating back to the third century B.C. but the majority datable during the first three centuries A.D. The funerary deposits comprised ceramics, bronze objects, coins, some remains of iron, gold, silver, and traces of wood and lacquer. Among the funerary ceramics may be noted the presence of a whitish or cream-coloured glazed ware which is of major importance because its provenance may be established—Ch'ang-sha and other sites in China being the source of this evidently imported ware.

1.   The sanctuary surrounding the fish ponds in the vicinity of Lach-truong (Pho-cat) and connected with arching bridges was probably dedicated to mediums (Shamanism?). *Cf.* Maurice Durand, *Techniques et Panthéon des Médiums Vietnamiens* (Dô'ng), pp. 46, 65 ff., *publ. de L'Ecole Française d'Extréme-Orient,* Vol. XLV, Paris, 1959.

Certain archaeological aspects and magico-religious implications connected with the form of tombs in the Lach-truong complex exhibit affinities with those of Ch'u:

(1) The tombs are of vaulted bricks and some with shafts of wood—now decayed—and some of a composite type, part wood and part bricks.

(2) As in the case of ancient Ch'u, the Lach-truong during the development of their culture experienced the influence of drugs introduced and practised by Shamanism and mysticism. The influence of drugs deeply rooted and intricately entwined with mysticism played a predominant and vital role in the presentation of symbols, inscrutable images, fantastic motives, the depiction of magic flights, and grotesque monsters.

(3) The Lach-truong, the Dong-son as well as the Oc-eo cultures had a widespread ramification throughout the Pacific Islands and their influences can be traced as far as to some Amerindians, especially those of the Inca civilization.

Consequently, through interdisciplinary research amongst the environmental factors pertaining to the Ch'u Silk Manuscript which exhibit some Western and some non-Chinese elements, we arrive at certain conclusions. By comparing the relics of the Lach-truong tombs with those found at the Ch'ang-sha and other Ch'u sites we may contribute something towards the elucidation of some of the problems before us.

First, we will discuss the contents of the tomb of the so-called 'Kneeling Man'—Tomb No. 3 of Lach-truong (Figure 1A). Thanks to some distant and obscure but deep-rooted traditions of taboo, the hypogeum itself as well as the rich and interesting deposits were found intact, untouched through the centuries by human hand. This

FIGURE 1. A: Tomb No. 3—the 'Tomb of the Kneeling Man'—Lach-truong (Thanh-hoa), Vietnam (after Janse, 1951: Pl.30); B: stone slabs and cone-shaped ink-grinders of ink-stands from Lach-truong tombs (after Janse, 1947: Fig.11). C: bronze figurine probably representing Zagreus, alias the infant Dionysos,, probably found in the Lach-truong cultural site (After photograph courtesy Coll. David-Weill, Paris; after Janse, 1947: Pl.11); D: cone as the symbol of Magna Mater engraved on a Syrian coin (see, Janse, 1961).

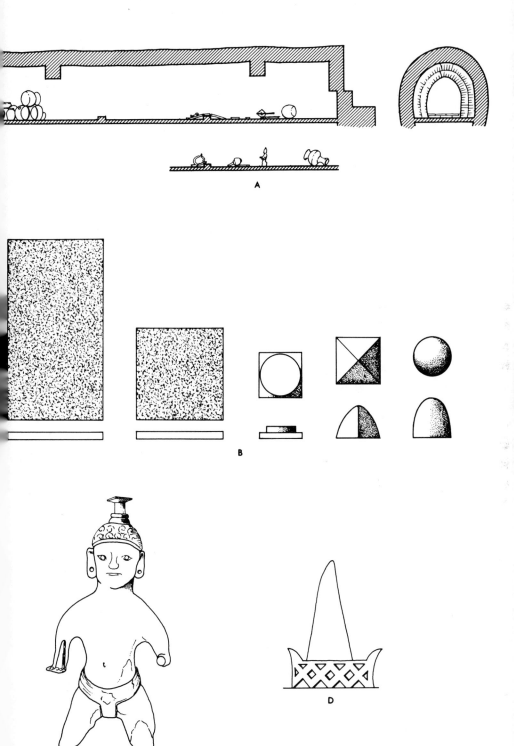

A

B

C

D

happy circumstance gave us the opportunity to excavate the tomb methodically. The specific arrangement of the relics probably indicate a strange play of imagery, as though in a system of regulatory interactions or interdependency on one functional unity of seemingly paradoxical ideas, and yet forming a coherent identity related to syncretism of the Oriental mysticism transplanted into the Greco-Roman world.

Close examination of some of the relics and the tomb structure as well leads inescapably into considering the Lach-truong culture as a ramification of the Ch'u culture.

1. Ink-stands

The presence in the tombs of such artifacts as ink-stands may be taken as tangible evidence pointing to the existence of some records or messages in a written media either on paper or silk and prayers intended for the spirits dwelling in the world beyond. Some of the ink-stands made of polished greyish stone slabs are provided with grinders serving the purpose of preparing India ink powder (Figure 1B). Some other ink-stands have a geometrical form possibly suggesting a hidden yet meaningful symbol. The ink-stands found in the tomb of the 'Kneeling Man' form a disk-shaped slab with a cone grinder, both items with certain implications: the slab symbolizing the sky and eternity; the grinder, the goddess Magna Mater. According to a myth, the infant Dionysos was offered a cone to play with before his dismemberment by the Titans. A bronze figurine (Figure 1 C) found in one of the tombs near Lach-truong is an anthropomorphic lamp probably depicting Zagreus (alias the infant Dionysos) holding a cone in his right hand and conveying the idea of resurrection. The cone symbol is also minted on a coin of Babylos (Syria) and dedicated to the goddess Magna Mater, the protectrice of the city (Figure 1 D).

The ink-stands, placed on a wooden frame (Janse, 1947: Pl. 67, 2) which would have been used to hold brushes and bamboo tablets stacked in a lacquered wooden box, were usually placed in the tombs as was the practice during the Han Dynasty.

A quite different type of ink-stand was found in one of the tombs of Lach-truong (Figure 2). It is a bronze tortoise holding in its

FIGURE 2. *Bronze ink-stand in the form of a tortoise from the tomb at Bim-s'on (Thanh-hoa), Vietnam-Han Period.*

mouth a sebila—a vessel common to both the Lach-truong and Ch'u cultural sites as well as to other sites in China but not known in the Dong-son culture. The three small cylinders affixed to the sides of the tortoise shell are intended for brushes. The large solid tube with a broken stem on its back was probably intended to carry a miniature box of scrolls. What is the symbolic meaning of this ancient bronze in the shape of a tortoise? Is the animal here to testify the art of writing? According to a Vietnamese tradition, the tortoise (*qui con rùa*) is one of four mystic and mysterious animals associated with magic power and longevity.[2] The creased design of the tortoise shell was originally believed to be signs or Chinese characters endowed with divinatory power. In historic times, the Vietnamese picture an ancient tortoise carrying on its back a box of scrolls and with its

2.   Liu An, the well-known philosopher of the 2nd century A.D., believed that the tortoise—supposed to have given the Chinese the gift of writing—lived for 3000 years.

203

mouth expelling volutes. These may represent an ancient conception of breathing as a vehicle for uttering magic words associated with mystic signs or with Chinese characters. The origin of the ink-stand is obscure and lost in the unknown but with some degree of certainty it may be placed in Han period China.

Besides the ink-stands, there are several other items that may be cited as examples revealing similarities between the Lach-truong culture and ancient Ch'u.

2. Ewers

These containers, made in earthenware, wood, bronze, or other materials, and widespread throughout Europe and China were used to contain red wine either for temporal or sacred libations and in communion rites. Figures 3 A and B represent two earthenware zoo-morphic ewers found in the province of Thanh-hoa. A similar type of ewer but with a carved design and made of wood and coated with lacquer has been found in Ch'ang-sha (Figure 3 D).[*] These ewers are similar to the Greco-Roman wine-pouring vessels called *askos* or *guttus* and frequently made of glass or silver (Figures 3 C,E,F). However, these vessels common in Southeast Europe, especially in

[*]   This type of vessel is usually termed *hu-tzu* 虎子; attention may be drawn also to their appearance amongst recently excavated Han period sites in Kiangsu (*Chiang-su-sheng ch'u-t'u wen-wu hsüan-chi*, Pl. 117; *cf.* also Pl. 54) but the appearance of this type of vessel seems most notable from the Six Dynasties and later. It is unfortunate that relevant data from excavations in the Eastern Provinces was not covered in the Symposium — Dr. Janse has touched upon several important decorative elements and vessel-types the significance of which cannot really be fully assessed until the Chinese data from recent excavations especially in Kiangsu is brought into the picture. [Ed.]

FIGURE 3.   A: pottery ewer in shape of crouching grotesque animal of Han period date found in a tomb at Bim-s'on. B: pottery ewer in shape of animal of white ware with light green glaze, found in Thanh-hoa (after photograph courtesy Cl. Huet, Brussels Collection); C: silver ewer of Parthian style, Sirkap, Pakistan; D: wooden ewer with carved décor covered with lacquer, found in Ch'ang-sha (after photograph courtesy Freer Gallery of Art, Washington, D.C.); E: silver ewer found in Syria, 1st century A.D. (after photograph courtesy Musée du Louvre, Paris); F: glass ewer (askos) of the treasure of Boscoreale, vicinity of Naples (after photograph courtesy Chicago Museum of Natural History).

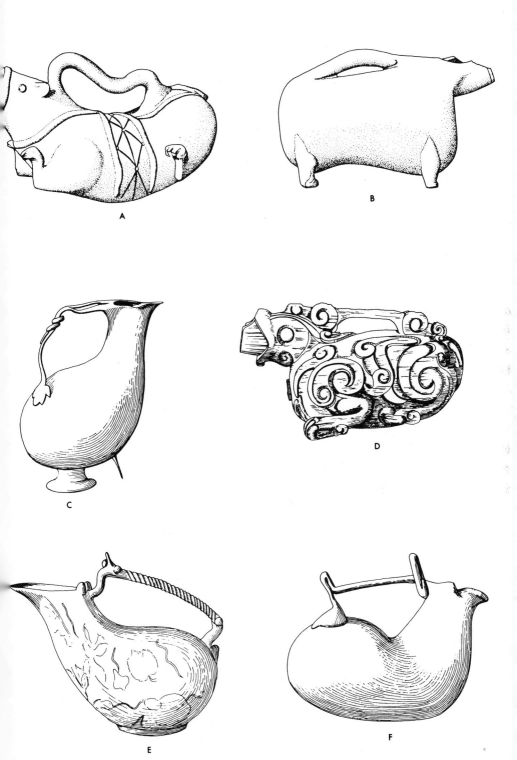

A

B

C

D

E

F

the Macedonian country, can be traced far back to remotest times. Most probably, they are an imitation of buckskin 'leather bottles'.

The historical records show that wine was shipped to India from the Greco-Roman world. Trade relations were known to exist between India and the Southeast Asia at the beginning of the Christian era. Consequently, it may be assumed with some degree of certainty that the the need was felt for reproducing such vessels that would contain the divine substance—the source of intoxication for the devotees partaking in the mystic rites.

Among the well known *askos* of the Boscoreale treasure (Figure 3 F) four silver pieces of the sebila type (Figure 4 C) were found which are common to both China and Lach-truong. The Boscoreale vessels were probably reproduced in Italy from the sebila which form originating in China and known as *yü-hsiang* (羽觴) served as a prototype. It should be pointed out that several of such items belonging to the Boscoreale treasure offer tangible proof of the existence of reciprocal trade relations between the West and East.

3. Cylindrical Jars

In the course of our investigations in the Thanh-hoa Province we discovered several cylindrical tripod-jars (Figure 4A).* They seem to provide sufficient evidence to support the theory that the earthenware items and bronze vessels were originally made in imitation of wickerwork boxes or bamboo.

The finding of cylindrical jars in tombs may confirm the contention that the objects were used for religious purposes. In Vietnam of today, the millennium-old tradition calls for such cylindrical red lacquer jars to be placed on the altars of temples. The

* This particular vessel is generally termed *lien* 奩 and functioned as a cosmetic casket. Both metal and lacquer versions have been excavated in considerable numbers. Pottery 'models', too, are not uncommon. [Ed.]

FIGURE 4. A: *cylindrical jar of white baked ware and glazed. Tomb No. 1, Lach-truong; B: cylindrical tripods of the Esperanze period, Guatemala (after Heine-Geldern, 1958: 209); C: sebila (yü-shang style) from the Boscoreale Treasure, silver.*

A

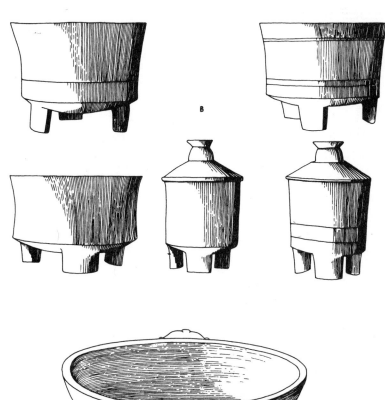

B

C

sacred objects are seen without cover. This occurrence may be explained by the mere fact that they are used for depositing joss-sticks. The ceremony of placing joss-sticks is usually followed by gestures of veneration and devotion and prayers. As a matter of fact, in the sanctuary of Tomb No. 4 of Lach-truong we discovered two cylindrical cream-coloured glazed earthenware jars without covers.[3] Other articles belonging to a group of artifacts used in funerary rites from Tomb No. 4 comprised a unique Roman-type iron lantern (Janse, 1946: Pl. 20a, b; 1951: Pl. 72); earthenware vessels apparently reproductions of ewers (Janse, 1947: Pl. 21,2; 1951: Pl. 59), and ceramic cups, presumably with wooden parts that had long been decayed. All these ritual implements seemed to have been placed on a rectangular tray or on a low wooden table that had decayed in the course of time.

Found also in Lach-truong Tomb No. 1 was a large cylindrical vase (Janse, 1947: Pl. 4) placed on a tray with a three-fish design (Janse, 1947: Pl. 6) which was found near the 'Sacred Fish' pool in a Buddhist shrine, Pho-cat. The centre band of the vase is decorated with a thin horizontal ridge and two opposite *t'ao-t'ieh* masks in low relief. The noses of both masks extend to form loops designed to hold mobile ceramic rings. Without any doubt, the rings represent an imitation of the original prototype—wickerwork boxes.

The type of cylindrical vase, the so-called *mystica cista* – a wickerwork box used as a sacred utensil – is portrayed hanging on the wall in a Greco-Roman relief (see Figure 8A). Its conical cover resembles the so-called Chinese 'hill-jars' [博山爐 *po-shen-lu*]. Similarities with some Lach-truong examples can also be observed.

4. Lamps

In one of the Bim-s'on tombs in Thanh-hoa we found glazed earthenware lamps on stems (Figures 5 A,B). On the quasi-conical

---

3. Robert Heine-Geldern has suggested that this type of cylindrical jar, known throughout the Pacific, originated in Amerindian cultures (Figure 4 B).

FIGURE 5. A: lamp of white earthenware covered with glaze, Tomb B.1, Bim-s'on; B: lamp of white ware, Han period. Tomb of Nghi-ve (Bac-ninh) North Vietnam (Tonkin); C: ceramic lamp covered with glaze found in Ch'ang-sha (after photograph, courtesy Yale University Art Gallery): D: ancient pottery vessel, Luzon, Philippines; E: pottery vessel, Colombia (after Heine-Geldern, 1958: 208).

foot, a row of perforated normal triangles, obviously conveying the idea of bright unity. However, another lamp displays not only rows of open triangles but also a series of rectangles, probably symbolizing man and his life. In regard to an identical lamp found in Ch'ang-sha (Figure 5 C) and one of those originating in Vietnam conjecture has been made that the two lamps may have been produced in the same kilns somewhere in the vicinity of Ch'ang-sha and probably at the same time (cf. Janse, 1947: Figure 44; 1951: 172 ff). As Heine-Geldern has observed there are somewhat similar pieces that have been found in the Philippines and in America (Figures 5 D,E).*

5. Incense-burners

In two of the tombs we excavated at Lach-truong (plundered in ancient times) we brought to light two conical earthenware lids, presumably parts of incense-burners (Figures 6 A,B). The top of one lid was partly broken and upon the other is perched a winged creature. These bird-like creatures attached to incense-burners and lamps are to be found only in the Lach-truong culture (cf. passim, Janse: 1947, 1951). They may represent the phoenix whose life span was believed to have been hundreds of years and also was able periodically to immolate itself; out of its ashes a new cycle would arise symbolizing the triumph of eternal life over death.[4] One of the lids is perforated with a double row of open triangles—the symbolic

---

* Comparison of the pottery forms with perforated long conical bases as presented here with the recently excavated examples from Lungshanoid cultures of the east coast area of China as far north as Ch'ü-fu-hsien 曲阜縣 in Shantung and southwards to P'ei-hsien 邳縣 in Kiangsu (K'ao-ku hsüeh-pao 1964.2) suggests a further line of enquiry with which Dr. Janse's valuable finds might be considered. [Ed.]

4. The Chinese bronze incense burner (cf. Janse, 1951: Pl. 7, 2) in the shape of a bird with mobile wings is certainly the symbol of the rising vapour—the lofty ideal. The tongue seen in the beak of the bird seems to indicate another meaning: 'the spoken word on wings' noted by Homer.

FIGURE 6. A, B: two ceramic lids of incense-burners found in two tombs of Lach-truong: C, D: a Greek pottery incense-burner dating from the sixth century B.C. agora excavations (after photograph courtesy American School of Classical Studies at Athens).

A

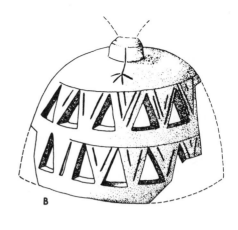

B

C

D

ternaries, the function of aspiration of vapour produced by burning frankincense. The two incense-burners found in Lach-truong have a somewhat different form but also are adorned with open triangles. One displays a row of perforated rectangles, probably conveying again the idea of the purpose of man and his life (see Janse, 1947: Pls. 83, 1; 97, 1).

The artifacts provided with a quasi-conical top and stem seen on a tray, described earlier, were probably an imitation of the Greek *thuribulum*. Some pieces of well-baked white ware (Figure 6 C) belong to the sixth century B.C.

The lofty spectre of a detached contentment, the spiritual oblivion closely approaching the deep-seated idea of salvation that could be evoked through psychedelic experiences under the influence of and stimulated by drugs, and well-known for several millenia in distant lands of the world, was the cornerstone of mysticism. The Scythians, according to Herodotus, had a ritual custom of throwing hemp seeds or flowers into a bonfire built on a heap of red-hot stones. The devotees partaking in the communion were entitled to a lungful of the narcotic inhalation.

Two bronze incense-burners (Figures 7 A,B) differ from the ceramic pieces mentioned previously. Both were found in the Lach-truong area but were probably imported from Ch'ang-sha. The upper part of the item is not on a stem but is carried on the head by a human figurine. This custom, unknown in China, was, on the contrary, widespread in the West, in India, and in Southeast Asia. Each human figurine has a pair of small stylized wings on the shoulders. We know that the wings are the attributes of the Psychopompus-god Hermes—the divine messenger, the go-between of gods and humans. One of the incense-burners represents a figure riding on a fantastic lion with a long beard of the 'chimera' type somewhat reminiscent of the prototype of stylized Bactrian art. Another bronze object with a similar chimera type was found in the Thanh-hoa province in Vietnam (Janse, 1947: Pl. 65a, b).

FIGURE 7. A: bronze thurifer found in Tomb No. 3 at Dai-khoi (Thanh-hoa); B: bronze thurifer found in Thanh-hoa. Both probably imported from China (National Museum of Hanoi).

In re-examining the purpose and intrinsic values of various funerary relics, we feel the necessity of bringing out some particular points and perhaps, too, some new facets of the repository of the 'Kneeling Man's' tomb and its structural features which could have a significant bearing on the problem. The tunnel-shaped brick hypogeum, similar to other constructions, lends the impression of an artificial imitation of a cave. In Taoist philosophy the vaults represent the Cosmos entity, enclosed between the sky and the earth, with the 'entrance' being the imaginary line separating the material and metaphysical worlds. The heap of bricks seen at one end of the hypogeum was probably a screen symbolizing the god Hermes, the protector. The arches, separating the compartments, are symbols of the magic filters of a spiritual nature—the purifying fluids. The stage was usually set either below or close to the arch—between the 'Sacred Centre' and the 'Chapel' as it was the case in the tomb of the 'Kneeling Man'. The rôle of the actors and the staging requisites of the drama remain the topics of further studies:

(1) The anthropomorphic candelabrum identified as the Asian god Dionysos (Figure 8 B).

(2) Pan, the minister of Dionysos, the minor god (Figure 9 A).

(3) The testimonial of the god Hermes is the stele, where his son Pan is seated.[5]

(4) A bronze vase used in libation or lustration (Figure 9 B).

(5) A bronze tripod stylizing the sun-bird, or phoenix (Figure 17).

(6) The ink-stands (Figure 1 B, 2).

(7) Bronze basin with a cup (cf. Janse, 1951, Figure 8).

(8) Four cymbals (cf. Janse, 1957-58, 1961, 1963 and Figures 1 A, 8 B and 10).

(9) A steam-pot—a kitchen utensil for boiling rice (cf. Janse, 1947, Pl. 16, 1; 1951 pàssim).

The bronze figurines personifying Dionysos, Pan and the testimonial of the god Hermes, the quartet of **Phrygian** musicians, the three mudras, and the three attendants (*dramatis personae*) constitute the entity of a far-reaching significance, for they are playing here the rôles assigned to them in the drama of Dionysos—the ever-perpetuating legend of death and resurrection. The primitive setting is adapted by drastic methods, accompanied by light, music, gestures, by the tradition-prone sacramental meal and by drinking the intoxicating red wine which is the everlasting

---

5. The Hermes' stele as a symbol of the god of speech is attested in the root of several words (cf. Joshua Whatmough, *Language, a Modern Synthesis*, p. 14ff, N.Y. 1960; cf. *Genesis* 24, 2, 9).

The stele related to Pan (in the tomb of the 'Kneeling Man') is similar to the symbol of Hermes found in the Mithraic Mysteries and representing several attributes of the god of Kronos. The piece found in the Mithraeum of Astia (Italy) is dated 190 A.D. Pictured on the stele are attributes of Hermes: the Caduceus, a cock, and a pine cone (cf. Franz Cumont, *The Mysteries of Mithra*, p. 105, Fig. 20, N.Y., 1956).

EX DONO DVCI SEORIIAE SEORTIAE

FIGURE 8. A: a Roman relief (first century B.C.) representing a priest of Magna Mater and his devices: mystica cista, cymbals, flute, etc. Museo Capitolini, Rome. After Neumann I, 1962, Fig. 15. B: anthropomorphic candelabrum (probably first century B.C.), representing a priest of the Asian Dionysos. From Tomb No. 3 ('The Kneeling Man') Lach-truong.

215

FIGURE 9. A: bronze figurine representing Pan seated on a stele, the testimonial of his father Hermes. Lach-truong, Tomb No. 3; B: bronze vase from same tomb.

emblem of communion with the god. On the other hand, Dionysos could be considered the counter-partner of Osiris, Bacchus, and other divinities of the Oriental mysticism. One could hazard a confident guess that Dionysos, adorned with one of his complementary epithets—the conqueror of Asia—carried the Dionysiac artists in a triumphal march all over Eurasia. A silver basin from Persia (Freer Gallery of Art, 64.10) dating back to the 2nd century A.D. depicts a scene where several actors perform around the effeminate Dionysos at rest.

The 'Kneeling Man' wears a loincloth or slip (Figure 8B) which may also be the symbol of his self-emasculation or it may be a barbarian process designated for religious purposes as a god, priest, or devotee of mysticism. A somewhat different aspect of bi-sexual behaviour was observed by the author a few years ago in the mountains of Tonkin where a sorcerer wore a bridal dress during a ceremonial dance.

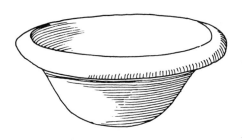

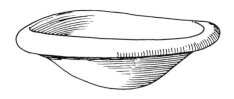

FIGURE 10. Cymbals found in Thailand (after P. Dupont, 1959: Fig. 260).

When studying closely the face of the 'Kneeling Man' we notice relief ridges projecting from the commissures of his mouth. Tentatively, we could call them twin-tongues. As god of wine, Dionysos was called 'the loosener of tongues'.[6] This peculiar element may be observed on at least one Chinese and also one Celtic relic. A Chinese semi-elliptic ceramic plaque from the Han period represents a grotesque human face with three ridges on either end of the commissures (Figure 11 A) which here again could be the forked tongue. The piece was probably the ornament of a tomb wall. The twin-tongue element is seen on gods and heroes and a particularly impressive reproduction is to be noted on the unique Gundestrup silver cauldron (Figure 11 B). The object, which dates back to the first two centuries A.D., was probably made in the Near East. It should be pointed out that the serpent horns represented on this vessel are the symbol of Zagreus, or the infant Dionysos.[7] The split-tongue element is present in the Ch'u Silk Manuscript.

Four small kneeling plastic figurines, forming a quartet of Phrygian musicians, are seen on the knees and on the loins of the

6. *Cf.* E. Royston Pike, *Encyclopedia of Religion and Religions,* New York, 1958, p. 125.
7. *Cf.* Salmon Reinach, *Mythes et Religions,* Vol.II (Paris, 1906), p. 58 and *cf.* the Phrygian conical headgear in Fig. 41. Note also J.E. Cirrlot, *A Dictionary of Symbols,* N.Y., 1962, p. 242.

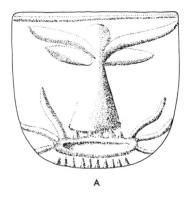

A   B

FIGURE 11. A: Chinese semi-elliptical ceramic plaque of a monster with three tongues protruding from the commisures of its mouth, Han period (after Janse, 1936: Pl.II, 3). B: One of the plates of the Celtic silver cauldron (Holy Grail?) representing the face of a god with a tongue projecting from the commisures; Gundestrup, Denmark—probably originating from the Near East–2nd century A.D. (after Müller, Le Grand Vase de Gundestrup, Pl.X).

statuette representing Dionysos (Figure 8B). One pair is playing double cymbals while their two companions blow on Phrygian one-reed flutes—not what is known as the Greek double reed, *aulos*. Two pairs of identical cymbals, as well as similar instruments, discovered in the tomb, were also found at the local site of Oc-eo, the Kingdom of Fu-nan in South Vietnam and in Thailand (Figure 10). However, no cymbals have been found in China dating before T'ang period. In all likelihood, together with the cymbals, two wooden flutes might have been placed in the tomb of the 'Kneeling Man', but these instruments, being of organic matter, would have decayed and disappeared in the acid soil. The musicians wearing the conical, Phrygian-type headgear, were probably itinerant actors coming from the Near East. Among the sacred utensils seen on the Greco-Roman relief mentioned earlier (Figure 8A) are a set of cymbals and Phrygian one-reed flute.

The form of the mobile sebila on a tray, held in the hands of the 'Kneeling Man' whom we have identified as Dionysos, reminds us of the semi-oval wickerwork bark still in use in Vietnam as a boat (sampan) as well as in southern China. Assuming that the sebila might represent a floating 'basket' it may then possibly be an invention of the Ch'u culture made prior to the Han Dynasty.*

The sebila, common to the Lach-truong culture, seems to have been originally made of wood and later on of some other material such as earthenware or metal. Basically, the sebila, embracing two different symbols, represents several other meanings. It was used chiefly in performing funerary rites as well as in temporal and ceremonial games. Curiously enough, the double meaning: boat and drinking cup is deeply rooted in several Indo-European words such as 'vessel' (*cf.* Janse, 1957/58: 30, 50). The funerary sebila found in the tomb of the 'Kneeling Man' is likely to carry a double symbol: that of a boat or bark and that of a drinking cup. The 'vessel' is believed to ferry the saviour—the sun divinity—at night over the perilous travel of its cosmic course over the underworld waters from Occident to the Orient.

The sebila, when used as a drinking cup, contains the wine of the 'god' in libation ceremonies of the myṣtae under the influence of intoxication and especially in sacred symposiums. The sebila in temporal usage as a vessel is known in China as well as in Korea in literary contests and games or in poetry writing when it is carried as a floating drinking cup. The literary game involving a play is found in two Chinese accounts: one dating back to the 3rd century A.D., the other to the 4th century, all dealing with the 'floating cup'. This kind of ceremony was still being performed during the T'ang period and can be seen in the miniature river found at the Royal Summer Palace, Po-sung Jung (700-875 A.D.) near Seoul, Korea. A wooden lacquer ornament comprising a sebila on a stem found in Ch'ang-sha which is now in the Freer Gallery of Art (FGA 49.1) may have been regarded

* The sebila or *yü-shang* 'winged cup' (*cf.* Chang-Kwang-chih's cited passage in the present volume, p. 31) is certainly well attested in Ch'u cultural remains pre-dating the Han period. [Ed.]

as a prize in such a contest. Several semi-oval silver cups similar to the sebila type found in Iran date from about the 6th century A.D. One of these vessels may have been used for drinking wine of the 'god' because it represents probably the image of the 'god' on a tray, also found in Iran. In both cases, the picture of the androgene god is framed by wine branches.

After the sun god had terminated the nocturnal voyage, the saviour 'Vessel' arrived for his return journey over the sky in three stages. On the upper arms and back, the 'Kneeling Man' carried three mobile (hinged) lamps symbolizing the light of the sun. The lamps are believed to be the expression of the mythical diurnal course of the sun god—from his birth on to resurrection—or the new life on the Oriental horizon—at dawn through the zenith and onto the occidental horizon—dusk—and finally the agony.

The aquatic birds, the swans, placed on the lamps in pairs and on the same level and identically stylized, represent the united emblem dedicated to Apollo, the counterpart of Dionysos (both at their sanctuary in Delphi). The swan in relationship with Dionysos signifies both hermaphroditism and the light as the function of the being 'unmover and mover', the deity of the cosmic orbit. The mystic belief was that the swan song of agony may be an incantation to overcome some secret or supernatural magic power. The chant of the swan before its 'incruente' (or bloodless) immolation is the dusk of light, like the flickering flame of a lamp, the dying of the sun-god, sacrificed for the salvation of mankind. This myth is probably relevant to some elements of the Lohengrin legend. With the third lamp placed in the centre or in the zenith, the stylistic *naga* head was added. The serpent embraces the symbol both of darkness and the light of resurrection, the sun probably dwelling in the sebila-boat. O. Almgren has reproduced a figure of a sinuous serpent on a mystic solar boat, as seen on ancient Swedish rock carvings which may be compared with a similar image represented on an Egyptian tomb of the 26th Dynasty (Figure 12).

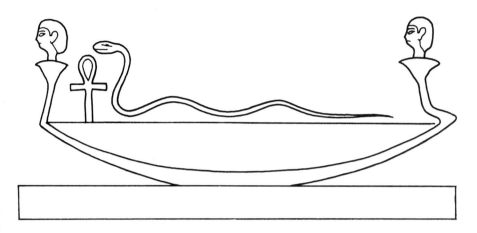

FIGURE 12. *A snake in a solar boat—Egyptian tomb of the 26th Dynasty (after O. Almgren,* Hällristningar, *Fig. 4).*

6. Vases

A bronze vase (Figure 9 B) we found in our excavations in Thanh-hoa was so brittle as to require very special care during the cleaning process and its restoration. At the Musée Cernuschi in Paris, great care was taken to remove the earth that filled the interior of the vase and to clean it. Two great experts on the staff of the technical personnel of the Musée du Louvre had tried first to clean it by putting it in a bath. Unfortunately, however, as the water dissolved the material the vase flaked and crumbled into pieces. The obvious reason is that the bronze alloy was, in the first place, very brittle and fragile as an eggshell. The explanation of the fact could lie in the peculiar techniques employed at the Ch'ang-sha site and later transferred to the Lach-truong culture. Hence, it may be assumed that similar objects may have disappeared simply due to their fragility, on one hand, and because of the carelessness of gravediggers both in China and Vietnam, on the other. The vase has a cylindrical neck on a globular body supported on a truncated foot and adorned with various geometrical patterns, some parts arranged in superimposed zones with a zoomorphic motive display on the body.

221

Another vase we found in one of the tombs of Lach-truong was of earthenware with a fine glazed coating (Figure 13). Two similar

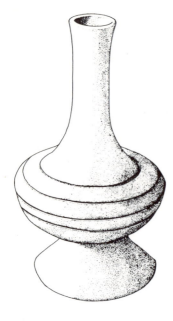

FIGURE 13. *Glazed pottery vase found in Tomb No.6, Lach-truong.*

earthenware flasks were found at the Ch'ang-sha site and were donated by Mr. John Hadley Cox to the Yale University collection. Vases of this shape are seen on an image in India (Figure 14 A), Abhiska of Cri, Udayagiri and two identical ones are carved on the stupa of Sanci (North India) shown as being used in a ritual pouring of lustrum above the head of goddess Cri. Identical scenes but without the vases may be observed on the silver cauldron of Gundestrup (S. Müller, Pl. VIII) and on a tympanum of a Cham temple in southern Vietnam (Figure 14 B).

This idea of the 'Lustrum in Heaven' rites can be seen reproduced on the tomb walls of the Wu-liang-tzu family (in Shantung) of Han date wherein there is a scene with two attendants of the ritual drama holding bases which probably contain lustrum. Earthenware vases of the same form are known in China up to the Ming period and have been used in ceremonies or for purely ornamental purposes (*cf.*

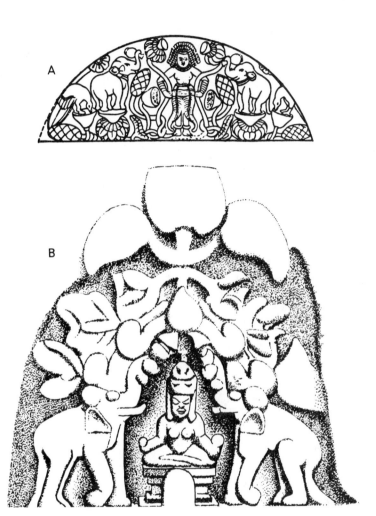

FIGURE 14. A: Abhisk of Cri, Udayagiri, India, representing two elephants pouring lustrum over the goddess Cri, and each holding a vase in its trunk (after Ananda Coomaraswami, Yaksas, Vol. II, Pl.44); B: possibly the same scene as in A, except that here the two elephants each hold an attendant in its trunk who pours lustrum over the goddess. Tympanum of a Cham temple, Dong-duong, Quang-nam, South Vietnam (Museum of Da-nang [form. Tourane] No. 597, Cf. Janse, 1935: Pl.IV).

International Exhibition of Chinese Art, Royal Açademy of Arts, London, 1935-36).

The geometrical pattern seem on the vase in superimposed zones (Figure 9 B) comprises a trellis, series of lozenges, sharp angles, and fretwork. These patterns are to be found on various relics originating in China, such as funerary bronzes, pottery, and bricks. The trellis pattern and lozenges appear either separately or combined and sometimes isolated lozenges are filled with trellis pattern (Figure 15).

FIGURE 15. *Lid of a bronze tripod showing lozenges filled with trellis pattern, Man-thon (Tho-xuan), Thanh-hoa, Tomb 1A (after Janse, 1947: Pl.117, 1, 3).*

These ornamental designs are symbolic of the magic net representing the firmament—the cosmic order. The net implies various facets of its use such as catching the sun from its orbit as with a snare, or ensnaring the enemies of the divinities and monsters like fish in a net. In all probability the trellis may mean a hanging net while the lozenges may indicate stretched meshes ready to ensnarl or capture. This idea has been widespread since time immemorial not only in Eurasia but also among the Incas (Frazer, 1919: I, 1, 316). The Sumerian god Tammuz was frequently addressed as the *Divine Lagmar*, meaning 'Lord of the Net'. According to Weston (1957) the epithet may be equivalent to the 'Fisher King' legend. The symbol was prevalent in the Babylonian, Egyptian, and Greco-Oriental cults, where the magic net was offered to Priapus and Dea Syria. Homer gives an account of the myth of Ares and Aphrodite who captured the god of fire, Hephaistos, in a golden net.

The trellis decorating the roof of a Persian temple probably symbolizes the cosmic net placed as a canopy but also represents the idea of the firmament. The same net symbol appears as an ornament on a large funerary brick of the Han Period (*cf.* Janse, 1936). The principal element of trellis is the net hanging over the crown of the cosmic tree. On the upper and lower sides of the brick, a series of interconnected lozenges represent the stretched mesh of the net as though intended for snatching or catching the highest prize.

Some bricks record the myth of trapping or capturing a solar bird. According to a Chinese myth, ten solar birds perched on the cosmic tree and scorched the land. A mythical emperor summoned the divine archer Heng-O and ordered him to shoot down nine of the solar birds. On the left of the cosmic tree (seen on the brick) is the archer. On the upper right in the scene is a bird which no doubt symbolizes the only remaining solar bird. Every day at dusk it flees the cosmic tree to escape possible immolation. The tiger, seen at the end of the scene, signifies darkness or night. The full meaning of this pictorial story told vividly on the funerary brick is the attempt to prevent the destruction of the solar bird during its noctural orbit (*cf.* Janse, 1951). The connection between the net and the firmament is further attested in the *Tao-te-ching's* 'Net of Heaven', where in substance it is said: ' . . . it is wide-meshed [lozenges?] but lets nothing through'. As the symbol of protection, the cosmic net is probably linked with the idea of the ritual parasol.

Finally, it may be noted that the net symbol may be linked with the art of ancient Ch'u. In one of the Lach-truong tombs (Bim-s'on Tomb No. 1 B) we discovered a truncated ceramic basin of the Ch'ang-sha type, well-baked and of whitish ware, resembling a tambourine. The walls on the outside have a trellis pattern; on the inside, the flat bottom is deeply incised with a geometric star-shaped figure with seven points (Figure 16). The number seven may well symbolize the mystic idea of magic power in the regulatory process of the world, thus meaning perfect order. In China, the seven stars (i.e.. the Great Bear Constellation and the Dipper) are sometimes engraved on jade *kuei* and symbolize the realm of time and space, the

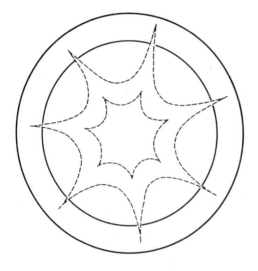

FIGURE 16. Incised geometric design of a symbolic star with seven points on inside bottom of a ceramic vessel (Tambourine?); the outside has trellis pattern (cf. Janse, 1947: Pl. 96, 1).

seven days of the week, and the seven directions. In a truncated ceramic vase from Bim-s'on, Tomb No. 1 B, the two symbols, the trellis and the geometric pattern of a seven-pointed star, are linked with the net. Upon the basis of similar ornamentation of mirrors found in the Ch'ang-sha site a possible relationship may be surmised (cf. Hu-nan ch'u-t'u t'ung-ching t'u-lu, Pl. 41).

The solid spout made in the shape of a long neck on the large bronze tripod from Tomb No. 3, Lach-truong resembles the head of a cock or possibly a pheasant (or a phoenix?). The three legs are each of a triangular cross section, distantly suggesting hoofs (Figure 17). The lid and the handle of the tripod are decorated with the same pattern as the flask (Figure 9 B) and the figurine of Pan (Figure 9 A): trellis, lozenges, fretwork, sharp angles, and fragments of galloping animals. A vase found in Ch'ang-sha exhibits the trellis pattern, the series of sharp angles, and a zone containing the motif of galloping animals (Figure 18). The zoomorphic motifs surmounting the animals in flight is likely to represent the mysticism connected with narcotic-induced visions or hallucinations well-known both in Taoistic and Shamanistic cults.

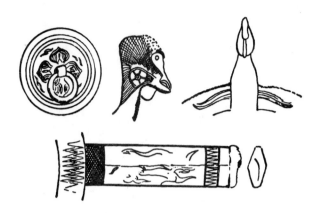

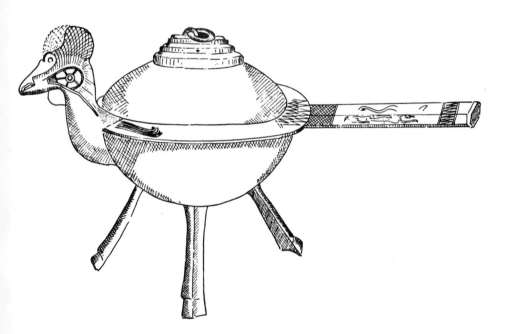

FIGURE 17. *A bronze tripod in the general shape of a bird and details of the décor. The piece is to be compared to the three-legged solar birds and the Hindu sun divinity taking over the day in three steps. The lid is shown with three steps. Tomb No. 3, Lach-truong.*

In discussing the unit system of the tomb of the 'Kneeling Man' attention was drawn to the symbolic stele terminating the figurine of Pan which is regarded as the testimonial of his father, Hermes, the

FIGURE 18. *A bronze vase from Ch'ang-sha showing the same decorative features as found in various Lach-truong relics (after photograph, courtesy of the Museum of Far Eastern Antiquities, Stockholm).*

god also worshipped in ancient China. The epithets of Hermes are: *spealeite* 'the man of the cave' and *psychopompus* 'the conductor of souls or spirits in the Underworld'. The main indication of his various functions are the small wings which appear either on his sandals, his helmet, or his shoulders and the *Caduceus*—his double-snake entwined staff—symbolic of his rôle as the 'messenger', the 'go-between of gods and men'. In the Ch'u Silk Manuscript it may be noted that one of the Peripheral Figures comprises a pair of intertwined serpents painted in two colours—red and blue. The two Lach-truong thurifers discussed earlier (Figure 7 A, b) each surmount anthropomorphic figurines with small wings sprouting from their shoulders. If both pieces were, as we earlier suggested, originally from China their style characteristics of both Iran-Hellenistic and Bactrian spheres would be of especial interest. We may further assume that they may represent the god Hermes. These together with the lampadary comprising the figure of Dionysos with musicians, *mudras*, and attendants and that of Pan with the testimony of Hermes all belong to a passion play of mysticism. The original drama in its performance has a predominant subject—the resurrection of the dead the bonds of the laws and the power of nature. The strong influence of the Greco-Roman Orient permeating the Lach-truong remains as demonstrated in this short study and the incidence of the several similar features attending the art of ancient Ch'u which likewise appear to have Western origins gives rise to many involved, interdisciplinary problems.

BIBLIOGRAPHY

Almgren, Oscar
    1926-27 'Hällristningar och Kultbruk (Gravures sur rochers et rites magiques)', in Kungl, *Vitterhets: Historia och Akademiens Handlingar,* Vol. 35. Stockholm.

Carter, George F.
    1959 'The Mystery of American Civilization. Did the Western Hemisphere Develop Spontaneously or were there Outside Influences? A Fascinating Argument Rages on', in *Viet-My,* Tap IV, So IV, Dec. 1959, Saigon (after the *Johns Hopkins Magazine,* Baltimore, Md.).

Cirlot, J. E.
    1962 *A Dictionary of Symbols,* New York.

Cottrell, Leonard
    1960 *The Concise Encyclopedia of Archaeology,* New York.

Cox, John Hadley
    1939 *An Exhibition of Chinese Antiquities from Ch'ang-sha,* Gallery of Fine Arts, Yale University, New Haven, Conn.

Dupont, Pierre
    1959 'L'Archéologie Mone de Dvāravatī', *Bulletin de l'Ecole Française d'Extrême-Orient,* Vol. XLI, Paris.

Durand, Maurice
    1959 'Technique et Panthéon des Mediums Vietnamiens (Dong)', *Bulletin de l'Ecole Française d'Extrême-Orient,* Vol. XLV, Paris.

Eliade, Mircea
    1960 'Spiritual Thread, Sutratman, Catena Aurea' *Paideuma, Mitteilungen zur Kulturkunde,* Band VII, Heft 4/6, Weisbaden.
    1961 'Recent Works on Shamanism' in *History of Religions,* Vol. 2, No. 1. Chicago.

Frazer, G. James
    1911-19 *The Golden Bough,* 3rd ed. London.

Ghirshman, R.
    1954 *Iran,* Baltimore (Md.)

Heine-Geldern, R.
    1945 'Prehistoric Research in Netherland Indies' in *Science and Scientists in the Netherland Indies,* New York.
    1946 'Research on Southeast Asia: Problems and Suggestions', *American Anthropologist,* Vol. 48. New York.
    1951 'Das Tocharer Problem und die Pontische Wanderung', *Saeculum,* Vol. II, 2. Vienna.

JANSE

1954   'Bronzegeräte auf Flores', *Anthropos,* Bd. 49, Fribourg.

1958   'Chinese Influence in the Pottery of Mexico, Central America and Columbia' in 33rd *Congres Internacional de Americanistas.* San Jose.

Janse, Olov R.T.

1935   'L'empire des Steppes', *Revue des Arts Asiatiques,* IX, Paris.

1936   *Briques et objects céramiques funéraires de l'epoque des Han,* Paris.

1947   *Archaeological Research in Indo-China,* Vols. I (1947), II (1951), Harvard University Press, Cambridge (Mass.). Vol. III (1958), Institut Belge des Hautes Etudes Chinoises, Bruxelles/Bruges.

1957-58 'Dionysos au Vietnam', *Viking,* Oslo.

1961   'Vietnam, carréfour de peuples et de civilisations', *France-Asie* (Asia). Tokyo.

1962   'Vietnamese Askos', *Dai-Hoa.* Hue.

1962a   'Quelques réflexions à propos d'un bol de type Mégaréen trouvé au Vietnam', *Artibus Asiae,* XXV. 4. Ascona.

1963   'The Origins of Traditional Vietnamese Music', *Asian Perspectives,* Vol. VI, 1, 2. Hong Kong University Press.

1966   'Complex Problems Raised by Excavations in Southeast Asia', *Symposium on Historical and Linguistic Studies on Southern China, Southeast Asia and the Hong Kong Region,* F.S. Drake (ed.), Hong Kong University Press, 1966. *Cf.* Bibliography of Chinese reports on the Mainland sites referring to Ch'ang-sha.

Malleret, Louis

1959-63 *L'Archéologie du Delta du Mékong,* published by l'Ecole Francaise d'Extrême-Orient. Paris.

1961   'Les dodécaedres d'or du site d'Oc-eo', *Artibus Asiae,* XXIV, 3, 4. Ascona.

1959   'La Civilisation de Dong-son', *France-Asie* (Asia), No. 160-1. Saigon.

Neumann, Erich

1962   *The Origins and History of Consciousness,* Vol. I. New York.

Salmony, Alfred

1954   'Antler and Tongue: An Essay on Ancient Chinese Symbolism and Implications', *Artibus Asiae,* Supplement. Ascona.

Schuster, Carl

1951   'Joint-marks—A Possible Index of Cultural Contact Between America, Oceania and the Far East', *Koninklijk Inst. voor de Tropen, Mededeling no X, XCIV Physische Anthropologie,* No. 39. Amsterdam.

1952a   'Head-hunting Symbolism on the Bronze Drums of the Ancient Dong-son Culture and in Modern Balkans', *Actes du Congrés Internationale des Sciences Anthropologiques et Ethnologiques,* Vol. II. Vienna.

1952b   'An Ancient Cultural Movement Reflected by Modern Survivals in the Arts of the Carpathians, the Caucasian Region, West China and Melanesia, and dated by the Dong-son Culture of Northern Indochina', *Actes du Congrés International des Sciences Anthropologiques et Ethnologiques,* Vol. II. Vienna.

Tarn, W.W.

1951   *The Greeks in Bactria and India,* New York.

Weston, Jessie L.

1957   *From Ritual to Romance,* New York.